Christopher Badcock

lectures at the LSE, where he teaches psychoanalysis and evolutionary science to psychologists and social scientists. He is also author of the classic introduction to Freudian theory, *Essential Freud* (1988), and of *Evolution and Individual Behaviour* (1991).

Praise for PsychoDarwinism

'Badcock writes with grace and intelligence, and has managed to produce a new and lively synthesis of Freudian and Darwinian theories. His book, even when it is contentious, is always interesting and thought-provoking.'

DR JOHN FORRESTER, co-author of *Freud's Women*

'Freud described something which Darwin explained: human nature. Yet Freudians and Darwinians have little time for each other these days. Christopher Badcock brings great clarity and knowledge to the uphill task of reconciling two great streams of thought. He is very persuasive.'

MATT RIDLEY, author of *The Red Queen*

'This is an immensely challenging book, which is a tribute to the enduring vitality which Freud's ideas continue to have. Badcock's work need not command ideological agreement, but it does succeed in provoking the kind of stimulating debate which is worthy of keeping alive the intellectual tradition which freud started.'

PAUL ROAZEN, Ph.D., author of *Meeting Freud's Family*

CHRISTOPHER BADCOCK

PsychoDarwinism

The New Synthesis of Darwin & Freud

Flamingo
An Imprint of HarperCollinsPublishers

Flamingo
An Imprint of HarperCollins*Publishers*
77–85 Fulham Palace Road,
Hammersmith, London W6 8JB

Published by Flamingo 1995
9 8 7 6 5 4 3 2 1

First published in Great Britain by
HarperCollins*Publishers* 1994

Copyright © Christopher Badcock 1994

Christopher Badcock asserts the moral right to
be identified as the author of this work

ISBN 0 00 686305 1

Set in Linotron Galliard by
Rowland Phototypesetting Limited,
Bury St Edmunds, Suffolk

Printed in Great Britain by
HarperCollinsManufacturing Glasgow

To the memory of
CHARLES DARWIN & SIGMUND FREUD,
fathers of PsychoDarwinism.

CONTENTS

ILLUSTRATIONS

'In the early days I made a number of altera-
tions in my views and did not conceal them
from the public. I was reproached on account
of these changes, just as today I am reproached
for my conservativeness. Not that I should be
intimidated by the one reproach or the other.
But I know that I have a destiny to fulfil. I
cannot escape it and I need not move towards
it. I shall await it . . .'

SIGMUND FREUD (1912)

PREFACE

'If my father were alive today, I don't think he would want to be a psychoanalyst.' This remark was made to me more than once by Anna Freud, Sigmund Freud's daughter and successor in psychoanalysis, in the year or two before her death in 1982. When on one occasion I asked her what she thought her father would want to be if he were alive today, she was less sure. However, that he would not wish to be a psychoanalyst she was adamant.

This, and other similar remarks by Anna Freud, greatly increased my uncertainty about what I wanted to be when the analysis I had been undergoing with her was abruptly terminated by her death. It had begun in 1979, at a time when she was well past the maximum age at which the analytic profession will allow an analyst to begin an official training analysis with a student. As a result, I faced the prospect of starting more or less at the beginning if I wished to qualify as a psychoanalyst, and of course with a new training analyst.

In any event, my interest in psychoanalysis had always been primarily scientific, rather than therapeutic. I felt that most big discoveries of the therapeutic method had probably already been made and that psychoanalysis as a profession had lost sight of its scientific goals in its scramble for success as a medical speciality. Indeed, I learnt that this was a view very much shared by Anna Freud, and that this was one of the main reasons why she believed that, had he been alive at the time, her father would not have wanted to be a therapeutic analyst. I dimly intuited that the work of Freud had an important rôle to play in behavioural science generally, but could not see precisely what it was.

Then something that happened in the following year resolved the issue. I came across a little-known paper by Robert Trivers that was in effect a summary of his work published up to that time. That paper was a revelation to me and instantly converted me to modern Darwinism as the only secure scientific foundation for behavioural science as a whole.

I realized that the methodological bias that had always worried me in the social sciences – the tendency to take a collectivist point of view that ignored individuals and their interests – had been solved in modern Darwinism with the discrediting of 'group-selection' and the discovery of the rôle of the individual gene in the evolution of social behaviour (this will be fully explained later). 'Our destruction of group-selection thinking', observed Trivers, 'has removed the chief prop from the comfortable belief that the dominant interests naturally rule in everybody's self-interest. And we uncovered a series of submerged actors in the social world, for example, females and offspring, whose separate self-interest . . . we emphasize.'[1]

Such an unbiased, individualistic approach was fundamental to psychoanalysis, in large part because it relied on the individual's free associations for its material. As a result, Freud had long since discovered parent-offspring conflict as a fact, even if we had to wait for Trivers to explain its evolutionary basis. And long before Trivers, Freud's method of allowing the patient on the couch to free-associate had uncovered not merely submerged actors, but their submerged thoughts, feelings and desires. Among these actors women figured very prominently, and later developments were to give a voice to children in much the same way – in large part thanks to Anna Freud's pioneering work in child-analysis. When I subsequently read all Trivers's publications in detail, I began to see that much of what he had to say related to many of Freud's findings, and that here was the real future for Freud: a synthesis with modern Darwinism that today I call *PsychoDarwinism*.

I devoted the next decade to the task of unifying Freud and Darwin, publishing a number of books along the way. This book represents the most complete synthesis that I have been able to achieve to date, and is much more than a mere summary of my earlier publications.

I begin with an introductory chapter devoted to the neglected subject of the many parallels and continuities to be found in the work of Darwin and Freud. Here I am indebted to Lucille Ritvo's book, *Darwin's Influence on Freud*. The next two chapters are an introduction to modern Darwinism. I must thank Dave Johnson for permission to use his computer program EVOLV-O-MATIC in illustrating the first, and to Ronald Beloin's Symbiosis 1.2 for illustrations in the second. I present a modern Darwinian view of the question of consciousness in the next two chapters, using an analogy based on the Macintosh™ computer operating system in the second. In the fifth and sixth chapters I present the essentials of my own work on reconciling Freud's findings related to sex with our modern, Darwinian understanding of it. In the seventh chapter I propose a new solution to one of the oldest and most confused questions in human behavioural science – that of incest and its avoidance. Finally, I devote the last chapter to suggesting some new answers to another central issue of Darwinism as applied to human behaviour. This is the question of how selection at the level of the individual gene can be related to the complexities of actual human behaviour, with all its cultural and environmental influences. I take sex rôle determination as my key example, and show how Freud's findings provide an exemplary solution to the problem of how genes relate to behaviour in a complex environmental context.

Some readers may be surprised to find that there are no chapters devoted to culture as such, or to psychopathology. The reason is simple. Both subjects proved to be too big and too complex for this book. Consequently, I plan a future volume, parallel to this one, to discuss them at the length and with the detail that they deserve. Here I limit myself to outlining the essentials of the Darwin-Freud synthesis, rather than applying it as such. However, my treatment of the incest question provides an example of what can be expected from a PsychoDarwinist approach to such complex issues.

I must thank my wife, Lenis Badcock, and my colleagues, Helena Cronin, Alan Lloyd and David Spain, for many helpful suggestions for improving the text. I must also thank my students, especially Kirsti Edmonds and Mike Haywood. Thanks and acknowledgements are also due to Jean Aitchison, Bruce Alexander, Robert Axelrod, David Barash, Morris Berman, Alan Bittles, Chris Brand, David Buss, Robert and JoAnn Campbell, Charles Crawford, Martin Daly and Margo Wilson, John Davey, Richard Dawkins, Paul Ekman, David Haig, William Hamilton, Bill Irons, Robert Kruszynski, Peter Loizos, Bobbi Low, David MacKnight, John Maynard-Smith, Randy Nesse, John Price, Daniel Rancour-Laferriere, Matt Ridley, Michael Ruse, Warren Shapiro, Keith Sharp, Roger Short, Stuart Sutherland, Peter Sykora, Robert Trivers, Eckart Voland, Brant Wenegrat, George Williams, Daniel Wilson, Glenn Wilson and Jan Wind. Finally, I owe a special debt of gratitude to my agent, John Brockman, and to my editor, Philip Gwyn Jones.

CHRISTOPHER BADCOCK,
April 1994.

INTRODUCTION

The aim of this book is to present a new synthesis of Darwin and Freud. But such a thing seems impossible. Three objections in particular spring to mind. First, today people think of Freud in connection with Lamarck's discredited theory of evolution, rather than with Darwin. Second, just about everyone – but Darwinists perhaps more than most – see Freud's sexual findings as absurd, especially his theory of infantile sexuality. Third, Freud is normally regarded as a believer in 'nurture' rather than 'nature'. Since Darwin emphasized nature as a major determinant of human behaviour, this seems to rule out any reconciliation of the two.

Nevertheless, we shall see that things are not as they seem. In part, this is because Freud has been extensively misunderstood, misrepresented and misinterpreted, particularly on the nature/nurture issue. Furthermore, I shall try to show that many of Freud's findings make sense in terms of factors that have only emerged within the last two decades and at the cutting edge of modern Darwinism. For example, we shall see that Freud's central discovery, the repressed unconscious, has been rediscovered in modern evolutionary thinking and demonstrated in laboratory experiments. In later chapters we shall see that much of what Freud discovered about so-called 'infantile sexuality' makes surprisingly good sense in terms of the recently developed theory of parental investment. I shall argue that even seemingly bizarre ideas like castration anxiety and penis envy look completely different when placed in the context of our best recent insights into the evolution of behaviour. The fact that Freud could not possibly have known about these developments, and quite certainly lacked a clear enough understanding of Darwinism to have been able to anticipate them, suggests that his findings, although widely ridiculed and disparaged until now, may come to be seen in a very different light in the future.

But even if you *could* reconcile Freud and Darwin, why *should* you? Of what possible use is such a thing?

There are three good reasons for attempting the synthesis of Freud and Darwin. First, if Freud and Darwin are as compatible as I shall claim, it means that current attitudes towards both must be fundamentally wrong in certain respects. If I am right, Freud must have been much more 'Darwinian', and Darwin more 'Freudian' than either have appeared to be up until now. This in itself is important, and suggests that there are aspects of both men's work that have been overlooked or misunderstood. Given the prominence of Darwin and Freud, such errors or omissions surely ought to be corrected if they exist. A precedent for this might be the case of Darwin's contemporary, Mendel (1822–84). When his work was rediscovered at the beginning of this century (having been overlooked earlier) it was wrongly interpreted as disproving Darwin, and set back the so-called 'modern synthesis' of Mendelian genetics and Darwinian evolution for some time. But today Darwinism is unthinkable without Mendelian genetics.

A second reason follows directly from this historical example. Because Darwin was ignorant of the true principles of genetics his theory was bound to remain controversial, incomplete and dubious as long as it lacked this vital ingredient. But once the synthesis of Mendel and Darwin was complete, modern Darwinism became the only credible scientific theory of evolution, and the basis of biological science in general. If we accept that human beings are the product of evolution, then it follows that their psychology must be Darwinian in some sense. This is the second good reason for the Freud-Darwin synthesis: it aims to place Freud's findings on the best scientific foundation that exists in behavioural science, which is modern Darwinism.

A third reason for attempting such a synthesis is also suggested by the case of Mendel. Psychology is critically important to the application of Darwinian insights to human behaviour, as most modern Darwinists agree. Just as Darwinism had to have a correct understanding of genetics to make its claims to explain evolution in general credible, so Darwinian attempts to explain human behaviour in particular cannot do without the right psychology. So the third, final and most important justification for a Freud-Darwin synthesis comparable to that of Mendelian genetics and Darwinian evolution achieved earlier this century is that it could hold the key to the ultimate problem for evolutionary explanation – human behaviour.

With one or two notable exceptions, modern Darwinism has become associated with the so-called 'elastic leash' model of how genes control behaviour. According to this view, incest (to take the prime example) is avoided by a genetically-determined mechanism that pulls individuals away from committing it rather as someone walking a dog might pull it away from something by means of the leash. Apologists for this view are quick to point out that the leash is highly elastic and that, as in the real world of dog-walking, environmental factors can intervene to frustrate the effects of the leash. Nevertheless, the model is one of fairly straightforward genetic determinism, albeit with an elastic fudge-factor built in.

The model of human behaviour found in Freud is quite different, and much more dynamic. Later chapters will be devoted to explaining this model of the mind (which some modern Darwinists have also advocated[1]). Its main virtue is that it is not one of relatively simple, if flexible, determinism. On the contrary, Freud found human nature to be fundamentally *ambivalent*: that is, riven by deep conflicts of feeling and contradictory intentions. Such an approach easily explains all the facts about incest and finally solves a strategic problem that has blocked progress in Darwinian thinking about human psychology for a hundred years. The solution suggests that human beings are not like dogs on elastic leashes, but much more like children caught between divorcing parents: now tugged this way by love for one, now that way by feelings for the other, and seldom if ever able to reach a single, settled or static solution. If Darwinism ever expects to be taken seriously by human beings as an explanation of themselves, it will have to incorporate a much more sophisticated psychology than the human-puppet-on-an-elastic-string-pulled-by-genes picture that we have been offered so far.

As I shall now try to show, Freud can provide the psychology that Darwinism needs if it is to explain the particulars of human behaviour just as Mendel, despite first appearances, was able to provide the genetic basis of Darwinism in general. If I am right about it, a new 'modern synthesis' is now needed between Freudian psychology and Darwinian evolution that will connect evolution by natural selection with the complexities of human behaviour just as the earlier synthesis founded it on the principles of genetics. I call this new synthesis *PsychoDarwinism*. My aim in this book is to show how it can be achieved.

Darwinian expressions

Another point worth making about what passes for Darwinian psychology today is that it has little if any connection with Darwin's own psychological writings. The chief of these, *The Expression of the Emotions in Man and Animals,* was published in 1872 and despite being a bestseller at the time was described a century later as a 'historical dead end' and has been almost totally ignored, even by modern Darwinists. Indeed, on the rare occasions when modern works do cite Darwin's book they often get the title wrong, suggesting that their authors have not actually read it. Practically no-one now discusses the content of Darwin's book, perhaps because it is concerned with the emotions – an aspect of behaviour almost totally ignored by twentieth-century academic psychology and seldom considered even by those who regard themselves as Darwinists. So let's begin by correcting a common oversight and consider what Darwin has to say.

Darwin's book is organized around three fundamental principles. The first, the principle of 'serviceable associated habits', is illustrated by this example: 'When a dog approaches a strange . . . man in a savage or hostile frame of mind he walks upright and very stiffly; his head is slightly raised . . . his tail is held erect and quite rigid; the hairs bristle . . . the pricked ears are directed forwards, and the eyes have a fixed stare.' (See figure 1.) 'These actions . . . follow from the dog's intention to attack his enemy, and are thus to a large extent intelligible. As he prepares to spring with a savage growl on his enemy, the canine teeth are uncovered, and the ears are pressed close backwards on the head . . .'[2]

This nicely illustrates the *serviceable* aspect. An example from human behaviour that shows the element of *association* that is often present would be scratching your head when in doubt or perplexed about something. You can't actually relieve such feelings by directly scratching your brain or thoughts in the way in which you might directly relieve itching of the skin by scratching, but Darwin's deduction is that you are acting *as if* you could, and thereby attempting to remedy the feeling of being perplexed. Such an action is serviceable only by way of association. Serviceable associations become *habitual* by normally being expressed in such situations. According to Darwin, a man 'rubs his eyes when perplexed, or gives a little cough when embarrassed, acting in either case as if he felt a slightly uncomfortable sensation in his eyes or windpipe . . .

FIGURE 1: Dog approaching another dog with hostile intentions.
By Mr. Riviere.

A man . . . who vehemently rejects a proposition, will almost certainly shut his eyes or turn away his face; but if he accepts the proposition, he will nod his head in affirmation and open his eyes widely . . . I have noticed that persons in describing a horrid sight often shut their eyes momentarily and firmly, or shake their heads, as if not to see or to drive away something disagreeable; and I have caught myself, when thinking of a dark or horrid spectacle, closing my eyes firmly.'[3]

The Expression of the Emotions in Man and Animals appeared when Sigmund Freud (1856–1939) was still undergoing his secondary education and at a time when Darwin's theories were being widely popularized in the German-speaking world. Writing much later in his *Autobiographical Study,* Freud remarks that 'the theories of Charles Darwin, which were then of topical interest, strongly attracted me, for they held out hopes of an extraordinary advance in our understanding of the world.'[4] By contrast to the main stream of twentieth-century psychology, which ignored Darwin, Freud applied Darwin's principles directly in his treatment of *hysteria* – essentially a state of disordered emotions.

Freud found that 'In taking a verbal expression literally and in feeling the "stab in the heart" or the "slap in the face" after some slighting remark as a real event, the hysteric is not taking liberties with words, but is simply reviving once more the sensations to which the verbal expression owes its justification. How has it come about,' he asks, 'that we speak of someone who has been slighted as being "stabbed to the heart" unless the slight had in fact been accompanied by a sensation in the region of the heart which could suitably be described in that phrase and unless it was identifiable by that sensation?' Freud replies to this rhetorical question with examples similar to those of Darwin quoted just now: 'What could be more probable than that the figure of speech "swallowing something", which we use in talking of an insult to which no rejoinder has been made, did in fact originate from . . . sensations which arise in the throat when we refrain from speaking and prevent ourselves from reacting to an insult?' Freud leaves the reader in no doubt that he has Darwin's book in mind when he adds that, 'All these sensations and innervations belong to the field of "The Expression of the Emotions", which, as Darwin has taught us, consists of actions which originally had a meaning and served a purpose. These may now for the most part have become so much weakened that the expression of them in words seems to us only to be a figurative picture of them, whereas in all probability the description was once meant literally.'[5]

So much for Darwin's first principle. As to the second, let's return to the dog illustrated in figure 1 and 'suppose that the dog suddenly discovers that the man he is approaching, is not a stranger, but his master; and let it be observed how completely and instantaneously his whole bearing is reversed.' (See figure 2.)

'Instead of walking upright, the body sinks downwards or even crouches, and is thrown into flexuous movements; his tail . . . is lowered and wagged from side to side; his hair instantly becomes smooth; his ears are depressed and drawn backwards . . . and his lips hang loosely.' In other words, the reactions of a friendly dog, unlike those of a hostile one, are not directly intelligible in terms of what Darwin called serviceable actions, such as a readiness to attack an enemy, but 'are explicable . . . solely from being in complete opposition or antithesis to the attitude and movements which . . . are assumed when a dog intends to fight, and which consequently are expressive of anger'.[6] This constitutes the principle of *antithesis*.

Freud observed something similar in one of his hysterical patients. This was a woman among whose symptoms were '*tic*-like movements, such as clacking with the tongue and stammering, calling out the name "Emmy . . . Keep still! Don't say anything! Don't touch me!"' Freud

FIGURE 2: Dog approaching another dog in a humble and affectionate
frame of mind. By Mr. Riviere.

found that these symptoms were the result of 'the putting into effect of
antithetical ideas . . . Our hysterical patient, exhausted by worry and
long hours of watching by the bedside of her sick child which had at
last fallen asleep, said to herself: "Now you must be perfectly still so as
not to awaken the child."' According to Freud, 'This intention probably
gave rise to an antithetical idea in the form of a fear that she might
make a noise all the same that would wake the child from the sleep
which she had so long hoped for.' Furthermore, 'In our patient's state
of exhaustion the antithetic idea, which was normally rejected, proved
itself the stronger. It is this idea which put itself into effect and which,
to the patient's horror, actually produced the noise she dreaded.'[7]

The mechanism of antithesis in human psychology comes out most
clearly in what Freud would later term *reaction-formation*. A graphic
example was once recounted to me by Anna Freud. She had analyzed
a young woman who had come to treatment following an incident in
the street. The woman was responsible for her aged mother's care, and
had taken her out one bitterly cold winter's day. Passers-by had called
the police when she was seen to be wrapping scarves and mufflers so
tightly around her mother's neck that the old lady was turning blue
from asphyxiation! Yet the dutiful daughter was adamant that all she
intended was to protect her mother from the cold. Analysis revealed
latent death-wishes against the aged parent, who was robbing her

daughter of her youth and opportunity to live a life of her own. The conscious wish to save her mother from the cold stood in antithesis to the latent wish that her mother should be dead much as the tail-wagging of a dog signals the antithesis of the antagonism represented by its opposite. But in this case the action of winding things around the old lady's neck found a motive in both antithetical ideas: consciously and subjectively it expressed caring, protective behaviour, but unconsciously and in its objective effects it represented an attempted strangulation.

Freud's chief insight into the mystery of hysteria was a direct extension of Darwin's third principle of the expression of emotion. This Darwin attributed to 'direct action of the excited nervous system on the body independently of the will, and independently, in large part, of habit. According to Darwin, 'The frantic and senseless actions of an enraged man may be attributed in part to the undirected flow of nerve-force.'[8] Darwin gives many other examples of this third principle, including a lot more from human experience, ranging from trembling with fear, to perspiration, palpitation, blushing, laughter and crying. Although many of these expressions involve elements of the first two principles, their particular intensity often derives from what Darwin called 'nerve force generated in excess'.

Freud thought that it was a comparable excess generation of nerve-force independent of consciousness that underlay the symptoms of hysterics. 'Some of the striking motor phenomena' exhibited by the patient mentioned above

> were simply an expression of the emotions and could easily be recognised in that light. Thus, the way in which she stretched her hands in front of her with her fingers spread out and crooked expressed horror, and similarly her facial play . . . Others of her motor symptoms were, according to herself, directly related to her pains. She played restlessly with her fingers or rubbed her hands against one another so as to prevent herself from screaming. This reason reminds one forcibly of one of the principles laid down by Darwin to explain the expression of the emotions – the principle of the overflow of excitation . . . We are all of us accustomed, when we are affected by painful stimuli, to replace screaming by other sorts of motor innervations. A person who has made up his mind at the dentist's to keep his head and

mouth still and not to put his hand in the way, may at least start drumming with his feet.[9]

These examples show that Freud, by contrast to most twentieth-century psychology, was heavily indebted to Darwin. Indeed, according to a recent study, 'psychologists did not see it as their task to investigate the mind at all in the way that Darwin did . . . Behaviourism turned its back on all such studies; the belief was that if we were ultimately to understand our minds, it would only be through understanding our behaviour. A Darwinian psychological approach goes in exactly the opposite direction; the adaptive significance of our behaviour may be obscure but we have some hope of understanding it by understanding our minds.'[10] In 'tracing the legacy of natural selection' in human nature Darwin

> didn't do it in the style in which today's Darwinians typically go about it. But his approach could turn out to be a fruitful way for us to study ourselves. It is what we might nowadays characterize . . . as 'psychological' rather than 'ethological' or 'sociological'. Darwin is interested in our emotions rather than our actions. Whereas the majority of today's Darwinian investigations of human nature might look at the incidence of homosexual behaviour, comparative divorce rates, social hierarchies, aggressive encounters, family relationships, Darwin was more interested in feelings, in feelings of love and hate, of jealousy and generosity, of pride and shame, or resentment and gratitude, of sympathy and spite.[11]

Such an understanding of the mind, with an emphasis on the emotions, is also characteristic of Freud. Indeed, I would claim that Freud's psychology was much closer to Darwin's own approach than is that of present-day Darwinian psychologists. The latter share the mainly cognitive bias of academic psychology and seldom if ever consider the emotions in the way in which Darwin or Freud did. PsychoDarwinism represents a natural synthesis of two very similar views of human nature, both of which stressed the emotions, and both of which attempted to understand human behaviour by first understanding the mechanisms of the mind.

It has been the Freudian tradition in psychology, rather than any other, that has followed Darwin's example of observing infants as a means of studying the expression of the emotions. Indeed, psychoanalysis has institutionalized it to the extent that today observation of infants is a requirement of psychoanalytic training and a whole subdiscipline of child psychoanalysis has emerged. Darwin also suggested that a prime insight into the expression of the emotions could be gained through studies of the insane. Here no-one could deny that Freud and his followers in the psychoanalytic movement have been at the forefront of attempts to understand mental illness and to establish new standards of humane treatment. Freud had a unique opportunity to observe the mind in both its normal and abnormal states as recommended by Darwin. Indeed, Freud's study of Michelangelo's *Moses* fulfilled Darwin's disappointed hope of also enlisting 'the great masters in painting and sculpture, who are such close observers'.[12] Writers on Freud have made much of his motives in undertaking this short study, and perhaps they have a point. But anyone familiar with *Expression of the Emotions* would immediately recognize it as precisely what Darwin had in mind, concerned as it is with the interpretation of the complex emotions expressed in that great work of sculpture.

In later chapters we shall see that the one or two modern psychologists apart from Freud who have continued the Darwinian tradition in psychology have made advances that, when placed in the setting of our best current understanding of the evolution of behaviour, converge on Freud's principal discovery – the dynamic unconscious. We shall see that the expression of the emotions (or rather, the need *not* to express them so as to deceive others) is the key to solving the riddle of consciousness, and that Freud's model of the mind lends itself surprisingly well to a modern Darwinian view of our psychology. But before we consider that, there is another, preliminary issue that must be considered.

Lamarckian stigma

According to present-day thinking, there are two principal theories of evolution: that of Charles Darwin and that of Jean-Baptiste Antoine de Monet (1744–1829), better known to us as Lamarck. Darwin's theory is based on the principle of natural selection and is demonstrably correct. Lamarck's theory is based on the inheritance of acquired characteristics, which is now known to be false. Freud was a lifelong believer in the inheritance of acquired characteristics. Therefore Freud's evolutionary thinking is wrong, and anything but Darwinian. According to this view, Freud was a confessed PsychoLamarckian, and most certainly not a PsychoDarwinist.

Let's put the question of Freud's so-called 'Lamarckism' on one side for a moment and concentrate on Darwin. There is some considerable truth in the view that Darwin's and Lamarck's theories of evolution are completely different and that modern research has vindicated Darwin, but discredited Lamarck. Nevertheless, a serious confusion has occurred over what is meant by the term 'Lamarckism'.

If we ask what Darwin understood by the term, we find Lamarck writing as follows: 'If an animal, for the satisfaction of its needs, makes repeated efforts to lengthen its tongue, it will acquire a considerable length (anteater, green woodpecker); if it requires to seize anything with this same organ, its tongue will then divide and become forked.'[13] This is completely different from Darwin's own theory of evolution by natural selection, which does not involve any such willing or effort to evolve.

Exactly the same is true of another aspect of Lamarckism that Darwin regarded as 'nonsense': his belief in the inevitability of organic 'progress' towards some 'higher', 'more advanced' or 'superior' forms. Darwin was far too knowledgeable a naturalist to be able to credit such a view and explicitly denied that any particular kind of progress was implied by the theory of natural selection (see below, pp. 27–9). So far, it seems, the modern view that Darwin and Lamarck are implacably opposed is wholly correct.

What people today actually mean when they speak of Freud's Lamarckism is not evolution-by-the-will-with-inevitable-progress, but his belief in the inheritance of acquired characteristics. Because this belief has been discredited by modern genetic research, it is assumed to be contrary to Darwin's own view. Freud's stubborn belief in it is conventionally regarded as proving that his theories are wrong, have nothing to do with Darwin, and should be rejected. But this overlooks the important fact that, if Freud was a 'Lamarckian' because he believed in the inheritance of acquired characteristics, then so too was Darwin.

Indeed, Darwin went out of his way to emphasize his Lamarckism in this respect, remarking that 'even in the first edition of the "Origin of Species," I distinctly stated that great weight must be attributed to the inherited effects of use and disuse, with respect both to the body and the mind'.[14] In *The Descent of Man* he claimed that 'some intelligent actions – as when birds on oceanic islands first learn to avoid man – after being performed during many generations, become converted into instincts and are inherited'. He also believed that 'the vocal organs would have been strengthened and perfected through the principle of the inherited effects of use'.[15]

Even when Darwin did mention natural selection in this context, it appears only as an alternative to Lamarckian evolution: 'some instincts have been developed simply through long-continued and inherited habit, other highly complex ones have been developed through the preservation of various pre-existing instincts – that is, through natural selection'. But notwithstanding this recognition of natural selection, he candidly admits to seeing no real alternative to Lamarckism where habitual actions are concerned: 'That some physical change is produced in the nerve cells or nerves which are habitually used can hardly be doubted, for otherwise it is impossible to understand how the tendency to certain acquired movements is inherited'.[16]

Despite ridiculing Lamarck's concept of evolution-by-will where physical adaptations like tongues or necks are concerned, Darwin seems to credit the idea where psychological factors are concerned, explicitly stating regarding instincts that 'it was necessary to show that at least some of them might have been first acquired through the will in order to satisfy a desire, or to relieve a disagreeable sensation'.[17] His observations of one of his own children even led him to 'suspect that the vague and very real fears of children, which are quite independent of experience, are inherited effects of real dangers and abject superstitions during ancient savage times.'[18]

Given Darwin's belief in the inheritance of acquired characteristics, and given that psychological factors like instincts or reflexes are demonstrably inherited, it did not seem absurd to say that they must first have been acquired before they could be inherited and to assume that, before they were inherited as instincts or reflexes, they were intentional acts. Darwin explicitly states this when he says that 'it seems probable that some actions, which were at first performed consciously, have become through habit and association converted into reflex actions, and are now firmly fixed and inherited'. Only when an originally voluntary action had become converted into an inherited reflex through frequent repetition did Darwin see the mechanism of natural selection taking a hand in its evolution by way of preserving variations of it that were beneficial.[19]

It begins to seem, then, that Darwin was not merely a 'Lamarckian' if we take that term to mean a believer in the inheritance of acquired characteristics, but that, at least where psychological factors were concerned, he was even an evolution-by-will Lamarckian. Whereas it seemed patently absurd to him to believe that a long tongue evolves because an animal wills its tongue to become longer, it did seem credible to him that willed actions such as avoiding painful stimuli might eventually become inherited reflexes. Just wishing you were thinner when you see yourself in the mirror cannot have a direct effect on your body fat. But if you decide to go on a diet, that exercise in will-power can make you slimmer – at least if you stick to it. Intention can produce direct results in behaviour in a way it never can in body parts like fat or tongues. This is probably the reason why Darwin's Lamarckism is much more prominent in *The Expression of the Emotions* than in any other of his works and why he explicitly accepts evolution by will as well as the inheritance of acquired characteristics in his psychological writings. Indeed, this may be one of the chief reasons why Darwin's work on the emotions is so often cited, but so seldom read or quoted. It may be that the unmistakable Lamarckism of his psychological writing makes his book on the emotions seem strange and dated, and best passed over in silence by modern writers who conceive of Darwinism and Lamarckism as mutually exclusive.

As far as Darwin's belief in the inheritance of acquired characteristics is concerned, the obvious explanation of this is that in Darwin's lifetime the true nature of inheritance was still obscure, thanks to the fact that Mendel's discovery of the laws of genetics remained unknown to the wider world until after the turn of the century. In Darwin's day a belief in the inheritance of acquired characteristics would not have struck anyone as distinctive of Lamarck, because it was so widely believed, and had been so since time immemorial. Only in the twentieth century, following Weismann's realization that an organism's genetic endowment could not be changed by its body or experiences, did the meaning of the term 'Lamarckism' begin to undergo the change that has resulted in it coming to be primarily associated with the doctrine of the inheritance of acquired characteristics. But Weismann's position was at first widely rejected in favour of the traditional view, and by no means immediately accepted. To Darwin and to Freud, 'Lamarckism' meant evolution-by-the-will-with-progressive-improvement, *not* the inheritance of acquired characteristics that it usually means today.

If we now finally turn to Freud, and ask where all this leaves him, we can clearly see that his much despised and denigrated inheritance-of-acquired-characteristics Lamarckism is yet another feature that unites him with Darwin. Far from putting him in a different tradition of evolutionary thinking as has often been supposed in recent years, Freud's 'Lamarckism' in fact places him squarely in the tradition of Darwin's own writing on evolution and psychology. Indeed, historical research has shown that Freud acquired his characteristic Lamarckism from the writings of Darwin, and not from those of Lamarck. Rejecting Freud because his thinking on evolution is contrary to that of Darwin is, therefore, a perverse judgement if Darwin's own writings are taken into account. On the contrary, we might more accurately conclude that Freud's psychological work resembles Darwin's in a further way that distinguishes it from other schools of thought in our century: by being Lamarckian, at least in the sense in which that term is normally understood today.

Of course, it is true that Darwin died in 1882, when Mendel's discovery of the laws of genetics was still unknown to the wider world. Freud, by contrast, died in 1939, at much the same time that Darwinism and Mendelism were being unified in the 'modern synthesis' that I mentioned at the beginning. However, Freud lost contact with mainstream biology at much the same time that he began to develop his distinctive psychological researches. And as I mentioned earlier, even when Mendelism was rediscovered early in the twentieth century, it was at first taken to discredit Darwin, rather than to vindicate him. Only after the decisive unification of Mendelian genetics with natural selection in the 1930s did the realization begin to dawn on the wider public that inheritance of acquired characteristics was no longer a tenable scientific belief. But by this time Freud was in his seventies and eighties. Since then, Darwin has been forgiven his Lamarckism, but Freud's has been left hanging, albatross-like, around his neck.

The reason for this is that Darwin's work has become part of the modern synthesis of evolution by natural selection and Mendelian genetics, but Freud's has not as yet undergone any such scientific refurbishment. The effect of the modern synthesis on our perception of

Darwin has been to clear away his many personal confusions about how heredity and selection worked and to erect in its place a new, clarified version of his fundamental insight that today we think of as 'Darwinism'. The fact that Darwin evidently believed that a woman's children by a second husband could inherit characteristics of her first does not prevent us from thinking nowadays that modern genetics is an integral part of Darwinism.[20] Well may modern Darwinists knowingly remark that 'Lamarckians are traditionally fond of calluses' (because calluses can be acquired and seemingly inherited), and then contrast this with the 'Darwinian' who 'has a ready answer' in terms of natural selection (as opposed to the inheritance of acquired characteristics).[21] But the truth is that Darwin himself was not ready with such an answer. On the contrary, his own response was the traditional Lamarckian one: 'In infants long before birth', he wrote, 'the skin on the soles of the feet is thicker than on any other part of the body; and it can hardly be doubted that this is due to the inherited effects of pressure during a long series of generations.'[22]

Darwin, it seems, was not as Darwinian as modern Darwinists might have wished him to have been. We forgive, forget and overlook Darwin's own errors and confusions because we find his fundamental insight into natural selection to be correct, and with the benefit of hindsight see how profoundly well it agrees with modern knowledge that he never had. But we should not lose sight of the fact that Darwin's own views were not always as Darwinian as they could have been. On the contrary, we can now see that the antithesis between 'Darwinism' and 'Lamarckism' that is so often used to discredit Freud is a very recent creation and that historically things were not so straightforward.

Of course, I am not trying to imply that because Freud resembled Darwin in his Lamarckism Freud was any less wrong. Clearly, both Freud and Darwin were misled by Lamarckism. What I am trying to point out is that to dismiss Freud merely because he is stigmatized as 'Lamarckian' in certain respects is no more fair to him that it would be to dismiss Darwin's *Expression of the Emotions in Man and Animals* just because it is similarly Lamarckian in presentation. If we are prepared to make allowances for Darwin in this respect I see no reason why we should not make similar ones for Freud. Darwin's work on the emotions is of value as a wonderfully closely observed study of the subject, despite its blatant Lamarckism. In my view, similar remarks apply to Freud.

Indeed, they apply even more to Freud because Freud's Lamarckism is nothing like as central to the main body of his work as Darwin's is to his writings on psychology. As in the case of Darwin's study of the emotions, it may be that Freud's descriptive findings are far more important than his theories about them. To dismiss all of Freud merely because its author can be convicted on a charge of Lamarckism seems hasty, to say the least.

Freud's Lamarckism and confusion over the whole question of evolution make the agreement between his findings and some of the most counter-intuitive insights of recent Darwinism all the more astonishing. They suggest that, far from being the unscientific, crack-pot theorist that he is often taken to be, Freud may have been the discoverer of major new facts about human behaviour whose true interpretation had to await theoretical advances in biology that were not to take place until he had been dead for several decades. The first two chapters will be devoted to explaining these developments. Only when Darwin is correctly understood is it possible to begin to grasp the true insights of Freud.

UNIVERSAL DARWINISM

Evolution by natural selection – the essence of Darwinism – is one of the simplest and most elegant scientific ideas ever conceived. Yet, perhaps for that reason, it has also been one of the most extensively misunderstood and misrepresented. PsychoDarwinism is even more likely to be misconstrued if the fundamental Darwinian mechanism on which it is based is not correctly understood. My aim in this chapter is to explain the key concept of Darwinism, evolution by natural selection, as clearly as I can. I shall do so in the first place by giving an example of natural selection in a context that is completely different from the one in which we might normally expect to meet it. In the second part I shall show why many of the assumptions and associations that people make in connection with Darwinism are misplaced, and in no way essential to the fundamental principle. Finally, we shall see how natural selection can be applied to solving the mystery of the evolution of very complex and improbable structures, such as living organisms. Darwin's key discovery involves more than merely presenting a theory about the evolution of life on earth and becomes an insight into a much more basic concept. This is what we might term *universal Darwinism*. By this I mean evolution by natural selection independent of organisms and local conditions – Darwinism as a universal truth.

Automatic evolution

A major problem that stands in the way of anyone who attempts to explain Darwinism is that everyone already knows so much about it – or, at least, thinks that they do. Darwinism, after all, has been with us since 1859, and has been controversial throughout. The result is that Darwin is a household name, and has its own set of automatic associations. One of the most common of these is the phrase, 'survival of the fittest'. This is often ascribed to Darwin, and still widely believed to sum up the essential idea of natural selection. But 'survival of the fittest' was coined by Herbert Spencer (1820–1903), not by Darwin. It has all kinds of unfortunate associations, and like so many other recieved ideas about evolution, is likely to mislead much more than it is to inform. Nor is this an isolated or untypical example. Over the course of time Darwin's supremely simple idea has acquired accretions and additions of all kinds that obscure it almost to the point of invisibility.

As a result, there is a need to get back to the essentials of the idea in a way that avoids these distracting and misleading augmentations. One way to do this is to abstract the fundamental logic of Darwin's insight and to simulate it in a medium that is ideally suited to the task. This can be done by modelling the basic mechanism of evolution by natural selection on a computer. By removing it from its more familiar context, evolution by natural selection can then be seen in its pure form, purged of the distracting clutter that has collected around it for over a hundred and fifty years.

One of the best computer simulations from this point of view is

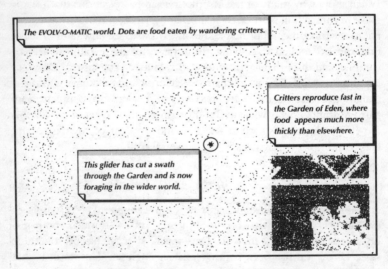

FIGURE 3: Glider and jitter-critters forage in the EVOLV-O-MATIC world.

called EVOLV-O-MATIC. Thanks to its simplicity it is ideally suited to demonstrate the essentials of evolution by natural selection. In EVOLV-O-MATIC, the world is represented by the computer screen and food appears in the form of black dots. Figure 3 illustrates an EVOLV-O-MATIC world that is divided into two regions: the larger part, in which food dots appear randomly at a constant rate, and a 'Garden of Eden' in the bottom right-hand corner. Here a food dot appears for each one in the larger world, making this a much more densely provisioned region, given its smaller area. The EVOLV-O-MATIC world is inhabited by 'critters', little bug-like creatures who move about and eat food dots as they pass over them. Such critters can be seen in figure 3 and in enlarged form in figure 4. Food eaten adds to the critter's energy, which is then spent in moving and reproducing. Reproduction occurs when the energy level of a critter reaches a critical level, death occurs when it falls to zero.

Each critter has a set of 'genes' that control its movement. Offspring inherit the genes of the parent, except in one value that is randomly varied, thereby introducing what we might term 'mutations'. Figure 4 illustrates the movement genes of critters in the EVOLV-O-MATIC world depicted in figure 3. The numbers associated with each arrow can vary from 0 to 15 and represent the probability that the critter will choose that direction next after the one in which it is currently moving. On the left of figure 4 are the movement genes of the critter in the middle of figure 3. The high value in one direction and the one-sidedness this gives to the weighting of its movement means that this is what we might call a 'glider'. Gliders tend to run in long, straight lines until hitting the edge of the world and being reflected off it. For example,

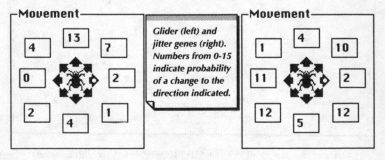

FIGURE 4: Glider and jitter genes.

figure 3 shows that this glider has cut a number of long, straight swathes through the Garden of Eden. On the right of figure 4 are the movement genes of one of the critters in the bottom right-hand corner of figure 3. The much more even spread of values right around the clock indicates that this is what we might term a 'jitter-critter'. The high probability that it will change to another direction after any particular one means that it is likely to turn repeatedly, rather than favour any one particular direction for any length of time.

Figure 3 illustrates an early stage in an EVOLV-O-MATIC simulation, with just one glider and six jitter-critters. Figure 5 shows a much later stage in the same simulation. The original glider has reproduced, and so too have the jitter-critters, producing two, almost evenly balanced populations: gliders who roam over the whole world with relatively straight paths, and jitter-critters who appear to be confined to the paradise in the bottom right-hand corner. But how did these two populations arise in the first place? Clearly, there are three possibilities: because a user has to set up the EVOLV-O-MATIC world in the first instance, we know that I created the Garden of Eden.

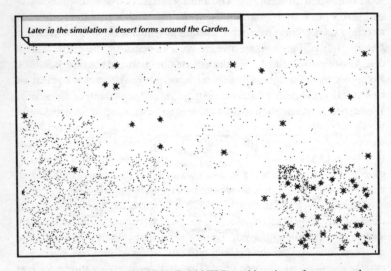

Later in the simulation a desert forms around the Garden.

FIGURE 5: A later EVOLV-O-MATIC world: a desert forms around the Garden of Eden.

This means that I might also have created two original critters, one with genes set for gliding and one with genes set for jittering. We might call this 'special creation'. Alternatively, I could have set up the world but merely created critters at random positions in it and with randomly determined genes. If so, there are a further two ways in which I may have arrived at the outcome observed. I could have simply killed off any randomly occurring critter that did not fit my requirements for gliding and jittering by way of the symbolic thumb that EVOLV-O-MATIC obligingly provides for the purpose. This we could call 'artificial selection'.

However, I could have saved myself the trouble of such culling and left critters to fend for themselves. Experiment shows that this usually has the observed result: the more jittery critters tend soon to expire in the wider world because they quickly exhaust the food dots around them. But any critters lucky enough to find themselves in the Garden of Eden survive because the food there is so much more concentrated. Indeed, only really jittery critters have any long-term hope of survival and reproduction there because any tendency to range more widely will sooner or later take them out of paradise and into the sparser, wider world, where they are likely to starve. This explains the appearance of the 'desert' around the Garden in figure 5. This is caused by the intense foraging of jitter-critters that spill out of the richer area of the Garden but soon exhaust the more meagre food resources around it and then die. Exactly the reverse applies to critters with gliding proclivities. Because they tend to range far and wide, they survive well, getting a bonus when they enter paradise, but surviving perfectly well outside it. We might call this possibility 'natural selection', because in this case it would have been the naturally occurring conditions in the world that would have determined the outcome, rather than any conscious intention on my part. It would be a kind of 'automatic' selection – a form of evolution that came about spontaneously, without any intention of any kind, but simply as a result of the given conditions.

The important point to notice here is that the reader has no way of determining which of the three – special creation, artificial or natural selection – actually occurred. This is because the outcome – one type of critter 'adapted' to the Garden and one to the rest of the world – is exactly the same in all three cases. In other words, what might look at first sight like conscious design could just as easily be the outcome of selection, and that selection could equally well have been artificial or natural.

So which was it? Indeed, is there any way in which the reader could know how the EVOLV-O-MATIC world illustrated was produced in the first place? Clearly, the answer lies in the *history* of the world in question. If my readers could examine the past of this EVOLV-O-MATIC world they could easily establish what occurred. In the case of special creation they would see two critters created by design. In the case of selection, they would see many random critters appear. If selection were artificial they would see unwanted critters being intentionally exterminated until only the desired ones remained. If selection were natural they would see critters perish without outside intervention until only two remained who were able to survive: the ancestral glider and jitterer.

In fact, the history of the EVOLV-O-MATIC world illustrated would show that it was the outcome of natural selection. I created nineteen critters at random, of which seventeen soon perished without progeny. This is because most were fairly jittery in behaviour, given that movement genes are determined by chance and so tend to make critters move randomly. Since starting position is also a question of luck, the odds are stacked against a critter being created in the Garden of Eden. However, one that did appear there survived and reproduced, thanks to the lush food supply. Soon afterwards, a glider chanced to appear in the wider world and survived, thanks to its wide-ranging pattern of foraging.

From this we can conclude that, although the outcomes of special creation and natural or artificial selection may be indistinguishable in the sense that all three result in critters apparently 'designed', 'adapted' or 'fitted' for their way of life, an examination of the history of the world ought to settle the matter decisively: if special creation is the explanation, a single creation-event can be predicted producing critters designed to survive. If artificial selection had occurred I would be seen intentionally culling many randomly-created critters. Finally, if natural selection had occurred, a probably protracted period of apparently wasteful random creation had to take place before natural conditions weeded out all of those save the survivors observed.

What I am calling artificial selection here is in fact very similar to what human beings do when they intentionally breed organisms or selectively cull them. As to the two other possibilities, Creationists believe in special creation, with organisms being purposely 'designed' for the world by some creator. Darwinists, on the other hand, appeal to the hard evidence of fossils to justify their conclusion that there is a history of apparently wasteful evolutionary development prior to the present. For them natural selection, rather than divine creation, explains the evolution of all organisms, including human beings.

But applying natural selection to our own evolution raises an emotional obstacle that ought to be mentioned. This becomes immediately clear if we imagine ourselves as critters for a moment. Special creation is fine, even flattering – how nice to think that you were designed specially for the world by the creator! This makes you feel good about yourself and about the creator who created you. You see yourself as a designer-organism, specially crafted for existence by a higher being. But natural selection is an outrage. If we were critters ourselves we would be shocked by my wanton destruction of life. We would want to know why I could not have created two critters for certain survival, rather than mindlessly make nineteen of which seventeen were doomed to die. And even if you are one of the lucky survivors, this makes life into a lottery, with natural factors quite beyond your control deciding the outcome.

Of course, we are not critters, and so this may seem ridiculous. Where simulated creatures on computer screens are concerned, we can be wholly objective. But where our own creation is at issue, things are different. Here we may not be so unemotional and, if asked to believe in natural selection, might easily react like my imaginary critters. This probably explains much of the appeal of Creationism in particular and non-Darwinian ideas about evolution in general. But the reason for this might simply be that our emotions evolved to equip us for survival, just as we have seen critters' genes do. This might make us value our own existence above all else and resist anything that appeared to disparage it, as evolution by natural selection might seem to do. Our need to safeguard our own survival might lead us to place a much higher valuation on our lives and see much more significance in them than was objectively justified. Our response to Darwin's insight into evolution, in other words, is probably in part an evolved one – and almost certainly is in so far as it expresses our emotions about it. Paradoxically, evolution by natural selection may have created emotional resistances to

23

the understanding of itself in our minds, and this may be a major psychological obstacle that Darwinism has to overcome.

But the paradox is more apparent than real. This is because natural selection is not concerned with making itself understood to human beings. On the contrary, the problem is making human beings understand natural selection, and here emotional repugnance may be an additional difficulty. But this is only part of the problem. As we shall now see, positive as well as negative feelings have led people astray where questions of evolution are concerned, and nowhere more so than where they concern our place in nature.

Evolution without the F-word

Another common reaction to the emotional shock of evolution is not to deny that natural (as opposed to supernatural) agencies created us, but to believe that evolution is an improving or perfecting mechanism, one that produces species progressively 'more fit', 'more advanced' or 'more highly evolved' than others. Like special creation, these value-judgements make you feel special and superior if you can convince yourself that you are one of the supreme achievements of progressive evolution. And if you are a human being this is easy. The fact that your species may have evolved only very recently and may rely on many others 'below' it in the evolutionary scale appears to underline the correctness of this conclusion: human beings are the ultimate species, the 'fittest', 'most highly evolved' and 'best adapted' of all! Even though you may not be able to bring yourself to believe that you were specially created for the world, you can at least see yourself as a supreme achievement of evolution understood as a progressive, perfecting mechanism. Indeed, with no creator to provide competition, you can regard yourself as a veritable god of creation, the supreme being and ultimate end of evolution!

But however that may be, I doubt if our EVOLV-O-MATIC simulation would suggest to anyone the idea that gliders were 'better', 'more fit', or 'more evolved' than jitter-critters, or vice versa. 'Fitness' in particular is a term that evolution by natural selection can do without. The problem with it is that it has all the wrong connotations. 'Fit' suggests in the first place the idea of organisms being crafted by evolution to match a natural setting like a statue might be designed to fit a niche on a building. In nature such niches are seldom completely static, and an important part of the environment is the presence of other organisms.

The world illustrated in figures 3 and 5 provides an excellent example. It started off with two founding individuals, a glider and a jitter-critter. At first, gliders proliferated in the wider world and jitterers were restricted to the Garden of Eden. However, the original glider and jitterer were not extreme examples of their type and before long a number of gliders mutated in the jittery direction and became confined to the Garden of Eden by the desert. (Readers will recall that one gene varies every time a critter reproduces, thereby producing variation on which selection can act.) These ex-gliders continued to mutate in paradise and eventually out-reproduced the original jitter-critters. Some of the original jitterers, by contrast, found themselves in relatively lush areas of the wider world where they survived long enough for natural selection to act on them in the reverse direction, and eventually their descendants began to glide much better than the original gliders, whom they gradually displaced. Eventually the populations or species reversed: jitter-mutants had now become the gliders, and glider-mutants the jitterers. Had the other species not been present to compete with it, each could probably have produced perfectly viable jitter and glider subspecies. But competition from better adapted individuals of the other species led to a reversal of rôles, with jitterers eventually becoming the gliders and vice versa.

Today all animals depend on oxygen in the atmosphere in order to breathe. But most of that oxygen was not there in the beginning, when the earth first formed. The oxygen we breathe is in reality an atmospheric pollutant released by green plants. It is a dangerous, reactive gas that causes fires, rust and oxidation of all kinds. If all life vanished from earth today it could not begin again spontaneously as it almost certainly did in the past, thanks to the destructive effects of oxygen, which would immediately react with the basic elements of biochemistry to abort the rebirth of life. The atmosphere, to take only one part of our environment, is not a pre-existing niche into which life has been designed to 'fit' like a glove on a hand, but rather something that life itself has profoundly altered.

A second unfortunate connotation of the words 'fit' and 'fitness' is with personal health and vigour. It suggests that natural selection makes organisms more fit in the sense in which a healthy person is more fit than a sick one or in which regular exercise might make someone fitter.

To an extent natural selection does do this, but the problem is that individual fitness is not what evolution by natural selection is all about, despite Herbert Spencer's slogan, 'survival of the fittest'. The bottom line for evolution by natural selection is not the 'fitness' of the individual organism, but that organism's ultimate reproductive success. No organism, however individually fit it might be and however perfected might be its personal health and vigour, could affect the outcome of evolution by natural selection if it could not pass on the determinants of its success to its offspring by way of its *reproductive* success.

Admittedly, individual fitness in the sporting or medical sense is often important in contributing to an organism's reproductive success, but the fact remains that reproductive success is all that matters as far as evolution by natural selection is concerned. Fitness is a means to an end, not an end of evolution in itself. To that extent, 'survival of the fittest' is a misleading and unfortunate phrase. Indeed, this is why 'fitness' in Darwinian writing has had to be defined as a technical term, and qualified by adjectives like 'Darwinian', 'true' or 'heritable'. But for our purposes the terms 'fit' and 'fitness' – the F-words of evolution – are best avoided altogether and the much more accurate phrase, 'reproductive success' substituted instead. This is the usage I shall follow in this book, the justification being that this is how natural selection itself operates.

What EVOLV-O-MATIC demonstrates most clearly is that natural selection is ultimately and only a question of differential reproductive success. Furthermore, this is a *quantitative* measure, not a qualitative one. What the evolution of our gliders and jitterers showed was that what was actually evolving was not the critters themselves so much as the genes that controlled their movement. Selection selected for these and these alone because it was only these numerical values that distinguished critters one from another. Indeed, our critters were in reality little more than combinations of numbers that determined the behaviour of each particular critter.

As a manner of speaking we may wish to call gliders 'better' at foraging than jitter-critters in the wider EVOLV-O-MATIC world. But we could equally well call jitterers 'better' than gliders in the Garden of Eden. Such comparisons are purely relative and ultimately founded on quantitative values that are objective facts, not subjective value-judgements. Indeed, we could even say that gliders were 'more independent', 'more adventurous' or 'more courageous' than jitterers. But again, this prejudicial, anthropomorphic way of speaking would only have objective meaning by way of the objective, quantitative fact on which it was based. And certainly, we would not be in any way encouraged to see gliders or jitter-critters as 'more highly evolved' or 'superior' to each other in any kind of absolute terms – particularly when, as in the simulation recounted above, one species evolved into the other and vice versa.

Unfortunately, confusion on this point affects many who should know better. For example, in his recent book, *Wonderful Life,* Stephen Jay Gould quotes Darwin confessing that 'After long reflection, I cannot avoid the conviction that no innate tendency to development exists'. Here Darwin's use of double negatives gives the impression that he was driven to this conclusion against the conventional view of his time, which was highly Progressivist. By this I mean that most Victorians believed along with Herbert Spencer that evolution was an-ever-on-and-upward progress towards something better. Darwin's position could hardly be more clear or his words more categoric. Yet on the next page Gould quotes Darwin again saying that 'The inhabitants of each successive period in the world's history have beaten their predecessors in the race for life, and are, insofar, higher in the scale of nature; and this may account for the vague, yet ill-defined sentiment, felt by many paleontologists, that organization on the whole has progressed.' Gould concludes that Darwin was one of those referred to in this remark, and that he was confused and ambivalent on the issue, pulled one way by 'social preconceptions' to accept Progressivism and pulled the other way by 'the logic of theory' to reject it.[1]

But what Darwin says here need not be interpreted that way. To see why, consider the following analogy. Suppose that you were standing on the stage of a theatre. Outside there is a large crowd of people wanting to get in to see some spectacle. Seats are allocated on a one-price, first-come, first-served basis, and the doors are opened. What will happen? Obviously, the first to get seats will want them at the front of the stalls, normally the most expensive in a theatre. Once these are filled, boxes, and the centre and back stalls will begin to fill, as will the front rows of the dress circle. When stalls, boxes and dress circle are filled, higher circles will be filled, until eventually only the 'gods' – the highest seats, most distant from the stage – will remain. But are the gods the best seats, and would anyone with a free choice choose such a seat? Of course not. The gods only got filled because the rest of the theatre was full already.

This suggests an arresting parallel with evolution, and is the basis of the idea to which Darwin alludes in Gould's quotation. The first comers of organic evolution to the earth found a completely open environment and filled the easiest and most accessible parts first – the equivalent of the stalls in my theatre analogy. These were the first, very simple organisms, descendants of which are still found in vast numbers everywhere on earth. Later comers had to do a little more to survive, so they evolved separate nuclei in their cells, or became multi-cellular – the equivalent of those filling the circles in the theatre analogy. Eventually all these environments were filled and it was more likely than before that large, complex, 'higher' organisms would find new ways of exploiting what remained – often by preying on organisms 'lower' down the scale. Eventually, and very late in evolution in relation to the beginning, human beings, the 'highest' of all organisms, appeared – to occupy the 'gods' in my theatre simile.

The point of this analogy is that no-one standing on the stage and watching such a theatre fill would make the mistake of thinking that higher seats were necessarily 'better' than lower ones. On the contrary, the evidence of their eyes would suggest the opposite: that it was the lower seats in the theatre, those nearer the stage, that were filled first, and the higher ones – including ultimately the gods – were only filled after all the lower ones were taken. In theatres in general the highest seats are simply not the best seats – the lowest ones are.

An objective view of organic evolution on earth would take a similar view. Life evolved into increasingly complex and elaborated forms only because simpler and more fundamental ones had evolved first and had already colonized most of the available environments for such organisms, leaving new-comers to find new, 'more advanced' and usually more complicated ways of existing.

The fact to which Darwin refers in the second quotation, which Gould thinks contradicts the first, is that it is a matter of necessity that complex organisms could only have evolved after simpler ones and that a requirement of natural selection is that survivors should have won out in the struggle for reproductive success over the organisms that they drove to extinction. But Darwin himself was quick to point out that this did not mean that evolution by natural selection *always* produced more complex, or more elaborate organisms. He was fond of quoting the example of the tape-worm as a species that could only have evolved after its hosts came into existence, and in order to exploit them, but that had lost or radically simplified many of the organs that its ancestors possessed. The result is an organism comprising little more than an elementary mouth, digestive system, and attached reproductive organs. Yet such parasites are 'highly evolved' in the sense that they have to be minutely adapted to their hosts, and are often so specialized that they can only exploit one particular species. So to the extent that tape-worms, for example, are adapted to human beings, and could only have evolved their specific adaptations for colonizing human beings after humans evolved, tape-worms are 'more evolved' than we are!

Far from evolution inevitably progressing towards some ultimate goal of undreamt-of complexity and perfection in the distant future, the best of our present knowledge suggests a quite different conclusion: one in which the sun finally depletes its nuclear fuel and begins to expand, ultimately engulfing the earth in approximately five billion years from now. The last organisms alive just before the final incineration are likely to be very similar to those that began it, the simple, unicellular bacteria – in all probability descendants of those that inhabit the deep oceans or live around thermal vents on the ocean floor. Life may well turn full circle in this respect, and if it could be described as having progressed, it would only be in the sense that it had departed from, and then returned to, its beginning.

This is the third and final reason for avoiding the word 'fit' and phrases such as 'survival of the fittest': they suggest value-judgements about the quality of what evolution produces and imply that it is a perfecting mechanism, one that aims to produce superior organisms ever more 'fit' or 'fitted' to their environments than those that went before. Such talk is non-Darwinian and unscientific because based on human, subjective value-judgements, not on objective, quantitative fact. This is important because we can now see that much criticism and prejudice against Darwinian thinking is unjustified, and based on a mistaken view of what the theory actually proposes. Darwinism properly understood can most certainly not be abused to draw purely qualitative value-judgements about individuals, sexes, races or species being 'more advanced', 'more highly evolved', 'more fit' or whatever. On the contrary, an objective, quantitative view would show that, in today's world

29

for example, many of the individuals and populations that enjoy the greatest reproductive success could most certainly not be described as 'the most fit' or 'most advanced' in qualitative terms. Only essentially non-Darwinian Progressivism could be the basis for the false claim that other individuals or populations with lower reproductive success were in some other qualitative sense 'more highly evolved'. Today, those who criticize modern Darwinism for what they imagine to be its implicit value-judgements about individual human beings, races, sexes or species say much more about their own ignorance and prejudice than they do about evolution by natural selection, which they cannot have understood.

Indeed, these criticisms of what people take to be Darwinism are probably the product of Darwinian evolution acting on our emotions to make us value and protect ourselves in competition with others. This is probably the real basis of social, sexual and racial prejudice based on pseudo-Darwinian rationalizations like 'fitness'. Thinking that you are a superior product of evolution may be an outcome of natural selection as it has shaped your subjective feelings about yourself, but it is certainly not an objective judgement that could be defended on scientific grounds. Such subjective value-judgements ought to be seen as expressions of the emotions about man and animals, rather than anything else. With this insight we can instantly dismiss almost a hundred and fifty years of misunderstanding and confusion about Darwinism and simply ignore the sterile controversies to which these errors gave rise. Instead we can go on to a new, deeper insight, one only very recently revealed by computer science, one that shows that Darwin's discovery goes beyond biology to become a much more general principle.

Recycling success

Looked at from the most basic point of view, we could say that EVOLV-O-MATIC was all about designing sets of rules that were most efficient at controlling the movements of critters. The output of these rules is the actual path followed by any particular critter. If I had to write the rules controlling critters' foraging patterns by setting the numerical values of their 'genes' for movement, I could probably quite easily design a glider or a jitterer by giving them values like those seen in figure 4. But if I had to design a glider or a jitter-critter that was better than another glider or jitterer, I might find the problem much more difficult because the difference between two reasonably effective gliders/jitterers would be much more subtle than the difference between any glider and any jitter-critter in general. I would probably have to resort to some quite complex mathematics to be able to predict what kind of critter would be best in competition with other critters of the same kind. At the very least, programming by trial and error would be time-consuming if I had to enter a set of values, try a critter against others, modify the values, and so on.

A much quicker and easier way would be for me to do what I did at the beginning, and merely create a large number of critters with totally random collections of movement genes, and let them compete until the best one emerged. The great advantage of this approach would be that, not only might it be much quicker, but it would not even require me to understand very much about the problem, except how to recognize a winner. Instead of programming my computer to solve complex equations, I could merely run EVOLV-O-MATIC and wait for the winning critters to emerge by natural selection!

The beauty of this idea is that, if it would work for designing critters in EVOLV-O-MATIC, it might in principle work for any engineering or design problem that had the same basic characteristics. The chief characteristic is that the problem should not involve a once-and-for-all, unique solution, like guessing the winning number in a lottery. A way of finding such a number could not evolve by selection of any kind, because it is a one-shot, right-or-wrong situation, with no prizes for anyone who got just the first digit of the winning number right, or the second.

But if lotteries did work that way, with the winning numbers revealed one digit at a time, designing a rule for finding the winning number would be easy, even if the final number were, shall we say, ten digits long (see figure 6). Suppose that the winning number were 7926477482. This is just one of ten billion (10,000,000,000, or 10^{10}) possible combinations. The chances of finding such a number in a one-step, once-and-for-all choice are one in ten billion, or totally negligible. However, suppose that you were able to guess one digit at a time. That would be easy: you would know that, whatever the winning, one-in-ten-billion number was, it would have to start with only one of ten digits. Your chances of getting the first digit of the winning number

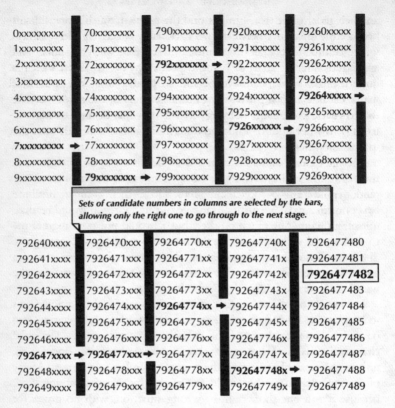

FIGURE 6: How to find a 1-in-10 billion number in ten steps.

right would then be, not one in ten billion, but one in ten. Only a maximum of ten guesses would be necessary to find out that the first digit of the winning number was 7. If we did the same with the second digit, no more than ten further trials would show us that the winning number began with 79, and so on, until we got the complete answer: 7926477482. In all, we would only have to try a hundred numbers (ten for each of ten digits) to get the correct answer. But even a hundred guesses on an all-or-nothing basis would have been overwhelmingly unlikely to produce the right answer because it would still leave us with only one hundred chances in ten billion of being right and nine billion, nine hundred and ninety-nine million, nine hundred and ninety-nine thousand, nine hundred of being wrong! No wonder, then, that real lotteries have to work on a one-shot, right-or-wrong-once-and-for-all basis, because finding the winning number would be too easy otherwise.

However, designing winning critters for life in the EVOLV-O-MATIC world is a different matter, and here we have already seen that partial, step-by-step solutions are possible. So we could start with many randomly created critters and let the world in which they live pick the winners by gradually selecting out the losers and rewarding the winners with reproductive success. Even if the chances of finding the winner were one in tens of billions, we have just seen that a step-by-step process of selection could readily find the answer in a surprisingly short time.

In the case of EVOLV-O-MATIC we have defined the problem as finding the correct set of movement genes. As we have seen, there are eight of these, each with a value ranging from $0-15$ inclusive, or sixteen in all. The total number of possible values that such movement genes could have is therefore 16 multiplied by itself eight times (or 16^8). This comes to 68,719,476,736, or some tens of billions of possible solutions, rather as our lottery example did. However, if as in the case of the lottery we could work towards a one-in-tens-of-billions solution by many small steps, finding the winning number would be a practicable proposition.

This example illustrates a second requirement of our method. This is that, not only should a step-by-step, gradual solution of the problem be possible, but we should also be able to select better solutions as they appear. In the EVOLV-O-MATIC world this is done for us by the environment, because critters that are better at foraging than others have more offspring, and so gradually squeeze out less efficient foragers in the competition for food. Nevertheless, we could do such selection manually, or set up a selection process that would do it periodically (for example, by eliminating critters with the poorest performance).

Finally, for best results we need to be able to recycle our solutions, in principle endlessly if necessary, so that gradual, step-by-step improvements continue until we have really good solutions. In the lottery example we did this by using each correct answer as the starting point for a new cycle of selection for the next ten candidate solutions. The outcome is a three-part process involving a trial, selection, and reproduction-with-variation. The resulting selection of new, varied candidates can then be recycled, in principle indefinitely. Furthermore, any form of information could become the starting point for this process. Such an approach as this is now increasingly used in finding engineering solutions, especially where computers can be used to generate variations that can then be selected on the basis of how near they come to an optimum solution.

Recently this approach has been used to obtain an artificial *enzyme*. Enzymes are complex biochemicals that act on other substances to produce some kind of reaction. (Much of the digestion that goes on in our stomachs, for example, is the result of the action of enzymes.) The enzyme in question was engineered to cut DNA, the organic chemical of which almost all genes in almost all organisms are made. The remainder use the very similar RNA, and the artificial enzyme is in fact a variant of RNA that occurs in nature. However, the ability of the natural enzyme to cut DNA is limited. Direct 're-engineering' of such an organic molecule was out of the question because of its sheer size and complexity, so a different approach was tried. Trillions of the enzyme molecules were subjected to a process that introduced random mutations. The resulting mutated molecules were then passed through a selection process that discriminated in favour of those that could cut DNA slightly more effectively than others. The resulting small number of 'improved' molecules were then used to 'breed' a much larger number of them, which were in turn subjected to further mutation, selection, breeding, and so on. Eventually, and after ten cycles or 'generations' of this process, an enzyme that cut DNA a hundred times more efficiently than the starting one was obtained. Furthermore, the winners in this evolutionary process had mutations in very unexpected places, and had been modified in ways that no human genetic engineer could possibly have imagined, let alone achieved by direct manipulation of the molecules.[2]

The method, in other words, was exactly like the one I used when I created critters at random in EVOLV-O-MATIC, or the one we imagined might have been used to find a one-in-ten-billion solution to a lottery, if you could guess just one digit at a time.

Here the trial, selection and reproduction-plus-variation cycle began with a biochemical – an RNA enzyme – that encoded chemical information in much the same way that critters' movement 'genes' encode the information that controls their foraging pattern. Selection, mutation and breeding from the resulting selected few were carried out artificially. However, all of these processes had occurred naturally to produce the original enzyme, and the essence of our best modern insight into evolution is that billions of years ago purely chance circumstances assembled the precursors of self-reproducing biochemicals that were the forerunners of today's DNA and RNA.

Both of these are made up of repeating chemical subunits, and, like the proverbial piece of string that they resemble in their spiral entwining, can in principle be any length. DNA – the principal genetic material in the vast majority of all living forms – is composed of two helical strands that are linked by inter-locking chemical bases much as the teeth of a zip fastener link two sides of a garment. There are four such bases, which are normally abbreviated as A, T, G and C. An A on one strand always forms a chemical bond with a T on the other, and a G on one with a C on the other. The result is that any possible sequence of bases on one strand – say CAT – must have a corresponding sequence – GTA – on the other. If one strand disociates from the other and new bases link to the exposed ones on each 'open' strand, an exact copy of each will have been made (see figure 7).

Essentially, this is the mechanism that underlies heredity in all living organisms. The sequences of bases contain information in the sense that triplets such as CAT or GTA spell out a code that is translated into some twenty-two amino acids, or into 'punctuation marks' in the code like 'stop'. These amino acids are in turn the essential elements of the proteins that make up all living organisms. According to Darwin's insight, the natural world plays the same selecting rôle that we saw the artificially-contrived EVOLV-O-MATIC world playing at the beginning of this chapter. The ability of DNA-like substances to produce copies of themselves in the way we have just seen, along with the fact that occasional mistakes in copying occur, ensures that the reproduction-with-variation part of the cycle also occurs. The result is actual genes producing further copies of themselves on which selection acts in turn, and so on, indefinitely.

In the past natural selection was usually only applied to organic evolution. Nevertheless, Darwin himself clearly understood that evolution by natural selection was a principle independent of what was selected. For example, in *The Descent of Man*, published twelve years after *The Origin of Species*, Darwin pointed out that 'The formation of different

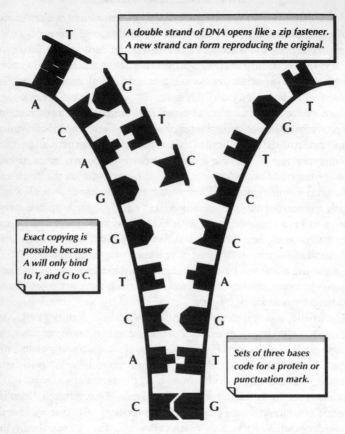

FIGURE 7: The genetic code.

languages and of distinct species, and the proofs that both have been developed through a gradual process, are curiously the same.' He realized that the cycle of variation, selection and reduplication of selected entities also occurred in languages. According to Darwin, 'We see variability in every tongue, and new words are continually cropping up; but as there is a limit to the powers of the memory, single words, like whole languages, gradually become extinct.' Darwin goes on, 'A struggle for life is constantly going on amongst the words and grammatical forms in each language. The better, the shorter, the easier forms are constantly gaining the upper hand.' Leaving absolutely no doubt about the fact that linguistic evolution was an example of Darwinian evolution in its most general form, he observes, 'The survival or preservation of certain favoured words in the struggle for existence is natural selection.'[3]

Darwin's extension of natural selection to human languages – a purely cultural phenomenon – answers one final fallacy about evolution. This is the frequently heard belief that human beings have 'stopped evolving' or are 'exempt from natural selection' because they live in cultures that have removed them from the 'natural' world, and therefore from the effects of natural selection. But clearly, other human beings and their culture are a very important part of our environment, just as other critters constitute an important part of the EVOLV-O-MATIC world. And if other humans and their culture have non-random effects on human reproductive success, this is just as natural for human beings as it would be for any other social species. The fact that termite queens have become so large and immobile that they cannot survive outside the mound – let alone get out of it – does not mean that they should be regarded as exempt from natural selection. Yet they live in an entirely termite-created environment, surrounded mainly by other termites on whom they are totally dependent for survival. Indeed, if termites could write about evolution, they would probably feel that they had as much right to claim to have 'stopped evolving' as human beings who, they might point out, live in buildings comparable to their own mounds and show levels of social co-operation that, if anything, fall short of the termite standard.

The truth probably is that the human-beings-have-stopped-evolving view is just another expression of an emotional response that tries to mitigate the effects of natural selection by conceding that although once we might have been subject to it, now we are exempt. It attempts to treat evolution like a criminal record – something that should not be held against your future, even if it does disfigure your past. To have any objective meaning, such a claim would have to prove that what we might call 'the human environment' either had no effect whatsoever on differential reproductive success, or had completely random effects (which comes to the same thing). But the main impact of the human environment is the presence of others, and as we shall now see, social behaviour can and does have dramatic consequences for the reproductive success of individuals.

EVOLUTION & CO-OPERATION

Evolution and co-operation seem to be contradictory ideas. We have just seen that the essence of evolution by natural selection is the reproductive success of individual organisms, often at the expense of others. Evolution and selfishness, by contrast, are easy to understand, and Darwinism has often been associated not merely with slogans like 'survival of the fittest' but also with 'nature red in tooth and claw'. It seems that, even if we reject the former because it fails to see that reproductive success rather than 'fitness' is at stake, the latter is still inevitable: evolution by natural selection will result in a pitiless struggle, if not for survival, then at least for individual reproductive success. We shall see in this chapter, however, that such a conclusion is by no means inevitable and that, far from selecting only for selfishness, natural selection can create exquisite co-operation. Perhaps most surprisingly of all, we shall see that it can only do so if we apply the fundamental insight of the last chapter: that selection acts on individual genes, and nothing else.

The fallacy of the free lunch

The question of how evolution by natural selection could produce anything other than total selfishness is often termed 'the problem of altruism'. In the eyes of many the problem resides in the very use of the term 'altruism' for anything other than human behaviour. Its use in relation to other animals – or even plants and organisms like bacteria – is regarded as 'anthropomorphic' and illegitimate because it attributes to other forms of life what should only be attributed to human beings.

We can remedy the problem in part by postponing for a while a consideration of how relevant evolutionary insights into animal altruism might be to human behaviour. For the time being we can define 'altruism' as a technical term, rather in the same way that terms like 'mass' and 'force' are given precise, technical definitions in physics. This defines them more accurately for use in science, where they have a restricted but much more definite meaning than in everyday speech. So let's do the same with 'altruism' and give it a precise, scientific meaning. For our purposes let's agree that 'altruism' is defined as *any act by one organism that promotes the reproductive success of another at a cost to the actor's reproductive success*.

To make the point unmistakably clear, consider the following 'thought experiment'. Suppose that we had a population of selfish organisms among whom an altruist as defined above appeared by mutation. By definition, that altruistic mutant would have to promote the reproductive success of the other, selfish members of the population at a cost to its own reproductive success. Since natural selection ultimately selects for reproductive success, it must select against such altruists to the point that they soon become extinct. Altruism, it seems, cannot evolve by natural selection if we conceive of that process in terms of an individual organism's reproductive success and if we define altruism in terms of sacrifices to individual's reproductive success. The logic seems inescapable.

But something must be seriously wrong. This is because altruism as we have just defined it is surprisingly common in the natural world. Social insects such as bees, wasps and ants, for example, show it to an extreme extent: the vast majority of individuals in such societies have no reproductive success at all, but rather labour altruistically for the queens and drones, who are the only ones who do have offspring. If natural selection is ultimately a question of individual reproductive success as I argued in the first chapter, how could it have produced entire castes of insect workers, soldiers and nurses who have absolutely no personal reproductive success at all? And if we insist on defining altruism as a technical term meaning a personal sacrifice of reproductive success by the altruist in favour of the recipient of the altruistic act, how can altruism so defined possibly evolve by natural selection?

It would seem that there are only two alternatives: either natural selection could not in fact produce such an outcome, or there must be some other way in which it could do so – one overlooked or excluded by the considerations above. After some reflection, we might consider a slightly different thought experiment that at first sight appears to get round the problem.

Consider the contrary situation to that in the first thought experiment. Suppose that there is a population of altruists among whom no selfish organism exists. By definition, all will benefit each other, and altruism, once established by the group, will continue to flourish. From this we might conclude that altruism can indeed evolve by natural selection, *but only if it acts, not on individuals as such, but on an entire group* – so-called 'group-selection'.

Anyone familiar with evolutionary writing a generation or two ago would have noticed that, far from being just a thought-experiment, group-selection was in fact the most common solution to the problem of altruism. Up to the 1960s it was widely believed that even if selection might act on individuals' 'fitness' it could also act on the 'fitness' of entire groups by way of benefiting all who made sacrifices for the good of all. It seemed obvious that the only way to explain the selfless sacrifice of insect workers was to conclude that natural selection regarded bee hives or ant colonies as 'super-organisms' and acted on them just as it appeared to do on individual organisms. After all, the individual organisms on which natural selection evidently did act could themselves be seen as vast societies of individual cells, most of whom did not reproduce themselves (in the sense of giving rise to other organisms) any more than insect soldiers or workers did. Like sterile castes of social insects, most cells in a sexually reproducing, multi-cellular organism fail to reproduce the organism itself and instead leave it to the sex cells, just as female workers in insect societies let drones and queens reproduce the colony. Entire societies, it seemed, could be the object of natural selection, and selection at that level would inevitably select for the self-sacrifice that made such 'super-organisms' possible. Group-selection was not only correct, but obviously correct.

Unfortunately, what is obviously correct is not always what is true, and common sense is sometimes a poor guide in science. The fact that we do not feel the earth moving, that dropped objects fall at our feet rather than to one side and that clouds, moon, sun and stars obviously move across the sky does not prove that the earth is stationary and the universe revolving around it. On the contrary, these apparently obvious proofs of a stationary earth and moving heaven belie the truth and only appear to show that the earth does not move. Today, with views of the earth from space to show us another perspective, the fact is universally accepted that the earth, and not the heavens, moves.

Much the same is true of group-selection. As a view of evolution it is just as wrong as an unmoving-earth-centred universe is wrong. To understand why, let's return to our second, apparently obvious thought experiment. We had a population of pure altruists, mutually co-operating for the general good. But now imagine that a selfish individual appears by mutation. By definition, the altruistic majority must favour the reproductive success of the selfish mutant. This is because we agreed to define altruism as a contribution to the reproductive success of another at a cost to the altruist, and this must hold good even if the beneficiary is totally selfish. After all, even in everyday usage, altruism is in the sacrifice, not in the benefit.

However, the similarly selfish offspring of the original selfish mutant will also be favoured by the altruists around them. The inevitable outcome will be that in each generation there will be more selfish individuals, until finally the altruists are driven to extinction. Once again, we seem to be able to conclude with total certainty that altruism as we have defined it cannot evolve by natural selection because, by definition, *the altruists will always promote the reproductive success of selfish organisms to the point of the altruists' total extinction.*

In other words, the group-selectionist solution to the problem of altruism is perennially vulnerable to what has become known as the 'free-rider' problem. This is the observation that if individuals pay a price in terms of their reproductive success to benefit the group or species, such a benefit will, by definition, reward others' reproductive success. Yet individuals who attempt to get the benefit without paying the cost will always be selected because their reproductive success will be favoured by the altruists defined as those who do pay. Gradually, natural selection would eliminate the paying population because of the cost to their own reproductive success and the benefit to that of the non-paying, free-riders. In short, altruism will encourage selfishness to the point that it is driven to extinction and only selfishness remains.

Trying to explain the evolution of altruism by appeals to group selection as an evolutionary mechanism is rather like attempting to design a perpetual motion machine. No physicist would take a machine that did not consume energy seriously for one moment because all such contraptions ultimately founder on the fact that they try to get something for nothing. Because energy can neither be created nor destroyed, but merely transmitted in various ways, and because its transmission always involves some irretrievable loss, no machine can recycle it with one hundred per cent efficiency, and so cannot move perpetually. Ineluctably, the tendency of energy to dissipate as heat, noise and friction takes its toll, and all such machines ultimately come to a stand-still.

The situation with altruism is similar: because natural selection is driven by reproductive success, a commodity like altruism has to pay its way, so to speak, in terms of its own reproductive success. Group-selection, like perpetual motion in physics, attempts to get something for nothing by assuming that the benefit to the group is in itself enough to explain the cost that altruism necessarily implies to individuals. Yet merely emphasizing the benefit to the group does not explain why individuals should pay the cost.

This is an important principle, and one that is often overlooked, especially in human behaviour. An incident that illustrates the point took place a few years ago at a leading school of the social sciences. A department there decided to entertain a retiring professor at a restaurant. The head of the department contemptuously dismissed advice from one of his staff who cautioned against his superior's plan of having one bill, with everyone paying equal shares. The subordinate was reminded that these were civilized people – social scientists who believed in groups and knew the value of social co-operation! But in the event the head of department found that, after seemingly having collected everyone's contribution, he was one short. Yet everyone claimed to have paid (and the colleague who had advised against this way of doing things took the precaution of drawing attention to himself as he did so, so that there could be no doubt that he at least had done so). Having unwisely taken cash, there was no way that the individual contributions could be checked, and so someone had a free lunch – ultimately at everyone else's expense.

This incident illustrates what we all know from common experience of life: that in reality individuals often put the cost to themselves before the benefit to others, no matter how civilized or mindful of the value of social co-operation they may seem to be. With free-riders perpetually ready to rob it, altruism is bound to leak away like energy does in real machines, so that in the evolution of behaviour in general as in economics, there is no such thing as a free lunch. Someone always has to pay for every lunch in the end, and in a similar way evolution by natural selection has to pay for its free lunches – altruistic acts.

Making a free lunch pay

If we had any remaining doubts about the free-lunch fallacy, we could test it using EVOLV-O-MATIC. What we would have to do would be to introduce a new 'gene' for critters, one for altruism as defined above. We could do this by deciding that every time two critters met, the one with the gene for altruism would 'feed' the other by transferring energy to it to the point that both critters' energy levels were the same. However, a 'non-altruist' would never lose energy to an 'altruist' – by definition, it could only happen the other way round.

What happens if we run this simulation? At first, our expectations are confirmed. A critter with the gene for altruism fares quite well to begin with, because critters are created with equal amounts of energy, so the altruist's first encounters with others cost it little. However, as time passes the differences between critters' energy levels begins to grow, and each time the altruist meets one with a much lower reserve than itself, it has to lose energy to the other. Yet others who have more energy than the altruist never repay it, so there is a tendency for altruists rapidly to weaken and die, often before they reproduce. And even if they succeed in reproducing, their offspring usually succumb to death quicker than those of the non-altruists, and so before long the gene for altruism is selected out, just as we would expect.

But this is not always what happens. Astonishingly, simulations with EVOLV-O-MATIC show that our expectations about altruism and natural selection are far from correct, and that, contrary to the apparently irrefutable logic of our thought experiments, altruists can indeed prosper in certain circumstances. For example, suppose that the altruistic mutant happens to be a glider. Gliders, as we have seen, only emerge occasionally, and usually prosper once they do, thanks to their efficient, wide-ranging pattern of foraging. If the altruist happens to be such a glider and few if any other gliders exist, it may not meet many other critters at all to begin with, especially if its travels seldom take it to the Garden of Eden, where the jitter-critters grow. As a result, it may reproduce before suffering much of a loss to its energy level, and its progeny may be similarly fortunate so that if they tend to meet anyone, it is one of themselves.

At first sight, this looks like group-selection, because it seems that a group or family of gliders is being favoured by their common attribute of being altruists. Just as in our second thought experiment, it seems that a group of altruists can indeed be selected as a group. But closer inspection shows that this is a superficial and misleading view. Let's look a little more closely at what happens to specific individuals in this simulation.

The first thing to notice is that if both parties are altruists, *both* do not in fact benefit in any one interaction. On the contrary, we have already agreed that the act of altruism in question always benefits the individual – altruist or not – with the least energy. Once energy levels are equalized, the couple part. Admittedly, rôles may – indeed, probably will – be reversed at some later stage, but the fact remains that, although individuals benefit each other, it is not because selection is acting on the entire group that they do so.

The reason two individuals may come to benefit one another as a result of at least two, and, in all probability, a much larger number of meetings, is that *both possess the same gene for altruism*. It is the gene for altruism present in the recipient that benefits if both parties to an exchange are altruists. This turns out to be the factor that completely overturns our expectations. Selection is acting, not on a *group* of glider-altruists as such, but on the *gene* for altruism that the members of the group share by common descent from its founder. Furthermore, the proof of this is obvious. What is it, we should ask, that makes a glider an altruist? The answer, as we have already seen, is simple: merely the fact that we gave it the altruism gene. It is only that gene that distinguishes the altruists from any other kind of glider.

The effect is even more obvious if the original altruist happens to be a jitter-critter. As we saw, such individuals only survive and prosper if they happen to find themselves in the Garden of Eden, and there they usually rapidly reproduce. If the altruist is the only jitter-critter, or one of very few such critters present in the Garden, its own progeny are often the ones with whom it comes into contact. If so, the result is exactly the same as it is in the case of glider-altruists who meet their own offspring: the gene for altruism, present in the offspring of the jitter-critter, benefits by the transfusion of energy. Indeed, both gliders and jitterers appear to benefit from the gene for altruism, as long as there are not too many non-altruists present to exploit them. This is because it tends to equalize the energy levels of individuals with the gene for altruism by virtue of the fact that an altruist who loses energy to a fellow altruist in one encounter may gain energy in another. The result is that the gene for altruism can be powerfully selected for in such circumstances.

What seems to limit its success is the presence of non-altruists in sufficient numbers to reduce the likelihood that altruists will encounter one another often enough to promote the overall reproductive success of the gene for altruism. But as long as an altruist is sufficiently fortunate to interact with other carriers of its gene for altruism, altruism can indeed be selected. The result is that even if jitter-altruists are not the only critters in the Garden, their tendency to stay in one place may mean that they interact more frequently with themselves than with non-altruists, to the benefit of their gene for altruism.

So, returning to our apparently irrefutable thought-experiments, what was wrong with our reasoning?

The answer is that we made a mistake about the *level* at which natural selection acts. We assumed that it selected individuals, but our earlier discussion of the essentials of Darwinism should have prepared us for the realization that in reality natural selection acts, not on individuals as such, but on the genes that they carry. In the case of critters in EVOLV-O-MATIC, these 'genes' are the numerical values controlling their performance parameters. If altruists could not pass on the 'gene' for altruism, or share it with relatives, our expectations would have been entirely fulfilled. But the fact that copies of the 'gene' for altruism could benefit from its operation in others completely overturns our expectations, and results in the surprising emergence of entire populations of altruists. In the case of living organisms genes need no quotation marks because, as we have already seen, these are indeed the entities on which natural selection acts.

The result is an astonishingly counter-intuitive insight. We can now see that it is only when we realize that natural selection in fact selects *not* at the level of the individual or at that of the group, but at that of the individual gene, that we can begin to explain social co-operation in general, and altruism in particular. What group-selectionist reasoning overlooked was the fact that selection acted at a more fundamental level than even the individual – that of the individual's genes. Paradoxically, it is only when we see selection operating at the most reductive, genetic level that we can begin to understand the evolution of co-operation at the highest, social level.

This is probably the reason why the problem of altruism could not have been satisfactorily solved in Darwin's own lifetime, or indeed at any time until the true nature of genetics was understood. Once it was, it was inevitable that, sooner or later, someone would make the momentous discovery that social co-operation of the most exquisite kind could only be explained in terms of natural selection of individual genes. This was first suspected by Darwinists like Haldane in the 1930s, but definitively solved by W. D. Hamilton in the early 1960s – almost exactly a century after the publication of *The Origin of Species*.

To see how Hamilton did it, consider the following example. Suppose that I have a gene (or many genes, it doesn't matter) that encourages me to sacrifice my life to save the lives of at least three of my children. To understand how such suicidal altruism can evolve in human beings we need first to take account of a genetic factor. This is that everyone has two complete sets of genes in the cells of their bodies. However, we only pass on one set in our sex cells, sperm or eggs. A fertilized egg has a double set of genes restored – one from each parent (see figure 8). Now comes the interesting point where altruism is concerned. If I do indeed have genes that encourage me to sacrifice my life for three of my children's lives, we can see that one hundred per cent of such genes is destroyed in my act of altruism. However – and this is the surprise – one hundred and fifty per cent of the genes for such a sacrifice is preserved. This is because each of my children receives half my genes. So the chances are that each carries fifty per cent of my gene or genes for self-sacrifice. Three times fifty per cent is one hundred and fifty per cent, which means that such genes enjoy greater reproductive success because of my self-sacrifice than they would enjoy had I not performed my act of suicidal altruism (see figure 8). The same is also true if it is siblings I save because they too share half my genes. Since all my other genes are in exactly the same position, they too benefit in the same way. As we saw in the first chapter, reproductive success is what natural selection ultimately comes down to, so we could say that my sacrificial act had been naturally selected because it conferred greater reproductive success on the genes that encouraged me to do it.

This is the essential insight into what is often called 'inclusive fitness', to use the F-word again. However, attempts to measure such 'fitness' in relation to individuals become extremely complicated, and even defining the term correctly is a headache that I would not want to inflict

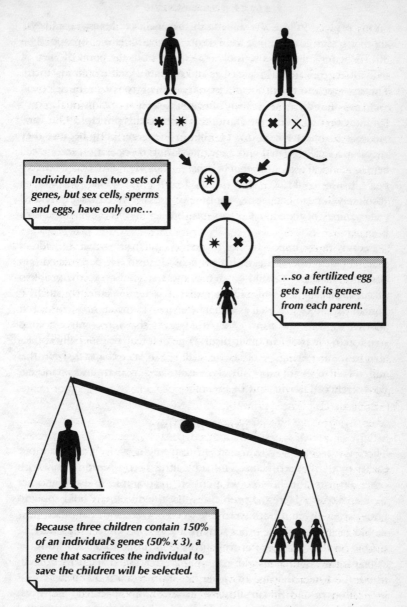

Individuals have two sets of genes, but sex cells, sperms and eggs, have only one...

...so a fertilized egg gets half its genes from each parent.

Because three children contain 150% of an individual's genes (50% x 3), a gene that sacrifices the individual to save the children will be selected.

FIGURE 8: How genetics favours self-sacrifice.

on my readers. In fact, the difficulties that inclusive fitness raises is yet another reason for avoiding the F-word altogether (see above, pp. 24–30). A better solution is to look at altruism from the point of view of individual genes and calculate costs and benefits of self-sacrifice to them. This approach to the problem also avoids the error of seeing selection as acting on individuals as such since multi-cellular organisms also owe the integrity and co-operation of their parts to this principle. Our various cells co-operate with one another in the larger body because they are all identically related and genes favouring co-operation in one cell benefit identical copies of them in others. In short, Hamilton's discovery that altruism could evolve at the level of the individual gene was an absolutely fundamental one, applicable not merely to closely related communities of individual organisms, but to multi-cellular organisms in general.

Because of the importance of relatedness in ensuring that individuals share the gene for altruism this form of altruism has been called 'kin altruism'. As such, it could be seen as the first solution to the problem of altruism, and we shall see later that it is fundamental to much in human psychology as well as social behaviour in the animal world. But another fundamental form of altruism exists that represents a second solution to the problem of altruism – one that may be especially applicable to human beings. And as we shall see in later chapters, both this and kin altruism are especially significant for a modern understanding, not merely of Darwin, but of Freud.

Diner's dilemma

There is a second way in which altruism might evolve and refute our earlier thought experiments. This is by altruists co-operating only with other altruists. But how could a critter, for example, know if another were an altruist? Here the problem is that the dilemma would apply to both parties: Even if both were able to co-operate with the other, how would each know if the other were ready to co-operate with itself?

One answer might be *kin recognition*: if altruists descended from the same parents could recognize one another, they could assess their likelihood of having inherited the gene for altruism from that parent. But this only works with kin altruism. Is there any other way in which reciprocal recognition might work? Indeed there is, but to understand it, we need to look a little deeper into the whole issue of social behaviour and to bring our discussion of altruism a lot nearer home.

Suppose that you and an acquaintance go into a restaurant for a meal. Looked at in the most basic terms, we might say that you and your partner could both obtain a benefit from such an event, and pay a cost. The benefit would be the meal, the cost, the bill. But each of you could face a choice, either to pay or not to pay. Let's call paying the bill *co-operating*, and not paying it *defecting*. Now, there are four possibilities, depending on whether you co-operate or defect, and whether your partner co-operates or defects. If you both co-operate, you both pay and you both eat. We could call this *reciprocity* because cost and benefit are equally shared.

But now suppose that you co-operate and pay, but your partner does not, perhaps by claiming not to have enough money, or simply refusing to do so. We could call this *altruism* on your part in the sense that you paid for your partner's lunch. Looking at if from your point of view, however, we could claim that what your partner had done was to perform an act of *selfishness* because what they got out of it was a free lunch. Finally, we could imagine a situation in which neither of you were prepared to pay anything and so neither got any lunch. This we might call *spite*(see figure 9).

If we now think about the relative value of these outcomes to you or your partner, we can see that a free lunch is always best – you get a benefit without a cost. This is better than a lunch with a shared cost, because, although you still get your lunch, you have to pay for it. But this is in turn better than no lunch at all, which although it imposes no cost, also carries no benefit whatsoever. Finally, the worst outcome is having to pay for someone else's lunch – a cost without a benefit to you. Translating these examples back into the terms we defined in the previous paragraph, we can see that selfishness (a free lunch) is better than reciprocity (both eating, both paying), but that is in turn worth more than spite (neither pays, neither eats), and that the worst outcome is having to perform an act of altruism (you pay, the other eats at your expense).

For reasons to do with the anecdotes usually contrived to illustrate it, this set-up is usually called a 'Prisoner's Dilemma' (figure 9). A frequently-voiced objection to it is that it can seem artificial and contrived. But if we think back for a moment to my earlier, real-life

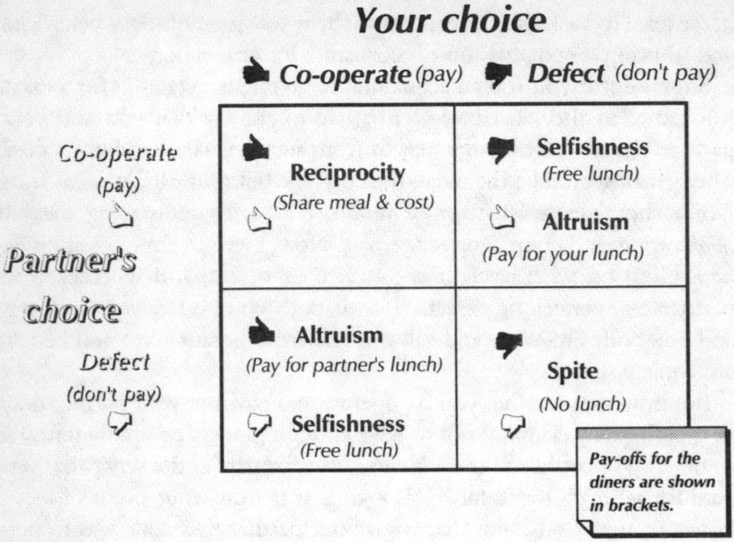

Your choice

Co-operate (pay)   **Defect** (don't pay)

	Co-operate (pay)	**Defect** (don't pay)
Co-operate (pay)	**Reciprocity** (Share meal & cost)	**Selfishness** (Free lunch) / **Altruism** (Pay for your lunch)
Defect (don't pay)	**Altruism** (Pay for partner's lunch) / **Selfishness** (Free lunch)	**Spite** (No lunch)

Partner's choice

Pay-offs for the diners are shown in brackets.

FIGURE 9: Prisoner's Dilemma.

example of the social scientists at the restaurant who found that one of their number had not paid we can see that there are plenty of situations that come very close to this model (see above, p. 42). In that case, the non-payer did in fact get a free lunch and the others present did indeed perform an act of altruism in the sense that they collectively had to pay for it. The fact is that people often do face conflicts about co-operating with others to the mutual benefit or defecting in their selfish interests, and it is important to recognize both sides of the basic dilemma, even if we would like to think that we would normally act in the social interest. The advantages of Prisoner's Dilemma is that it does present both sides, and balances them fairly, so that the outcome is not pre-judged.

We can relate this to our earlier EVOLV-O-MATIC simulation of altruism. First, let's recall what we saw there (see above, pp. 43–5). The situation described earlier depicted individuals with a gene for altruism. This means that they have to co-operate all the time. They are like one of the couple above who goes into a restaurant and is always ready to pay, no matter what their partner does. Let's call this the *Sucker*

50

strategy. (In the scientific literature it is more commonly called All C for 'always co-operate'.)

If we already have Suckers in our population – that is, critters with the gene for altruism – we can also see that we already have another type of critter playing the opposite strategy, what we might call by way of analogy *Defector* (known in the literature as All D). This is the remaining, non-altruist population – those without the altruism gene.

We have already seen how altruists and non-altruists fare in the EVOLV-O-MATIC simulation, but much depends on accidental factors, like where an altruist critter forages, who it happens to meet and so on. Again, energy levels are affected by things like the stage of the game at which an encounter occurs. To simplify the matter and help us get to the core of the problem of altruism, let's use a slightly different kind of simulation, one based on the Prisoner's Dilemma of the diners outlined above.

As in that case, two individuals have the choice to co-operate or defect, with the outcomes being ranked as we saw them just now. We could represent these pay-offs more simply if we just gave them points. It does not matter what the points are, as long as the relative ranking of pay-offs remains the same: selfish enjoyment of a benefit without a cost must be worth more than mutual payment and mutual benefit, which must in turn be better than mutual avoidance of cost without any benefit, while a cost to yourself that benefits the other must be the least valuable outcome (see figure 10). If we run a simulation on this basis the result is much as we would expect: Defector rapidly invades populations of Suckers, with Suckers only surviving as long as they mainly meet other Suckers. In other words, we find the outcome of our thought experiments above: Sucker altruists cannot resist invasion by selfish Defectors, and a population of Defectors could never be invaded by Suckers.

But now let's allow mutation to introduce new genes that can control behaviour in terms of co-operation or defection on a more subtle basis. How might this be done?

Robert Axelrod and Stephanie Forrest found a way of doing so.[1] Their solution was to devise a means that would allow a player to react to the other player, rather than merely co-operate or defect all the time. They did this by basing a player's response on the outcome of the last

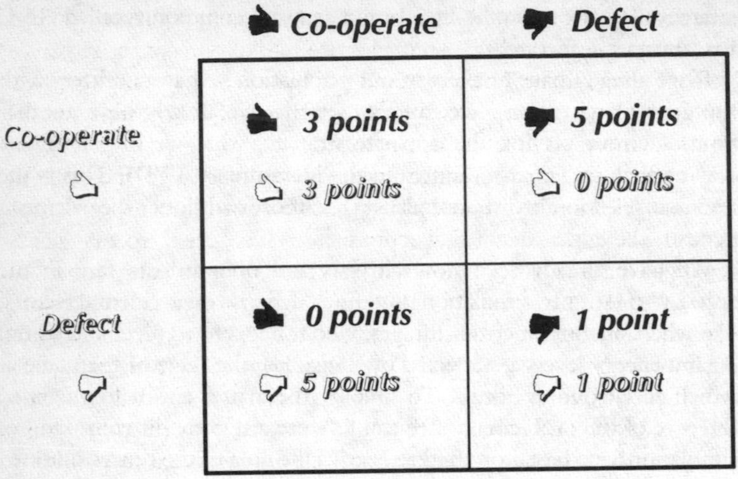

	 **Co-operate**	 **Defect**
Co-operate	**3 points** *3 points*	**5 points** *0 points*
Defect	**0 points** *5 points*	**1 point** *1 point*

FIGURE 10: Prisoner's Dilemma tournament points.

three interactions with the other player. It was like allowing our diners to retain a memory of what happened when they dined together on the last three occasions before this one. As we have seen, each interaction has four possible outcomes, depending on whether each individual co-operated or defected. If both co-operated, both paid and benefited; if both defected, neither paid and neither benefited; while if one co-operated by paying and the other defected, the paying partner was exploited by the non-paying, defecting one. Three repetitions of this produce 4 x 4 x 4, or 64 possible outcomes. Each could be encoded as a single item of information, with 'C' representing a co-operation and 'D' a defection. For example, Suckers could be regarded as having a gene comprising sixty-four Cs, while Defectors would have a string of sixty-four Ds.

These strings of Cs and Ds could be regarded as the basic strategy. Since each C or D in the sixty-four-digit-long string could be a D or a C respectively, the total possible number of combinations of sixty-four Cs and Ds is 2^{64} – that is, 2 multiplied by itself sixty-four times, or some sixteen quadrillion! Axelrod and Forrest comment that, if you had been evaluating the possible strategies at a rate of one per second since the beginning of the universe some ten billion or so years ago, you would only have exhausted two or three percent of the possible combinations by now, so great is their number.

A random set of such strategy genes was subjected to the cycle of variation, selection and reproduction that we saw in the previous chapter, with the added detail that reproduction was sexual, so that genes exchanged parts of their strings in the process of making copies of themselves. For example, a pure Sucker gene, with sixty-four Cs, might be paired with a pure Defector one, of sixty-four Ds, producing offspring with mixtures of Cs and Ds in their genes. The resulting genes were then subject to selection by being played against each other on the basis of the pay-off values given above: successful defection (defection when the other co-operated) got five points, mutual co-operation three each, mutual defection one each, with unsuccessful co-operation (co-operation when the other defected) getting nothing. Lower scoring genes were selected out, and the higher scoring ones then 'mated' by exchanging parts of their C/D strings, and thereby reproduced varied offspring, who were then played against one another, and so on.

As might be expected, most of these strategies turned out to be very poor players at first. Nevertheless, before long a strategy evolved that closely resembled one that had won two earlier tournaments that Axelrod had held for computer programs to play Prisoner's Dilemma. As it happened, this was the simplest of the computer programs entered and was called Tit-for-Tat. This strategy plays by always beginning with a co-operation, but then does whatever the other player did on the previous encounter. Figures 11 and 12 illustrate a simulation where Tit-for-Tat encounters Defector and Sucker in a territorial tournament in which players occupy spaces on a computer screen and play Prisoner's/Diner's Dilemma with up to eight neighbours, winning points as set out in figure 10 that determine their reproductive success. The surprising thing is that, although Suckers cannot resist invasion by Defectors and certainly cannot invade populations of Defectors themselves, Tit-for-Tat players can both invade Defector populations and encourage the co-operation of Suckers.

To see how and why, consider the situation in figure 11 (top). Here Suckers are indicated by a plus sign, Defectors by a minus, and the third

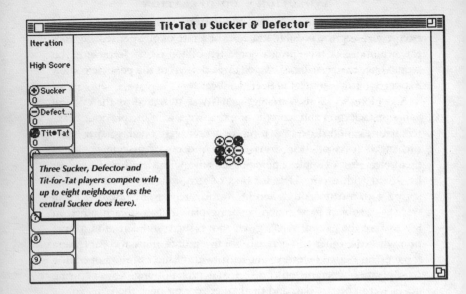

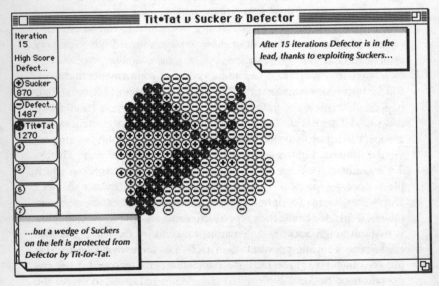

FIGURE 11: Tit-for-Tat versus Sucker and Defector in a territorial tournament.

players are Tit-for-Tat strategists. The starting position shows three of each, clustered in the middle. After 15 iterations (during which each player plays every other with whom it is in contact), Defector is in the lead, largely thanks to exploiting Suckers. However, a wedge of Suckers has survived on the left, protected by Tit-for-Tat players, who are in second place, as can be seen from the scores listed on the left of the lower half of figure 11.

By iteration 50 (figure 12, top), Tit-for-Tat has a commanding lead, and Sucker is now in second place, enjoying more reproductive success than Defector. However, Suckers remain only on the left hand side, where they have been protected by Tit-for-Tat players. They have not been able to make any headway on the right, where free space is still available. Nevertheless, an expanding wedge of Tit-for-Tat players can be seen colonizing the remaining vacant area faster than the Defectors who otherwise surround it. The reason for this is that Tit-for-Tat players enjoy greater reproductive success when they interact with one another – three points each – than do Defectors, who only gain one point when interacting with another Defector.

By iteration 1000 (figure 12, bottom), Tit-for-Tat has almost totally invaded the Defector population, which now only survives in isolated pockets in the bottom right-hand corner. Out of contact with Suckers to exploit, these Defectors are doomed to eventual extinction, but Suckers continue to flourish, thanks to interactions with one another, and with Tit-for-Tat. As these figures show, Tit-for-Tat both benefits Suckers and punishes Defectors, promoting its own reproductive success and that of any strategy able to co-operate with it to an equal extent. Gradually, Tit-for-Tat invades populations of Defectors and encourages the co-operation of Suckers with itself.

Contrary to those who thought that evolution by natural selection inevitably meant selfishness, aggression and spite, we can now see what is perhaps the most astonishing development of all: naturally selected co-operation gradually invading a population of selfish non-co-operators. Perhaps even more surprising still for those who equate evolution with slogans like 'weakest to the wall', the Tit-for-Tat players who achieved this never exploited the unconditional co-operation of the Sucker altruists. On the contrary, Tit-for-Tat protected and encouraged them, so that at the end there were more of them than there were Defectors.

The secret of the success of Tit-for-Tat is that it is a discriminating

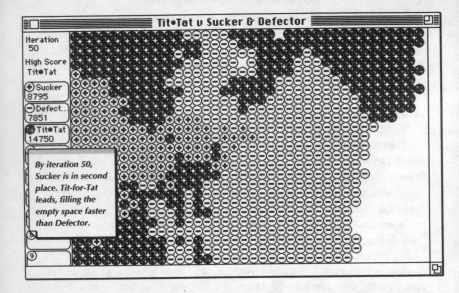

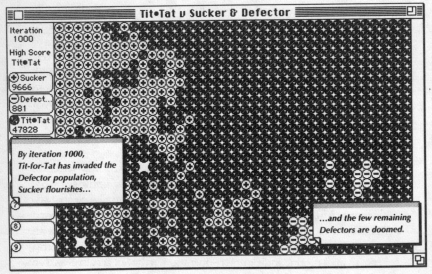

FIGURE 12: Tit-for-Tat takes the lead, and co-operation triumphs over selfishness.

kind of altruism, one whose basic rule is *co-operate with co-operation, but defect against defection*. Its readiness to co-operate with anything that will co-operate with it means that it rapidly reaps the rewards of mutual co-operation and does not exploit those more indiscriminately co-operative than itself. But its readiness to punish defection with defection protects it from exploitation by selfish players who capitalize on the co-operation of others.

Essentially, 'co-operate with co-operation' is the secret of the success of kin altruism too. There too, it is a question of a gene for altruism in one individual benefiting copies of itself in another. But in the case we are now considering the gene for altruism does not have to be present by common descent in the recipient of the altruistic act, so that genetic relatedness is not critical to its evolution. On the contrary, this type of altruism can evolve spontaneously between totally unrelated individuals. All that matters is that the co-operation of one should be reciprocated, or returned, by the other. Hence its name: *reciprocal altruism*.

Nevertheless, although identical copies of the same gene or genes for co-operation do not need to be present in reciprocal altruism, the genes controlling the co-operation of both parties must be benefited by the interaction in much the same way that genes for kin altruism must be benefited. In either case, we are not trying to get something for nothing by assuming that co-operation can evolve for the benefit of the group, society or species. On the contrary, we have seen how the inevitable cost of co-operation can be less than the benefit to the genes that underlie it.

But the most surprising thing of all to emerge from this chapter is the finding that, to understand social co-operation of the most elaborate kind, we need to see selection acting at the most basic level – that of the single gene. The so-called 'selfish gene' view of natural selection acting solely on individual genes was the inevitable outcome of Hamilton's discovery of the way in which genetics could favour the evolution of altruism. The consequence is that the most natural way of understanding altruism is from the point of view of single genes, and to see the gene sacrificing the organism to the benefit of the reproductive success of identical copies of itself in near relatives (figure 8). Looked at from this point of view, altruism is no more of a paradox than is the death of a living organism. Organisms may die, but reproduction ensures that genes are potentially immortal. And if the organism dies, or foregoes reproduction for itself, its sacrifice can promote the reproductive success of the genes it carries in common with near relatives.

This leads to a view of organisms as little more than the packaging or vehicles of their genes, at least as far as natural selection is concerned. Just as we saw at the beginning of the first chapter that critters in EVOLV-O-MATIC were little more than ciphers for the numerical 'genes' that controlled them, so naturally evolved biological organisms are essentially containers for their DNA. From this, ultimate point of view, sacrifice of individuals for the benefit of their genes is not so much a problem for evolutionary explanation as an insight into its most fundamental mechanism: natural selection at the level of the gene.

But how do individual genes affect behaviour? In a simple, uni-cellular organism like a slime-mould a single gene has indeed been found that seems to make slime-mould cells collect together into a slug-like organism that moves as if it were a single individual. A very similar gene has been found in human beings that seems to be implicated in cancer, suggesting that, at least at the level of the individual cell, we probably can speak of 'genes for co-operation' or 'altruism' (if cancer can be seen as 'defection' or 'selfishness'[2]). But the question of how selection at the level of the gene can influence human behaviour is a much more complex one, and it is to this that the remainder of this book will be devoted. We must conclude our consideration of natural selection at the level of the gene and move on to the mind.

CRYPTIC CONSCIOUSNESS

One consequence of seeing Darwinian evolution and co-operation as contradictory is a tendency to reserve an ability to act altruistically to human beings and then to claim that it evolved – if it evolved at all – by some other, preferably non-Darwinian means. But in the last chapter we saw that, contrary to first appearances, altruism rigorously defined can indeed evolve by Darwinian evolution in its most austere form: natural selection at the level of the individual gene. Now it is time to turn our attention to a second characteristic of human beings that – altruism aside – is even more frequently claimed to be distinctive: *consciousness*. As we shall see, its evolution may be much more closely allied with that of co-operation than might have seemed possible. And if evolution by natural selection can explain the one, there may be good reasons for thinking that it can explain the other. Finally, two other capacities that human beings often claim as unique to themselves – language and an ability to appreciate aesthetic harmony – will also emerge as parts of the explanation.

Why be self-conscious?

Few subjects have invited more argument and speculation than the question of the evolution of consciousness. But one or two sources of confusion can be cleared up immediately. The first is the question of what we mean when we speak of 'human consciousness'. There is a sense in which a Venus Fly-trap could be said to be conscious of a fly landing on it, because the landing of the fly causes it to close. The plant has responded to a stimulus, and to that extent we might be justified in calling it 'conscious' of the fly. But this is a very limited kind of consciousness and not at all what people usually have in mind when they speak of 'human consciousness'. Here they seem to mean

59

self-consciousness. By that term we imply, not only being conscious of something in the restricted sense in which a Venus Fly-trap might be said to be 'conscious' of something landing on it, but additionally *being conscious that you are conscious.* This is the sense in which I shall take the term 'consciousness' in what follows, at least in so far as it is applied to human beings. By saying that human beings have 'consciousness' I shall assume we mean that, not only do humans sense things, but they also sense that they sense them, and have a subjective awareness of being conscious − *self-consciousness.* You could say that human beings are self-consciously conscious in a way that a Venus Fly-trap is not.

Because we take this to be distinctive of our species and pride ourselves as pinnacles of creation, we tend to assume that such self-consciousness is generally involved in our mental pre-eminence in all things, but a moment's reflection is enough to show that this is not so. 'Self-consciousness' or the phrase 'feeling self-conscious' do not conjure up the towering intellect of an Albert Einstein, or the genius of a Leonardo da Vinci. On the contrary, they suggest inhibition and lowered capacity for achievement, rather than a heightening of our mental powers. Again, trying to be self-conscious of what you are doing when you run down stairs quickly is a distinctly dangerous exercise, since it almost always slows you down and tangles your feet, rather than improving your performance. A painful, if less dangerous, alternative is to concentrate on what you are doing when rapidly chewing a mouthful of nuts or some such food. The result almost always is that you bite your tongue. Where self-conscious interference with a reflex is concerned, Darwin was prepared to bet money on it: 'The conscious wish to perform a reflex action sometimes stops or interrupts its performance, though the proper sensory nerves may be stimulated. For instance, some years ago I laid a small wager with a dozen young men that they would not sneeze if they took snuff, although they all declared that they invariably did so; accordingly they all took a pinch, but from wishing much to succeed, not one sneezed, though their eyes watered, and all without exception, had to pay me the wager.'[1]

Clearly then, being self-conscious in the full human sense is not necessary to carry out many important actions that we perform every day. It seems that being conscious (as opposed to unconscious) of running down stairs, chewing, or being about to sneeze is not the same as being *self-conscious* of each of these actions in detail. On the contrary, self-consciousness of what we are doing in such situations often inhibits our doing them, rather than add anything of value. Indeed, detailed, conscious attention to what we are doing is usually evidence of our *not* having mastered the skill or operation in question, rather than the contrary. But when we are fully competent and have completely learnt skills like playing a musical instrument, speaking a foreign language or driving a car, we do not have much immediate self-consciousness of the often complex actions, judgements and responses that all these skills demand. We say that such abilities 'come naturally' and do not require the concentrated self-awareness that distinguishes the student or novice. We reserve the phrase 'feeling self-conscious' for situations where we feel awkward, ill at ease, or put on the spot.

Even tasks that do demand our full concentration, such as solving difficult problems or composing some complex communication, tend to make us concentrate on the problem, rather than be self-conscious about it. Sometimes people become so absorbed in these difficult tasks that they forget about everything else, including themselves. Some great intellects, such as Einstein, occasionally lapsed into states of abstraction in which they seemed to become totally absorbed to the point of forgetting everything else, including where they were and what else they might be doing – the complete opposite of being self-conscious. Indeed, in such situations it is hard to see how *self*-consciousness could contribute much. Such consciousness of yourself would seem to be a distraction from consciousness of, and concentration on, the problem. Indeed, you might even begin to wonder why we needed to be conscious of ourselves at all, given that being aware of the matter in hand can often demand our complete concentration, making awareness of ourselves at best irrelevant to it, or at worst something of a distraction.

There does, however, seem to be one activity that is both characteristic of human beings and almost always demands consciousness in the full sense of being conscious of yourself as a subject. This is speech in particular and verbal thought in general. Darwin noted that 'A long and complex train of thought can no more be carried out without the use of words, whether spoken or silent, than a long calculation without the use of figures or algebra.'[2] Furthermore, the use of words almost always demands full consciousness of yourself as the user. In part, this is because every properly formed sentence must have a subject – *I, you, he, she* or *it*, as the case may be if the subject is singular. Inevitably, this implies consciousness of who or what it is that is acting (or being acted on in the passive case), and such awareness is synonymous with consciousness in the full, human sense of being aware-that-you-are-aware.

Nevertheless, anyone who has ever tried to learn a foreign language, or even to improve their knowledge of their own language, soon realizes that actual speech involves the use of many complex rules and principles of which we are normally completely unconscious. If the only way to speak English were first to study grammar and vocabulary as conscious rules in the same way that many students have to learn foreign or dead languages like Latin or Greek, we might be justified in claiming that conscious attention was necessary for speech because that would be the only way to ensure that you were obeying the rules and making yourself understood. But no-one learns their native language this way, and even before they go to school most children have mastered the rudiments of self-expression in their native tongue. Yet even rudimentary expression implicitly follows complex rules of grammar and syntax that few speakers of the language could explain or even formulate. They are, in a word, *unconscious* of such rules, and speak, not by self-consciously applying principles, but by obeying implicit rules that they have never understood at a conscious level but are evidently able to obey at an unconscious one. In short, you do not have to understand what the subjunctive is in order to be able to use it in speech, and you can spend the whole of your life speaking in prose without ever knowing it!

Indeed, if conscious attention really were essential for the correct execution of complex, rule-following tasks, you might expect the opposite of what we find. Rather than people being unconscious of the linguistics of their speech, but fully aware of its meaning, you would expect them to pay careful conscious attention to linguistic rules, while remaining much less conscious of content – particularly in those many utterances where the meaning is much more simple than the language used to express it.

In other words, although the content of much that we say may demand consciousness on our part as Darwin observed, the ability to say it in words seems not to do so, at least in so far as the mechanisms used to translate thoughts into words are largely unconscious. But this only pushes the problem one stage further back, so to speak. Now we have to consider the question of why the content of human speech should demand consciousness, even if the mechanism of speech seems not to do so. We shall have to wait until the next chapter for a full answer to this, deeper question. But let's begin by considering the rôle of language in human self-consciousness.

Words and awareness

It is likely that language first evolved when our ancestors were still nomadic hunter-gatherers. The hunting and gathering stage of human evolution ended only about fifteen thousand years ago for the first human beings to leave it for settled agriculture during the so-called Neolithic Revolution. It came to an end within living memory for peoples like the Australian aborigines and !Kung San of the Kalahari desert in Africa (the '!' is a tongue-click). Since human hunting and gathering almost certainly began in the order of a million years ago, it follows that hunter-gathering accounts for at least ninety-eight per cent of history even for the first peoples to leave it, and even more for some.

Here it is tempting to speculate that a parallel may be found between the origins of human speech and one of the clearest examples of abstract communication among animals who also forage far and wide: the famous 'waggle dance' of the honey bee. The orientation of the outward, waggling part of this dance to the vertical gives the heading to the food-source relative to the sun, and between dances the bee in question lets its nest-mates taste the food that it has found. Perhaps this evolved from a simpler interaction in which bees pestered by others for a taste of their food provided it, but then made as if to return immediately for more, encouraging the others to do the same. Perhaps hominid hunters or gatherers returning with food that might immediately be claimed by others used a similar kind of ploy, gesturing in the direction in which the food could be found with one hand, while reserving it for themselves with the other. Encouraging grunts and other sounds might have accompanied these displays, paving the way to language proper, so that a costly act of altruism – sharing food with others – was partly replaced by a much less costly one: informing others where they could find food themselves. Free lunches and free speech may have much more to do with each other than we could ever imagine!

Here, as in the honey bee case, we see language in its simplest and most directly utilitarian form: 'There's game in them thar hills!' or whatever else the message may be. All such statements have one thing in common. This is that they can – at least in principle – always be checked by actually going and seeing if it is indeed so. Sometimes such statements may be wrong, or imprecise, but in principle they can always be compared with the reality that they depict. As a result, the value of such communications must have been very great to primal hunter-gatherers, just as honey bee communication seems to be critical to the success and survival of that species of foragers.

Presumably this is how language first evolved, as simple indicative statements that informed about food, danger, enemies, the weather and so on. The exchange of such information is likely to evolve on a reciprocal basis, so that if I am prepared to tell you where food I found today is located, I might expect you to tell me where you find water tomorrow, and so on. The cost involved in the communication is very slight – certainly much less than actually having to give you food – but the value to the recipient could be very great indeed. For example, even if I shared my food with you, you might only get enough for yourself. But if I tell you where I found it, you may be able to go there with others and all may find enough. It seems obvious that once even simple languages evolve, communication by words becomes extraordinarily useful.

If language originally evolved to make useful communications possible as a comparable form of communication evidently has done among honey bees, it may be that, having evolved for this, first purpose, language then became 'pre-adapted', so to speak, for a second. *Pre-adaptation* is a concept in evolution that means that something may originally be selected for one purpose, but then become selected for another, once the original selection has occurred. For example, the flippers of seals originally evolved as legs in the land-living form from which seals evolved. However, the flippers of penguins originally evolved as wings in the birds from which penguins are descended. In both cases limbs that had originally evolved for locomotion in air or on the land were pre-adapted for further evolution to suit them to water. The point is that the basic structure of a limb, whether for use in air, water or on land, can generally be the same, so that a limb evolved for one purpose can become a limb that is then further evolved for another, similar one, such as locomotion through the sea rather than through the air.

This is the sense in which we might see language as a pre-adaptation for the evolution of consciousness. Originally, we may suppose that language evolved for purposes of relatively simple and straightforward communication of the kind seen in the case of honey bees. Once evolved as such, however, language could then take on other functions, and be subject to selection for different adaptive outcomes. It may be that full self-awareness is normally required for speech, not because speaking in words is such a difficult task that there is no other way to do it, but because being able to speak makes self-consciousness possible. Speech, in other words, may be a pre-adaptation for consciousness, rather than consciousness being a necessary condition for speech.

This could come about because words are abstract representations of reality, not real parts of the outside world in themselves. Even onomato-poeic words like 'bang' and 'bump' are not the sounds themselves that they recall, but representations of them. Telling others that you felt some emotion such as fear does not mean that you have to be afraid when you tell them, or that they must feel fear in order to understand. In this case language is not an expression of the emotions so much as an expression *about* emotions. The emotion itself is indicated by speech, but not necessarily aroused either in speaker or hearer. The consequence is that abstract terms can in principle represent abstract realities, such as intentions, ideas, memories and emotions, just as surely as they can tangible realities, such as game, hills and the disposition of things in the real world. Words, in short, are pre-adapted for abstraction by being abstract themselves.

As a consequence, words can be used to represent things that are wholly abstract, and could never be seen, touched or sensed in the way in which an object might be. This suits them ideally for describing purely *psychological* things, such as motives, memories, emotions or thoughts. It is as easy to say, 'I am doing this for your benefit' as it is to say, 'There's game in them thar hills!' Both appear to be statements of fact, even though the first is about a purely abstract thing – an intention – whereas the second is about a wholly real thing, game in the hills. The essential difference is that, whereas the existence of game in the hills could be directly verified by going there and seeing, the existence of an altruistic intention cannot be directly observed because it is an abstract entity, not a material one. No-one could climb inside your head to inspect your intentions in the same way that they could go into the hills to see if the game was really there. You simply can't see a feeling, thought, intention or memory in the same way in which you can see things in the real world.

Indeed – and hallucinations aside – even the person experiencing these things cannot *see* them in the sense that they perceive them with their eyes. On the contrary, the most significant subjective realities we experience are our emotions, and they express themselves as feelings sometimes very similar to the way we might feel something in the real world through the sense of touch. Pain and pleasure in particular can sometimes be every bit as real as something felt by touch, and many other emotions come close to such immediate physical sensation. But even these feelings, real as they may be, are only felt by the subject experiencing them, and others may easily doubt their reality, or fail to appreciate their intensity simply because they are internal to the person concerned. Again, memories, thoughts and intentions can only be seen by the internal eye of imagination, and have no objective reality outside the mind of the person perceiving them.

This suggests that there is no way of verifying such abstract, subjective sensations because sight cannot extend to the inside of someone's mind and the sense of touch cannot connect directly with someone else's emotions. Nevertheless, we can *hear* ourselves speaking just as others hear us, and our thoughts, if formulated in words, can be heard even if never spoken. We can hear them purely internally, as unvoiced thoughts, thanks to being able to recall how the words used sound if spoken. As such, they sound in a purely internal space, our own consciousness, and here the ability to frame thoughts in words transforms the situation. Now we could verify a statement such as 'I am doing this for your benefit' because we could have heard ourselves formulate it in words, or at least in thought. As long as we were not aware of any contradictory thought, we could claim that such a statement was just as objective and just as true as any about the game in the hills. And if anyone questioned it, we could indignantly deny that any other thought ever occurred to us. If such a denial were the truth, it would begin to seem as if thoughts were like things and as if we could make statements about psychology in just the same way that we do about external, physical reality.

Indeed, we could extend this to include things that were subjectively felt, rather than heard – at least if they could subsequently be formulated in words. So emotions and intuitions could be given the status of 'facts' if we could formulate them in words as we might formulate a thought.

Thanks to being able to verbalize them, our inner, subjective senses in general might begin to play the rôle with regard to our psychological world that our external, objective senses do in relation to the real world. Then indeed the abstract possibilities of words would be realized and their prime function in human consciousness would be revealed. By giving us a means of describing an inner psychological reality they would allow us to become conscious of it by way of being able to communicate it to others. What may have started as simple communication about the disposition of objects in the outside world comparable to that seen in the case of honey bees may have evolved by these means into a medium that allowed statements about inner, subjective reality – what we otherwise know as consciousness.

Consciousness as a lie

The abstract nature of language would also have introduced another possibility that may be connected with the evolution of consciousness. This is the possibility of *deceit*. In the past there was a tendency to overlook this aspect of communication in evolutionary thinking because of the influence of group selection (see above, pp. 40–2). As long as communication is thought of in terms of its benefit to the group or species, mis-communication seems pathological and maladaptive. But the moment you begin to think of evolution in terms of the reproductive success of individuals and their genes, deception becomes intelligible, because if communication can be used helpfully and truthfully to the benefit of the recipient it can also be used to communicate deceptively or unhelpfully to the benefit of the misinformer.

The most obvious example of this is camouflage, which can be seen as deceptive misinformation. But many other examples exist. One that shows the value of misinformation to individual reproductive success most clearly is female mimicry in bluegill sunfish. In this species regular males are distinctively coloured and quite a bit larger than the females they entice into their carefully tended nests. However, there is a minority of 'transvestites', or 'female mimics': males who closely resemble real females in size and colouring. They never enter a nest first, but always wait until a genuine female has gone in and started to lay. Then, welcomed by the unsuspecting resident regular male as a second female conquest, the transvestite enters. But instead of adding to his collection of eggs, the female mimic releases vast clouds of sperm, fertilizing the eggs of the first female to have entered. Here the message sent by the mimic is not truthful, and not one dedicated to the 'good of the species' – regular males could look after that perfectly well. Here deception rewards the reproductive success of the deceiver so that, in evolution as on the stage, drag acts can pay.

Again, thinking about the evolution of consciousness has been deeply influenced by ever-on-and-upward-to-humanity Progressivism. Here the idea was that even if the seat of human consciousness was not in a god-given soul set just a little lower than the angels, at least it was a supreme achievement of evolutionary progress understood as a per-fecting – or at least improving – mechanism. Consciousness implies knowledge, and so the natural tendency was to think of human con-sciousness as a supreme form of knowledge, and to emphasize its tran-scendental, truth-revealing nature. But we have already seen Darwin denying such unwarranted conclusions, and our modern gene-selectionist view of Darwinism certainly has no room for them. Even if our species might metaphorically be seen as seated in the 'gods' in the theatre of evolution, there is no reason to think that our possession of self-consciousness necessarily implies our consciousness of supreme truth – least of all about ourselves (see above, pp. 27–30).

As we have just seen, to say, 'There's game in them thar hills!' is one thing, but to say, 'I had no idea there was game in the hills!' is quite another matter, even though from the point of view of syntax both statements are very similar. Saying that I did not know about the game in the hills may excuse me from the suspicion that, if I had known, I should have told others, rather than keep the resource to myself. But who is to know? Clearly, the abstract nature of language creates great opportunities for deceit of all kinds, especially if the statements in ques-tion are about a person's thoughts, memories, intentions or emotions. Such statements are rather like unaudited accounts because of the way they cannot be directly tallied with independent evidence. If you don't need to feel an emotion to describe it, be unable to recall something to say you have forgotten it, or wish something when you say you intend it, who is to know what you felt, forgot or intended? Language, it seems, may be a pre-adaptation, not merely for consciousness, but for massive fraud. 'In fact, it might even be claimed that the ultimate goal of language acquisition is to lie effectively' and that 'real lying . . . is the deliberate use of language as a tool . . . to mislead the listener.'³ Further consideration of the question of co-operation may indicate why this is likely to be so.

Although Tit-for-Tat turned out to be a winning strategy in Prisoner's Dilemma tournaments, the naturally-selected strategies that won the tournament described in the last chapter were in fact somewhat less nice than pure Tit-for-Tat (see pp. 51–5 above). Here *nice* means not being the first to defect. These naturally-evolved strategies tended to defect against the other player if they could get away with it. Tit-for-Tat never does this because it only defects to punish a prior defection by the other player and does so, in effect, to encourage a return to co-operation. But clearly, defection can pay if you can get away with it. As we have seen, a free lunch is the best outcome from the point of view of cost and benefit to any individual, and if that individual can get their partner to pay for their lunch then, in evolutionary terms, their ploy is a winning strategy. Indeed, entire classes of organisms, from tape-worms to mistletoe trees, have evolved to exploit such free lunches at the expense of their hosts.

One way of getting a free lunch is to mislead your partner into thinking that you cannot pay. A plausible lie, such as having lost your money, or having forgotten to go to the bank, might do the trick. But there is a problem with such deceptions, and this is that they can often be detected by the other, potentially exploited party. An ingenious series of experiments by one of the few twentieth-century psychologists to follow Darwin's own approach to psychology, Paul Ekman, showed how and why.

He investigated the means by which listeners could detect lies in what they were being told. Sometimes, the words themselves were enough, but often the voice was critical: 'The voice . . . is tied to the areas of the brain involved in emotion. It is very difficult to conceal some of the changes in voice that occur when emotion is aroused. And the feedback about what the voice sounds like, necessary for a liar to monitor how he sounds, is probably not as good for hearing the voice as it is for the words. People are surprised the first time they hear themselves on a tape recorder, because self-monitoring of the voice comes partly through bone conduction, and it sounds different.'⁴

According to Ekman, the best-documented vocal sign of emotion is the pitch of the voice. For about seventy per cent of people who have been studied, pitch becomes higher when the subject is upset. But studies show that pitch also rises when the subject is lying, probably as a result of the anxiety about detection that the deception induces. However, unusual flatness in the voice can also conceal deception, perhaps by way of compensation for this effect.

But the sound of the voice is not the only source of clues about the truth or falsity of what a listener is hearing. The face can also give away a lot. Here smiles are an excellent example. Ekman points out that there is a subtle difference between a false and a genuine smile. In the genuine smile, muscles around the eye contract, causing visible creases, as Darwin noted.[5] But the muscles in question cannot be voluntarily contracted in a false smile. The result is that insincere smiles tend to be somewhat exaggerated by way of trying to produce the wrinkles around the eyes characteristic of a sincere one through stretching the mouth into a more emphatic smile than would be the case if it were sincere. Ekman concludes: 'The face is directly connected to those areas of the brain involved in emotion, and words are not. When emotion is aroused, muscles on the face begin to fire involuntarily. It is only by choice or habit that people can learn to interfere with these expressions, trying, with varying degrees of success, to conceal them . . . Facial expressions are a dual system – voluntary and involuntary, lying and telling the truth, often at the same time.'[6]

If the face can give away so much, so too can the body:

> The body is a good source of leakage and deception clues. Unlike the face or voice, most body movements are not directly tied to areas of the brain involved in emotion. Monitoring of body movements need not be difficult. A person can feel and often see what his body is doing. Concealment of body movements could be much easier than concealing facial expressions or voice changes in emotion. But most people don't bother. They have grown up having learned that it was not necessary to do so. Rarely are people held accountable for what they reveal in their bodily actions. The body leaks because it is ignored. Everyone is too busy watching the face and evaluating the words.

In general he concludes that 'Liars usually do not monitor, control and disguise all of their behaviour. They probably couldn't even if they wanted to. It is not likely that anyone could successfully control every-thing he did that could give him away, from the tips of his toes to the top of his head.'[7] As that other psychologist in the Darwinian tradition, Sigmund Freud, also observed, 'He that has eyes to see and ears to hear may convince himself that no mortal can keep a secret. If his lips are silent, he chatters with his finger-tips; betrayal oozes out of him at every pore.'[8] To sum up, we might say that what these observations show is that self-conscious deception, like most other instances of self-conscious behaviour, does not produce improved performance in deceiving. On the contrary, *it seems that it is the consciousness that you are deceiving that is most likely to give the deception away.*

Reverting for a moment to Darwinian theory on evolution, we might conclude that a kind of 'arms race' might develop between means to deceive and means to detect deception. Such arms races have certainly occurred in other, more obvious examples of deception and detection-of-deception, such as animal or plant camouflage. Here selection rewards prey who manage to deceive their predators. But selection also rewards predators who successfully detect the prey, leading to a spiralling compe-tition much like the military arms races we know. The result is often an astonishing degree of successful deception in the prey, who is selected to be really well camouflaged to elude the sharpened senses of the predator who has to find it.

Recently Darwinists such as R. D. Alexander and Robert Trivers have suggested that a similar kind of arms race between deception and detection-of-deception may have evolved in human psychology, particu-larly over issues like co-operation. They have pointed out that, thanks to difficulties in hiding conscious deception like those revealed by Ekman's work, natural selection may have rewarded deceivers who did not know that they were deceiving, and thereby were less likely to give away clues of their deception. Put another way, we could say that, if liars were not self-conscious, they might be more effective in their lying. Lacking an awareness in themselves that they were deceiving, others would find it all the more difficult to detect signs of it. In other words, natural selec-tion might select for *un*self-conscious liars, or for deceivers who were not conscious of the fact that they were deceiving. If not aware that they were deceiving, such liars could lie with total sincerity and would not reveal subtle cues of deceit and anxiety about it. In a word, natural selection might reward deceivers who had become *unconscious* of their deception. If so, then consciousness – what you were aware of – would serve to hide, or screen, what you were *not* aware of. Indeed, such a consciousness might hide more than it revealed and we might be justified in calling it a *cryptic* form of awareness, one that evolved to deceive even more than to inform.

A useful analogy here might be from public relations. Imagine that you were the head of some business or public agency that you knew had done some wrong that would result in public criticism. If you wished to conceal the truth from the public, you would be best advised not to inform your public relations department of the full extent of the wrong-doing. This is because, even if you knew that they would do their best to conceal it, there would be a real possibility that under the full glare of public exposure someone might let slip a revealing word or make some other kind of gaff that would invite further scrutiny. Much better by far for them to know nothing whatsoever about the deception being practised and to be able to brief the press and public with complete sincerity. If you knew that your publicity department suspected nothing of the truth, there would be no way in which it could give it away inadvertently. Effectively, you would be applying a 'need to know' policy and not allowing those in the organiz-ation to be 'in the know' who might then inform the wider public, who would then be kept 'out of the know'.

According to this way of looking at things, the mind of the individual may be structured in a similar way, with some parts 'in the know' and some parts not needing to know for a similar reason. 'Being in the know' would mean being conscious, and 'not being in the know' would mean being unconscious. Deceptions in particular would be excluded from consciousness so that they could not betray the subtle cues that might give away the truth to others. Like a public relations department that had no inkling of any wrong-doing on the part of the organization it represented, the mind might evolve to deceive itself all the better to deceive others. The most effective liars would be those who had con-vinced themselves that their lies were in fact the truth. Having achieved that feat of self-deception, duping others would be all the more easy. Now they could lie in total sincerity!

Although, as you might think, experiments on self-deception are dif-ficult to devise and carry out, one particularly elegant one has been performed. The experiment used a lie-detector to measure galvanic skin response to voices. It established that skin response is heightened on hearing your own voice by contrast to hearing someone else's, and that response to your own voice increases with time, rather than declining as it does in the case of someone else's voice. The experiment compared experimental subjects' skin-response to the sound of voices with their conscious awareness of whose voices they were hearing, and found discrepancies in perception. The experiment showed that, of those individuals who failed to recognize their own voice, skin response was a much more reliable indicator of the truth than was their conscious awareness. As our earlier discussion of the rôle of speech may have led us to expect and as Robert Trivers comments, 'for most mistakes, the part of the brain controlling speech got it wrong, while the part controlling arousal got it right.'[9] This finding establishes that unconscious perception can occur while consciousness remains ignorant of it, much as in my public relations analogy above.

However, for that analogy to be really applicable, we would need to be able to show that such conscious unawareness was motivated, and not just a random error, or failure of conscious perception. In the analogy, the public relations department is not just uninformed of the truth, it is prevented from knowing it. To test this aspect of the situation, a second experiment was carried out in which subjects' self-perception was manipulated prior to a repetition of the first voice-recognition experiment. It is a common finding that we draw more attention to ourselves when we have something to be proud of than when we are ashamed of ourselves, and previous experimental work had established that subjects with high self-esteem are more ready to recognize their own voice than those with low self-esteem. The repetition of the experiment after manipulation of the subjects' self-regard by means of telling them how well or badly they had done at a verbal aptitude test showed that self-deception where voice recognition was concerned was indeed motivated. Those who were made to feel good about themselves by having scored well on the test were much more likely to recognize their own voices and, indeed, even to attribute their own voice to others. Those whose self-esteem had been lowered by doing badly, however, showed the opposite response: a tendency to avoid themselves and deny their own voices. Furthermore, when questioned after the experiment, those with lowered self-esteem reported enjoying hearing their own voice less and rated their own voices as less pleasant than the successful group did.

The authors of these elegant experiments conclude their paper concurring with the judgement that 'The discovery of a deceiving principle, a lying activity within us, can furnish an absolutely new view of all conscious life.'[10] The next chapter will be devoted to such a view – or model – of the mind. But before we leave the issue of awareness and deception there are one or two further questions on which the concept of cryptic consciousness can throw some interesting new light. One of these is important because, like subjective feelings of self-importance where understanding an objective fact like evolution is concerned, it stands in the way of an important insight (see above, pp. 23–4).

What I have in mind here is our credulity for group-selectionist ideas about altruism. In the last chapter we saw that from the scientific point of view group selection is about as credible as perpetual motion in physics. This is because it fails to count the cost to individuals of co-operation with the interests of others and effectively assumes that you can get something for nothing (see above, pp. 41–2). But that does not stop it being the way people often think – even people who should know better, like the social scientists who ended up paying for their colleague's free lunch. The fact that only one of them anticipated the problem is astonishing, given that all were supposed to understand human social behaviour. But this is typical. It is entirely normal for people to assume with what is often considerable naivete that others will bear the cost of group membership without hesitation, question or internal conflict.

Why is this so? The answer may be that it is in your own self-interest to deceive yourself about others' self-interest because then the others can all the more easily be pressured into acting against their self-interest. This is what we might term the 'Let George do it' principle. If we are all committed members of the family, group, society or species, and all count the benefit to the majority above the cost to us personally, then George is like us and George can pay. The fact that we personally are not going to pay on this occasion is just a detail for which we can always find infinite rationalizations: George has more resources of time or money, George is more competent to do it, likes doing it, is nearer to it, did not do it last time, etc. Furthermore, in any group larger than two the others we expect to contribute to the group without thought of the cost to themselves will always outnumber us, often by a very large margin. Since they can all benefit us personally by contributing to the cost of group membership, we have a personal self-interest in seeing them pay. To put it another way, we might say that free-riders rely on fare-payers, because otherwise there would be no rides at all! Paradoxically then, the very individuals who have most to gain by free-riding also have the greatest incentive to advocate payment by others.

In other words, self-deception about others' self-interest serves our own selfishness because it makes it easier for us to exploit others, expecting them to pay while we benefit. As a result, appeals to collective, group-selectionist feelings about social behaviour are probably an evolved bias in us, and one fed by entirely selfish concerns. (Indeed, to the extent that such ideas form the basis of the so-called 'social sciences' they may explain much of what is so unscientific about them in reality.) Believing in other people's altruism does not have to be naive credulity if its practical effect is very often to make it harder for others to refuse to act altruistically to our personal benefit. Since others will have the same incentive to adopt a similar attitude to us, a culture of admonitions to altruism and expectations of self-sacrifice will evolve, with everyone having a selfish interest in the altruism of everyone else.

Of course, such prejudices will sometimes impose costs on us too (as they certainly did on the head of the department in the restaurant case, who was caused intense embarrassment). Nevertheless, the overall benefit probably outweighs the cost in most cases, not least because it makes it all the easier for us to dupe ourselves about our own self-interest in not paying if we have first deceived ourselves about the self-interest of others. After all, if we would never suspect George of free-riding, why should we suspect ourselves? Like our personal consciousness, our social consciousness could be cryptic and could hide, not merely our own selfish and anti-social motives, but those of others too.

The second issue that considerations of social deceit and self-deception raises is interesting, in part because it is one of the most obscure and apparently far-removed from evolutionary considerations or scientific scrutiny. Furthermore, it is one closely related to expression of the emotions. The question I have in mind is what constitutes the basis of the feeling of aesthetic pleasure that people derive from art, literature and music.

If we take music first, it is worth noting Darwin's opinion that 'The perception, if not the enjoyment, of musical cadences and of rhythm is probably common to all animals, and no doubt depends on the common physiological nature of their nervous systems.' However, he adds that 'As neither the enjoyment nor the capacity of producing musical notes are faculties of the least direct use to man in reference to his ordinary habits of life, they must be ranked among the most mysterious with which he is endowed.' Nevertheless, Darwin was too good a psychologist to fail to notice that 'Music affects every emotion.' He goes on to conclude that our capacity to produce music and appreciate it may be a product of sexual selection (of which, more later), in part because 'Love is still the commonest theme of our songs' – something as true today as it was in 1871.[11]

But however that may be, an ability to detect rhythm and tone may have evolved in part because of their importance in speech, particularly in relation to emotion and to deception. As we saw Ekman remarking earlier, the voice is tied to the areas of the brain involved in emotion, and pitch tends to rise with emotion and to be an indicator of deception (see above, pp. 69–70). But the musical aspects of speech in general can tell a listener much about the psychological state of a speaker, and a sensitivity to them may have evolved in part for that reason. Specialized areas of the brain devoted to analyzing pitch, rhythm, intonation, tempo and cadence of speech in order to detect possible signs of deception may have been pre-adaptations (see above, pp. 64–5) for the appreciation of music.

However, aesthetic pleasure in general often seems to be related to the perception of harmony, proportion, rhythm and unity in the object, be it musical, literary, dramatic or artistic. Although discords and breaks in rhythm can be exciting and pleasurable for that reason, in the main it is harmony rather than dissonance, rhythm rather than the lack of it that we appreciate in music (compare atonal, arhythmic modernist music with popular music). Similarly in drama and literature, it is unity rather than disunity, integrity rather than disorder, consistency rather than chaos that we appreciate in plots, characters and descriptions. In the visual arts, internal harmony, pleasing proportion, unity of parts, all normally make for feelings of aesthetic enjoyment by comparison to the converse.

One possible reason why this may be so could be that harmony, integrity and lack of internal conflict are the hall-marks of truthful communications of all kinds, but of verbal ones in particular. Someone who is sincerely telling the truth is likely to convey a message that is simple, coherent and complete in a tone of voice accompanied by facial and other gestures that are appropriate to it and in harmony with it. Such a communication need arouse no suspicion or anxiety in the listener, who can feel relaxed and content as a result. However, someone who is not telling the truth is, as we have seen, likely to give it away by some internal discrepancy in the message or by some conflict between it and other signals that they might give out, either in voice, gesture or expression. The perception of such discordant signals, however subtle, is likely to arouse suspicion, anxiety and internal conflict in the hearer, who is put on their guard against the possibility of deception and the costs that may follow from it for them (such as paying for a free lunch). The result may be a tendency to feel enjoyment where an essential aesthetic integrity can be felt in something, but a lack of it where it is missing. Emotions originally evolved for directly judging words, appearances or gestures may in this way have come to underlie our indirect appreciation of these things in literature, art, music and drama.

Finally, it may be worth remarking that a chapter originally devoted to consciousness, the supreme attribute that human beings claim for themselves, has also taken in language, and ended up discussing aesthetics – two other things that are also usually regarded as unique to our species. But all three may have arisen out of evolutionary considerations that are most certainly not unique to humans. On the contrary, co-operation and defection, selfishness and altruism, deception and detection, are dilemmas that face most organisms that interact with others. It may be that human beings experience these dilemmas at a greater intensity than any other species, thanks to both a greater capacity to communicate and an ability to command so many of the earth's resources. But these are differences of degree, rather than of kind. Fundamentally, language, consciousness and aesthetics could well share a common origin in the evolution of human conflict and co-operation.

MODELS OF THE MIND

Talking about consciousness without mentioning Freud is about as defensible as discussing gravitation without Newton, or evolution without Darwin. Yet this does not prevent many writers from doing just that. In part, this may be because Freud is mainly thought of as having made discoveries about the *unconscious*, rather than consciousness. But Freud's findings about the unconscious have deep significance for our understanding of the conscious, and suggest that consciousness cannot be fully understood without understanding the unconscious too. Again, it is important to realize that Freud was not a philosopher or even a psychologist who set out to investigate human consciousness. He was a neurologist by training whose pioneering psychotherapeutic methods led him to make momentous discoveries about the nature of consciousness, even if consciousness in itself was not an issue that he had set out to explore in the first place.

The previous chapter has brought us up to date with thinking about the evolution of consciousness in modern Darwinism. The time has now come to consider how this relates to Freud's findings.

The mind as a Macintosh

Sigmund Freud died long before the age of the personal computer, but if he had had one, it is by no means unlikely that he would have noticed and perhaps commented on a number of illuminating parallels between it and his own understanding of the mind. There is certainly a precedent for this in a short paper he wrote on 'The Mystic Writing Pad'. This was a notepad comprising a clear sheet with further sheets underneath that adhered to a wax substrate to record marks made on it by a stylus in such a way that the sheets could also be separated to erase the marks. Freud's interest in this simple device was aroused by the way he saw it as illustrating some of his most abstract ideas about how consciousness (the ephemeral writing on the pad) resulted from the interaction of the perceptual system (the top sheet that receives the imprint of the stylus) and the long-term memory system (the underlying wax substrate). He justified drawing this analogy by commenting that all such aids are 'invented for the improvement or intensification of our sensory functions' and are modelled on them, mentioning spectacles, cameras and hearing-aids.[1] Had he lived in the age of the computer he might have gone on to add that computers generally resemble not just the senses but also the mind. Indeed, were he alive today he would find that hand-held computers with data-entry by stylus have succeeded the Mystic Writing Pad and that a pressure-sensitive screen can display data in the computer's memory, making it an even closer representation of his psychological model.

Hand-held computers of this kind often have a so-called 'graphic user interface' similar to the one used in the Macintosh computer on which this book was written. An *interface* is a region where two systems are in contact – in this case the human user and the computer's operating system. In the Macintosh version, the computer's contents are displayed as *icons*, or miniature pictures, which appear on an imaginary desktop. Files are represented in the form of *documents* that are organized into *folders*. There is even a wastebasket into which documents and programs can be thrown when the user wishes to erase them from the computer's memory. The user directs a pointer at an icon and selects it, whereupon it becomes highlighted, indicating that this is the item to be used. When the item is opened, it appears in a 'window', with a title, scroll bar and other means to identify and manipulate it (see figure 13).

Much of the success of the Macintosh was the result of its easy-to-use, intuitive interface. It solved the problem created by the fact that computers work in one way, but human beings in another. The user interface is critical as the point at which the human being who has to use the computer and the computer itself come into contact. In large part, the Macintosh solved this problem by hiding the detail of the computer's operating system behind the graphic fiction of the desktop and its icons. The computer screen never was a desktop in the literal sense – for a start, it was vertical, rather than horizontal – but the fact that it could be interpreted as one was all that mattered as far as using it as an interface was concerned. You could see it as a screen that concealed

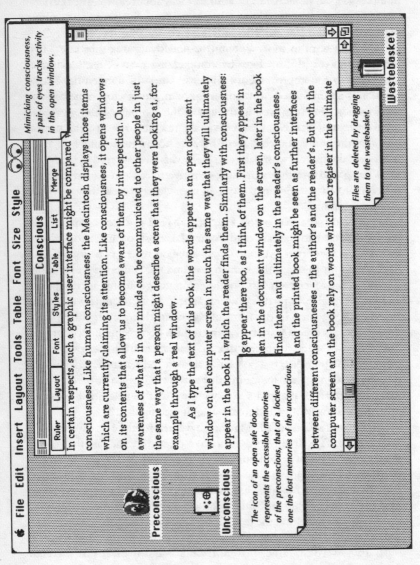

FIGURE 13: The Macintosh™ as a model of the mind.

unnecessary detail and complication from the user, but on which everything the user did need to know was shown in a convenient and intuitive way.

In certain respects, such a graphic user interface might be compared with human consciousness. Like human consciousness, the Macintosh displays those items which are currently claiming its attention. Like consciousness, it opens windows on its contents that allow us to become aware of them by introspection. Our awareness of what is in our minds can be communicated to other people in just the same way that a person might describe a scene that they were looking at, for example through a real window.

As I type the text of this book, the words appear in an open document window on the computer screen in much the same way that they will ultimately appear in the book in which the reader finds them. Similarly with consciousness: the words I am typing appear there too, as I think of them. First they appear in my consciousness, then in the document window on the screen, later in the book in which the reader finds them, and ultimately in the reader's consciousness. The computer screen and the printed book might be seen as further interfaces between different consciousnesses – the author's and the reader's. But both the computer screen and the book rely on words which also register in the ultimate interface – consciousness itself. By communicating my thoughts and feelings to others I allow them to understand what is in my consciousness so that it also registers in their consciousness. To this extent, my consciousness might be seen as a kind of psychological interface with the consciousness of others – a window into my mind. It is certainly the means by which others enter data to my mind, and I output data to their minds. (See figure 13.)

But there is a problem with such data transfers in general and with this kind of interface in particular. In computing it is apparent to everyone as the problem of data privacy and security. Let's take the Macintosh again as an example. Some years ago I had to share a machine with others and wished to store personal files on the computer's internal disk, rather than have to enter and erase them every time I used it. The problem was that if I just left them there, anyone could see them and access them. Because these were personal data, I did not wish that to happen. One way to prevent this was to encrypt the files. But this was not an ideal solution because they could still be erased by anyone, and encryption and decryption can be a time-consuming, annoying process. Another possibility was to hide my files among others, for example by giving them misleading or uninformative names. Here the problem was that, if I hid my files among someone else's, the owner of the files would probably immediately realize that they did not belong, and might open or erase them. And in any event, hiding numerous files with uninformative or misleading names in many different folders was a headache when it came to finding them again.

The solution I adopted was not to encrypt my files but to use a special piece of software to partition the hard disk in question into two parts: a public, open sector that anyone could use, and a private, hidden part that only I could access. Of course, I could not physically partition the disk by any mechanical means. What I did was to create invisible files that, contrary to the norm on a Macintosh, could not be seen on the desktop and could therefore not be found by casual users. Now my files were both private and secure, because no-one could even see them, let alone open or erase them!

This suggests a further parallel with the human mind, rather in the way in which the 'Mystic Writing Pad' suggested parallels to Freud. We could now say that, if consciousness can be the equivalent of the windows of the human, psychological interface, in which input/output data and current attention of the operating system were displayed, there could also be invisible files, closed windows, hidden partitions, or reserved sectors of memory, just as there can be in a computer. If we call the open windows *the conscious*, we might then call these closed, inaccessible parts *the unconscious*. We could suggest that this unconscious region would correspond to those contents of the mind that would be best kept secret because, all other things being equal, their display in consciousness would not promote the reproductive success of those who did reveal them in this way. We might predict that, if consciousness is a psychological interface with the psychology of others, it should only contain those aspects of the individual's mind that would either do no harm to them when revealed or might positively benefit them by being revealed. But other aspects of their minds, such as selfish, cheating, or anti-social motives, memories or emotions, might be best consigned to the invisible part – the unconscious. Effectively it would be the subjective, human, psychological equivalent of the computer privacy/security problem. It would be the way natural selection had arranged the human psychological interface to be open to others where this was desirable, but closed to others where it was not. And for reasons explained in the last chapter, this would also mean that self-consciousness would be treated similarly: you would know what it was in your self-interest that others should know, but not what it was in your self-interest that they should not know (see above, pp. 67–77).

To return to the question of the privacy of my files, my action was not as unprecedented as it might appear in the Macintosh operating system. There are other files that routinely never appear on the desktop. The desktop file itself, for example, which contains the data about what the desktop shows, is normally invisible and inaccessible to the user (simply because it is always in use when the desktop of which it is a part is visible). Again, specific system files that contain the instructions for the computer's operating system either cannot be seen at all, or if they can, cannot usually be directly opened as a window by the user (again because they are normally in use). Furthermore, we could also observe that, just as the Macintosh operating system keeps many of its most fundamental files inaccessible to the user, so might the human one. The reason that computers normally do not allow open access to their operating systems is that the user could do so much damage to them if they were easily accessible. Such systems are complex pieces of software that, like the intricate workings of a delicate time-piece, are best not tampered with because almost any interference, however slight, would probably be harmful. So we might expect that the human, psychological operating system (whatever that may be) would similarly be kept unconscious and beyond the reach of tampering by its user. Like the user interface in a computer that keeps the complex detail of the operating system hidden and only reveals information of direct relevance to the user, consciousness would hide the greater part of what was happening in the mind.

The unconscious, then, would comprise two types of 'invisible files' (to pursue the Macintosh analogy). On the one hand would be mental contents that could, in principle, be conscious, but were kept unconscious because of their socially undesirable nature. On the other hand would be elements of the mind that were never conscious but remained permanently in the unconscious, thanks to being part of the psychological operating system, so to speak.

But, like the invisible files in a computer, both these aspects of the unconscious would probably share their storage medium with the conscious, accessible parts (in the Macintosh case, the same disk). As my secret partitioning exercise showed, it is not necessary to assume any physical partitioning of the memory medium. All that is necessary is that certain data should be rendered inaccessible by way of the software interface.

However, not all of the inaccessible system software of a Macintosh is held in invisible or normally inaccessible files on disk. Some of it is in a form of built-in memory called ROM, which stands for *Read Only Memory*. As this term suggests, the memory in question can only be read, not rewritten. It is 'hard-wired' in the sense that it is permanent, and cannot be altered once it is installed during fabrication of the computer.

Here again an instructive analogy might have occurred to Freud. Along with what was unconscious through having been excluded from consciousness and what was permanently unconscious, there was a third part of the unconscious that Freud variously called 'the archaic heritage', 'primal phantasies' or simply 'phylogeny' (what today we would call 'evolution'). This is an aspect of his writing that has been systematically ignored and disparaged for fifty years, but is of such importance for PsychoDarwinism that it cannot be overlooked. Were he writing today, he would probably have pointed out that, just as computers have some of the most basic parts of their operating system 'hard-wired' as ROM, so we could regard the genetic code as a comparable form of read-only memory, a kind of DNA-ROM. Certain genes might code for parts of the human, psychological operating system just as the ROM chips in a Macintosh carry parts of the operating code for the system software. Such read-only memories would, of course, be totally unconscious and would indeed be located in a storage medium (DNA) presumably completely distinct from that in which other parts of the unconscious might be registered (and today we are still unclear about how memories are stored in the brain and have only the vaguest idea about how such a DNA-ROM would actually work).

The analogy, though, would remain a good one: indeed, having gone this far Freud – who was not one for half-measures – would probably go the whole way and point out that the remaining form of computer memory, *Random Access Memory,* or RAM, was also analogous to an aspect of human memory. RAM is so called because it is a volatile form of active memory that only exists while the computer operating system is loaded and powered-up. It vanishes on shut-down or with the loss of power, and represents a kind of short-term, working memory where the computer stores information currently needed for what it is doing. For example, suppose that I want to move some text in the manuscript of this book as I am writing it. I can cut the relevant part out and it will disappear from the document window and reappear at the point where I insert it. Where was it in the meantime? The answer is: in the RAM (specifically in a part of it called 'the Clipboard' reserved for such cutting and pasting by the Macintosh operating system). As such, RAM seems to correspond quite closely to the short-term, conscious memory I would use for example if, instead of being able to rely on my computer to remember cut-and-pasted text for me, I had to remember it myself. Just like my computer, I would have to store the data somewhere temporarily until I could use it, but would be content to forget it as soon as the operation involving it was done.

My motive for elaborating this analogy is the same as Freud's in the case of the Mystic Writing Pad: to give concrete expression to an otherwise abstract idea – in this case, Freud's insight into the structure of consciousness. This led Freud to define consciousness more carefully than is the case in everyday speech. He defined *the conscious* as *that which currently occupies awareness*, and nothing more. As such, the conscious would correspond to the active window on a computer screen, and, in so far as memory was also involved, to parts of the computer's RAM. This is a very much narrower and more precise concept of the conscious than we might normally entertain, but it has the virtue of being expressed in terms of psychological reality – actual moment-to-moment awareness – rather than in vaguer terms.

However, this definition creates a new problem, because it seems to exclude much that might be included in consciousness more broadly defined. This led Freud to invent a second term to cover what was left out by the first. *What was not currently in conscious awareness, but might be voluntarily recalled to it at any moment,* Freud termed the *preconscious*. This covers most of what otherwise might be called 'conscious' in everyday terms, and would correspond to the accessible, read/write memory on the computer's disk – files that could be opened by the user if necessary but were not currently displayed in an active window. An example might be my telephone number, something that is not always in my conscious awareness, but which I can recall easily whenever I need it.

Finally, one further category would be necessary if we had already defined the conscious as current awareness and the preconscious as what might potentially be conscious. Clearly, this would have to be contents of the mind neither conscious nor potentially conscious, but wholly unconscious. In this special, Freudian sense, the unconscious is defined as *that which could not be voluntarily recalled to consciousness*. In a computer it would correspond partly to invisible, partitioned or inaccessible files, and partly to the hard-wired ROM of the operating system – all of which could not normally be opened as a window on the desktop. (See figure 13.)

In human psychology an excellent example of unconscious awareness was provided by the voice recognition experiments I mentioned at the end of the last chapter. There we saw that some subjects definitely recognized their own voices by the evidence of their skin conductance, but remained totally unaware of the fact in their subjective consciousness. In a word, they were *unconscious* of it. A further example that comes even closer to the computer example is provided by so-called 'blindsight'. This is a condition found in people with damage to the visual areas of the brain. They have been found to be able to point at targets or track them with their eyes while at the same time vigorously denying that they can see anything. Again, although they have no conscious awareness that they are looking at an object, they can often correctly guess what it might be if encouraged to do so. Indeed, blindsight is routinely used to distinguish hysterical blindness (that is, blindness caused by purely psychological factors) from 'true', total blindness. These findings prove that, even though blindsighted subjects have no conscious awareness of seeing anything, they do in fact see unconsciously and that visual perceptions register somewhere in their minds, even if they cannot voluntarily access them.

I once exploited a similar effect to improve my shooting skills. Experience shows that no human being can hold a gun perfectly still for any significant period of time. Even lying prone and propping a rifle cannot prevent the sights drifting slightly over the target. I found that if I aimed the rifle as best I could, squeezed the trigger to the point where only a very small additional pressure was necessary to fire, a purely emotional feeling reliably informed me when my sights were dead on target. I found that if I fired then, and only then, my shooting was a lot better than otherwise and that I could aim to an accuracy that exceeded what I could consciously see. The likelihood is that, even in normal visual perception, some data do not enter consciousness. It may be that these additional data were critical to very accurate aiming and unconsciously accessed by me when I allowed my emotions rather than my reason to tell me when to fire. Effectively I was probably using a kind of blindsight as a means of achieving greater accuracy. This suggests that the unconscious region of the mind may have more complex relations with the conscious than my computer analogy suggests. It is to a more detailed model of the unconscious and its relation to consciousness that we must now turn.

A new ID for Freud

Of course, the human mind is not a computer, any more than it is a 'Mystic Writing Pad'. Freud's use of the latter was purely as a model for certain aspects of the mind, and my use of the Macintosh in the previous section was intended in exactly the same sense. It provides a convenient analogy for what Freud himself called the *topographical* description of the mind.

The voice-recognition experiments mentioned in the last chapter are an illustration of mental topography at work. In those experiments some subjects recognized their own voices by evidence of their skin-conductance, but failed to recognize them consciously. This finding suggests that those subjects understood that they were listening to their own voices in one part of their minds, but did not do so in another part. The only way to explain how two contradictory pieces of knowledge can exist simultaneously in one and the same mind is to assume that they exist separately in some sense. This is the essence of the topographical view of consciousness. It treats the mind as divided or partitioned, rather in the same way that I partitioned the shared hard disk that contained my private files.

Here 'mental topography' means an attempt to describe the mind in terms of imaginary spatial localization as if it were a landscape or a complex surface. I emphasize the word *imaginary* here, because Freud adamantly resisted any attempts to localize psychological functions in brain physiology. To pursue the useful analogy of the previous section, we might say that Freud's concern was with the *software* of the mind, not with its *hardware* – the brain. (Even today, we know so little about the latter that we could hardly go much further than Freud could. Nevertheless, what we do know suggests that his caution was well-founded, and that, thanks to what appears to be extensive parallel processing and subdivision of basic processes such as perception, speech and memory within the brain, there is little likelihood that complex phenomena like consciousness can be traced to a single centre or localized at any one point.)

Freud's first model of the mind is, then, a software model, not an attempt to map brain anatomy. It divides mental contents into three regions that might be seen like geological strata, lying one on top of another. In the Macintosh analogy I used in the previous section, we saw that the three subdivisions of consciousness could be compared to three kinds of file in a computer: open files (the conscious), accessible files (the preconscious) and inaccessible or invisible files (the unconscious) (see figure 13). The analogy was an apt one because it showed that, just as inaccessible system files, hidden files and readily accessible ones might be interleaved in memory storage on the same disk, they were distinguishable in terms of how easily or otherwise they could be opened by the user, who played the rôle of conscious volition. Freud's first model is much the same: it envisages the essential difference between the three states of consciousness in terms of how easily or otherwise their contents can be recalled to consciousness, and it is this that determines the topography of consciousness.

The first topography is so called because, in the course of the 1920s, it was followed by a second, the famous id-ego-superego model. However, it would be quite wrong to imagine that the three new terms were simple substitutes for the three previous ones and that the id equals the unconscious, the ego the conscious and the superego the preconscious. On the contrary, the three terms from the first topography remained in use to describe the three subdivisions of consciousness. The new terms were intended to add a new dimension, so to speak, one that concentrated, not on different levels of consciousness, but on different *agencies* within the mind. (What the new terms actually replaced were labels for the conscious-preconscious and unconscious as *systems*, rather than simply as topographical regions, but the details need not concern us here.)

An agency of any kind is defined by what it does – by its function. The so-called 'second topography' is like a map of the mind that includes, not just the contours and layers of consciousness like the first one, but additionally the function of definite localities, analogous to talking about watersheds, riftvalleys or flood-plains in land topography. All of these have topographical, or layered, spatial, relationships, but they also show qualitative differences of function, watersheds dividing precipitation, for example, while valleys concentrate it and flood-plains distribute it. In each case the topography underlies the function. Similarly with the three agencies of the second topography. Each has a characteristic topography that is defined in terms of its function or rôle in the internal economy of the mind.

First, the id. In Freud's original German, this is *das Es,* literally, 'the It'. In the medico-Latinized English translations of Freud's works this is rendered as the Latin pronoun, *id.*

One major argument in favour of the concept of the id is that it helps to clear up confusion about the use of the term 'unconscious'. Clearly, this can mean two, slightly different things: it can mean 'not conscious' where conscious is defined as we saw Freud defined it earlier – as *that which currently occupies conscious attention.* This would mean that my telephone number, for example, was unconscious whenever I was not thinking of it. But we have also seen that this would make it 'preconscious', because the definition of that was *what can be voluntarily recalled to consciousness,* and clearly, even if I am not thinking of my telephone number at any one moment, I can recall it instantly at another. In order to distinguish the currently unconscious preconscious from the totally, permanently unconscious it would be helpful to have a different term for the latter. Here the new model provides a solution. The id is the unconscious as a state of permanent unconsciousness. Although not all that is unconscious is part of the id, all that is the id is totally unconscious.

But this merely defines the topography of the id. What is its function? The previous discussion of the Macintosh analogy provides the answers. First, Freud thought that the id comprises permanently unconscious instinctual drives that ultimately arise in the body, but provide the instinctual foundations of the mind. We might say that it comprised the permanently inaccessible system files of the organism, ultimately encoded in the DNA-ROM of the genes. However, we have also seen that part of what is unconscious is what has been forced down into the unconscious from above, rather than rising up into it from below like instincts. The *repressed* unconscious therefore constitutes the second major part of the id.

Repression is one of the key concepts of psychoanalysis, and one of the most widely misunderstood. In large part, this is probably because people take it to mean what it does in everyday speech, where 'repress' is a transitive verb, with one subject and another object. Repression, according to this view, is something done to one person by another. But in Freud's writing 'repression' is a technical term, and is much more reflexive in the sense that repression describes something that you do to yourself, for your own good reasons.

Once again, the voice recognition experiments provide a good example. You will recall that a second experiment showed that subjects whose self-esteem had been artificially lowered by telling them that they had done badly on a test were less likely to recognize their own voices at the conscious level than were the subjects whose self-esteem had been heightened (see above, pp. 72–3). A Freudian account of the same thing would be that those with lowered self-esteem were more likely to *repress* the recognition of their own voices. Furthermore, the experiment makes it quite clear that they did so for their own reasons. Their state of lowered self-esteem may have been artificially engineered by the experimenters, but the subjects' tendency to repress recognition of their own voices was something that only they themselves could bring about. It was a defensive reaction to the situation engineered by the experiment, rather than something the experimenters did.

Freud's original word for what later became known as 'repression' (*Verdrängung* in German) was 'defence' (*Abwehr*), and in many ways this seems a preferable term, given the widespread misunderstanding that 'repression' seems to have caused, at least in English. Indeed, by 1926 he was advocating a return to it himself.[2] The defensive nature of the repression in those who did not recognize their own voices because of lowered self-esteem is explained by the observation that people generally are more likely to be self-effacing if they have failed at something, rather than succeeded (see above, pp. 72–3). You simply do not want to draw attention to yourself if you think that you have been unsuccessful, but would rather people did not notice your failure.

This illustrates the second characteristic of the specifically Freudian concept of defence, or repression. As we saw, the first is that the repressed is topographically distinct from the conscious. As Freud himself put it, 'the essence of repression lies simply in turning something away, and keeping it at a distance, from the conscious.'[3] The second characteristic of Freud's concept of repression is that it is *dynamic*. By this I mean that defence involves conflict, and that a definite force is required to repress what was or might have been conscious and to make it instead unconscious. The second voice recognition experiment showed that the subjects' defence against recognizing their own voices was motivated by their lowered self-esteem. This defensive self-avoidance was dynamic in the sense that it both had a definite motive and prevented recognition of their own voices becoming conscious by keeping such recognition unconscious. So the experiments demonstrated that the Freudian unconscious is topographically distinct from the conscious and that it is also dynamically repressed (or defended against). When joined with the permanently unconscious, instinctual foundations of the mind, this repressed unconscious constitutes the id.

A number of modern Darwinists have commended Freud's second topography. Edward O. Wilson, author of *Sociobiology*, declared that 'psychoanalytic theory appears to be exceptionally compatible with sociobiological theory',[4] and David Barash was among the first to explore the extensive overlap between Freud's discoveries and modern Darwinism.[5] Robert Trivers credited Freud with coming upon 'sexual overtones in parent-offspring conflict'[6] and pointed out a possible evolutionary rationale for infantile regression (see below, p. 133), as well as making the observations described earlier about repression (see above, pp. 71–7). Indeed, according to one author, 'Pierre van den Berghe seems alone among the sociobiologists in categorically rejecting psychoanalysis.'[7]

The attraction of Freud's model of the mind for many modern Darwinists lies in the prominent rôle it gives to biological drives. Freud himself formulated highly abstract theories of general classes of instincts, ultimately dividing into two: life instincts versus death instincts. But, as we saw in earlier chapters, our modern insights into evolution show that selection acts on individual genes. We might, purely as a manner of speaking, say that EVOLV-O-MATIC gliders had an 'instinct' for gliding, just as our jitter-critters had a 'drive' for jittering. But in reality we saw that what they actually had was eight directional genes, whose composite effect was to produce the observed 'instinctual' behaviour. Today there is every reason to think that what Freud and his generation a hundred years ago would have called an 'instinctual drive' is in fact behaviour coded in an organism's genes.

Again a computer example may help to explain. Every five minutes while I was writing this book, the normal process of outputting my typing to the screen and displaying it there was interrupted for a second or two while a subroutine in the word-processing application I was using made a back-up of the document on which I was working to disk. This was annoying, but necessary, because its aim was to safeguard against accidental loss of data by ensuring that if the system crashed because power was interrupted or some other such event occurred at most only five minutes' work would be permanently lost (along with all the other memory in RAM). The temporary interruption in function was caused by the back-up subroutine claiming a share of time on the computer, temporarily excluding outputting from the keyboard. We could say that my word processor had 'an instinct' for making back-ups every five minutes, and if it were an organism this is precisely how Freud and others of his time probably would have described it. Today we might say that an organism that did this would have the equivalent of the software code that made my word processor do this – a gene.

Nevertheless, Freud's concept of drives motivating behaviour is still a useful one, even if today we would want to see them as possibly arising from individual genes and certainly being the outcome of a process of development ultimately encoded in DNA. Here again, computing provides a convenient parallel, because both 'drives' and 'drivers' are found. A computer *drive* is a piece of hardware that reads a memory-storage medium, such as a magnetic or optical disc, tape or CD. A *driver* is a program the computer uses to control and prepare data for an output device, such as a printer. Freud's concept of psychological drives nicely echoes both meanings. On the one hand, drives could be seen as translating data ultimately stored in the DNA-ROM just as a CD-ROM drive on a computer retrieves data encoded on the compact disc. On the other hand, drives might be seen as a psychological equivalent of output drivers. This is because they motivate and control the behavioural output of the organism expressed in thought, feeling and action. So we might retain the term 'drive', but now regard it in the new light cast on it by the computer analogy: we could see it as being an output ultimately directed by the genetic code.

What significance does this have for Freud's id? Freud himself was always ready to rethink his ideas in the light of new facts or theoretical advances and commented regarding the second topography that 'Such ideas as these are part of a speculative superstructure of psychoanalysis, any portion of which can be abandoned or changed without loss or regret the moment its inadequacy has been proved.'[8] In the spirit of this comment we could rename the id to indicate a new awareness of the rôle of individual genes and furthermore to dissociate this useful term from outdated nineteenth-century biological thinking. So, let's rename Freud's id, the *ID*, where 'ID' is an acronym for something like Internal Drives. This is close enough to the original to remind us that it is essentially the same as Freud's id, but different enough to indicate that we are not importing all his assumptions about instincts. (In what follows I retain *id* if I am referring to Freud's original concept but otherwise use *ID* in this revised sense.)

A further virtue of this approach is that it immediately makes sense of Freud's finding that the id was *chaotic*. This is because genes that influence behaviour need not be organized in their relations to one another in the ID, any more than computer software need necessarily be organized as such in the memory medium in which it is stored. For example, modern computers can run several programs at once, and are almost always running at least two: the system that supports the computer's basic operations, and another program that is performing the current task, such as a spreadsheet or word-processor. What is important here is not that it should be possible to blend both system and word-processor or spreadsheet into one integral piece of software, but that the computer should be able to allocate time and capacity to each as and when the need arises. The result is that the code for each exists as a discrete entity, and each runs by turns, rather than as a unified organization. Presumably just the same applies to genes for behaviour. They do not have to form a coherent entity in the ID, but might make competing and even conflicting demands on the organism for 'run-time' in the central nervous system. Consequently the ID would be seen as the repository of many different programs for behaviour, not all of which need be compatible or conformable in any way, at least as long as they remained there. Like the genetic code itself, it would appear as a complete jumble of many different genes whose coherence lay in how they were expressed, not in how they were stored.

This insight would also explain another finding regarding the id on which Freud insists as much as he does on its chaos, namely its *timelessness*. Given the very slow rate at which evolutionary change occurs at the level of the genetic code, such a finding is not surprising if we equate the foundations of the ID with the human DNA-ROM. Genetic research shows that change by mutation at the level of the individual gene is very slow and cannot occur faster than once a generation, even if it is a radical change. The result is that, although certain genes may indeed be seen to change quite profoundly over a few generations, as far as the individual organism is concerned the genetic 'clock' ticks just once a generation because it receives all its genes at the moment of conception and can only pass on a mutation in itself when the time comes for it to reproduce. We certainly now know that some of the most basic genes go back billions of years and reveal similarities between some found in human beings and micro-organisms such as yeast. In this context, finding that the ID is timeless by human standards is yet another indication that its roots reach deep down, not merely into the unconscious, but also into the evolutionary past. (Indeed, although Freud wrongly believed in 'Lamarckian' inheritance (see above, pp. 10–16), this interpretation of his finding suggests that the timelessness of the id results from the fact that genes are passed on unaltered (mutations aside) by the organism that carries them.)

But the id for Freud was much more than merely a chaotic repository of the past. It was an active, dynamic agency of the personality, which sought above all to influence behaviour. Freud found that these internal drives expressed themselves principally as feelings of pleasure and pain, which are among the most palpable and important subjective sensations that we have. Yet, as so often seems to be the case, Darwin anticipated him: 'I have been accustomed to looking at the coming of the sense of pleasure and pain as one of the most important steps in the development of mind ... The sort of progress which I have imagined is that a stimulus produced some effect ... and that the effect radiated at first in all directions, and then that certain definite advantageous lines of transmission were acquired ... Such transmission afterwards became associated in some unknown way with pleasure or pain ... definite lines of action would be found to be the most useful, and so would be practised.'[9] Expressed in more up-to-date terms, what Darwin appears to be saying here is that what is normally felt as pleasure is likely to be the outcome of behaviour that, all other things being equal, would normally favour the reproductive success of the organism. So being fit, warm, well-fed, sexually-fulfilled, secure, loved by relatives and esteemed by friends would tend to be pleasurable to a human being and would serve to promote the reproductive success of the genes that contributed to those outcomes. Contrariwise, what is painful or unpleasurable is usually the outcome of behaviour that would not generally promote the reproductive success of the individual, all other things being equal. Unpleasure in general and pain in particular would be the sanctions that the ID could use to punish the organism if it failed to satisfy it, just as pleasure would be the reward for gratifying its demands. As a result, we can see the pleasure-pain principle much as Darwin evidently did, with pleasure being the carrot and pain the stick with which natural selection seeks to influence the behaviour of the organism.

. . . and a new EGO

The view of the ID as a psychological agency representing the individual's genes raises the issue of how the ID expresses itself and to what its drives are directed. The answer is to be found in the second of Freud's new agencies, the ego. Once again, a vernacular German term – *das Ich* – has been rendered as the first person singular Latin pronoun, *ego*. Unlike the id, which is wholly unconscious, the ego as conceived by Freud in his second model of the mind spans the whole range from conscious via preconscious to unconscious.

Of course, the term was in use long before Freud and even in his writings is somewhat ambiguous. This is because it sometimes seems to mean 'the self' as a whole, mind and body. But sometimes Freud uses 'ego' in a more restricted, technical sense to mean the managerial agency of the personality, charged with responsibility for voluntary thought and movement, as well as having important unconscious activities. Here again, it might be advisable to follow the precedent set by my redefinition of the ID and adopt an acronym that clears up this confusion.

The ego as a decision-making agency needs to be clearly distinguished from the ego as the self. I suggest that the former be represented by

EGO standing, perhaps, for Executive and Governing Organization (and again use *EGO* where I refer to this, newer definition, but retain *ego* when I want to allude to ways in which Freud's original concept differs). The virtue of this is that the new EGO becomes self-evidently the agency to which the ID directs its drives and demands. In part, this is because the EGO is in direct contact with the outside world via inputs from the perceptual system, and makes outputs of various kinds through its ability to control voluntary thought and action. This means that consciousness defined as whatever occupies current awareness is a unique peculiarity of the EGO, which to this extent is the only agency capable of consciousness as such. Like the Macintosh operating system, it would be an *event-driven* system, meaning by that term that it essentially responded to stimuli, either from outside (sensory data from the real world) or from inside (the drives of the ID or parts of itself expressed as emotions, feelings, thoughts, intentions or memories). Again like a computer operating system, it would have to discriminate among competing demands for its time and attention and would be charged with allocating its own resources of perception, thought and action to the various tasks involved in meeting those demands. (See figure 14.)

This insight might explain why the EGO is characterized by unity, rather than the chaos characteristic of the ID. Freud found that our feeling of personal integrity – of having a single, unified personality – was an attribute of the ego. This makes sense if we see the EGO as a managerial agency charged with executing the programs of the ID. The reason is that an agency that has to run programs must be concerned with their compatibility and coherence in execution. For example, it cannot expect to run two contradictory programs at once and still expect its actions to amount to anything consistent. Contradictory feelings or motives – *ambivalence*, in a word – does not result in coherent, consistent action, but rather tends to paralyse the EGO's decision-making functions, because it can seldom serve two contradictory intentions at once. The real world in which the EGO has to function dictates that you can keep your cake or you can eat it, but you can't keep your cake and eat it at the same time. So although cake-eating and cake-keeping genes could perfectly well co-exist in the ID, two such contradictory programs could not often be run simultaneously by the EGO without contradictory or self-defeating results. Like the single body that all genes have to share (at least temporarily), the EGO would be a central managerial

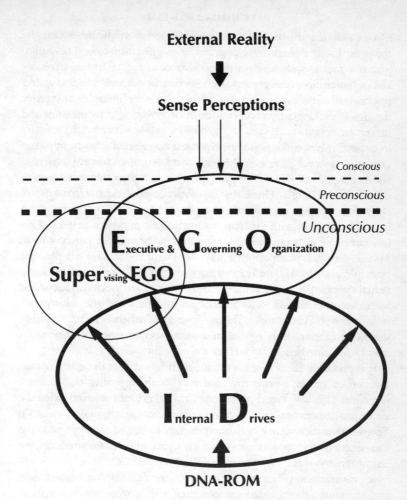

External Reality

Sense Perceptions

Conscious

Preconscious

Unconscious

Executive & **G**overning **O**rganization

Supervising **EGO**

Internal **D**rives

DNA-ROM

FIGURE 14: A PsychoDarwinist model of the mind.

agency through which all behavioural programs demanding action had to pass. The EGO's sense of unity and integrity would reflect its central, unifying rôle for the whole organism and all its constituent genes, fated as they are to share it as a key part of the psychological operating system on which they collectively rely for their ultimate reproductive success.

Such considerations explain why, at least ideally, Freud regarded the ego as obeying the *reality principle,* in contrast to the id, where he thought that the pleasure-pain principle reigned supreme. The reality principle meant acceptance of the hard facts of life, of logical necessity and of limitations to what could be achieved. In practice it meant giving priority to sense perception and objectivity over internal, subjective feelings – sticking to your diet instead of giving way to pleasure and eating the cake.

In part, this was for reasons I have just mentioned – you can't keep your cake and eat it, not in the real world at least. However, there is another aspect of the reality principle that is a direct consequence of the pleasure principle. This is that, in motivating individuals to maximize their own reproductive success, the pleasure principle may drive them into direct conflict with the reproductive success of others. It is a notorious fact of life that one person's pleasure may be another person's pain. To put the same point another way, we might say that, if the pleasure principle and the ID are concerned with the self-interest of the individual's genes, the reality principle and the EGO are inevitably identified with the problem this raises in relation to others and the self-interest of *their* genes. Furthermore, the self-interest of others is something that the EGO cannot safely ignore in a social species where co-operation may be a major benefit, as well as a significant cost.

It is probably for this reason that Freud found that there was a sub-division of the ego primarily concerned with opposing the pleasure principle. This was Freud's third and final agency of the mind, what we know as the *superego,* (Freud called it the *Über Ich* – literally, 'over-I'). To maintain consistency with the previous two, and to emphasize the fundamental, normal function to which I have just drawn attention, we might rename it the Supervising EGO, or *SuperEGO.*

My justification for calling it the *Supervising* EGO is that Freud found that the superego regarded the ego itself as if it were another person. In some extreme forms of psychopathology the SuperEGO shows itself quite clearly in the form of 'hearing voices'. The voices in question do not come from outside – they are clearly delusions – but the person afflicted with them hears them well enough. Very often they express criticism, scorn or contempt for the person in question and sometimes comment on their behaviour rather in the manner in which an outside observer might: 'Patients of this sort complain that all their thoughts are known and their actions watched and supervised; they are informed of the functioning of this agency by voices which characteristically speak to them in the third person ("Now she's thinking again", "now he's going out"). This complaint is justified; it describes the truth. A power of this kind, watching, discovering and criticizing all our intentions, does really exist. Indeed, it exists in every one of us in normal life.'[10] The agency in question is subjectively known to us, Freud concludes, as our *conscience*. As such, part of the SuperEGO might be regarded as preconscious. However, like the larger EGO of which it is a part, most of the SuperEGO is unconscious. Indeed, Freud found that it had deep and complex interrelations with the unconscious ID and that this explained how well informed the SuperEGO usually is when making its critical evaluations of the EGO. (See figure 14.)

These virtual voices show in the clearest possible way the working of the conscience, or SuperEGO, as a secondary, additional EGO that has the specific task of evaluating, observing and censoring the primary EGO. If we think back to the earlier discussion of the evolution of co-operation we can begin to see how and why such a self-critical agency might evolve by natural selection. There we saw that others will monitor our behaviour in co-operative interactions, but also that cheating will often pay.

A sense of conscience understood as an internal critic of your own behaviour need not necessarily be assumed to evolve to serve the interests of others. As Robert Trivers has pointed out,[11] feelings of guilt could evolve in your own interest if it was important for you to be able to judge in advance how others would react to your behaviour and to have a sense of how they would respond to any cheating you might be tempted to try. A conscience would give advance warning of the moral reactions of others and, all other things being equal, could pay for itself in evolutionary terms by its benefit to the individual in doing so. It would be an aspect of the reality principle that applied reality judgements to your own behaviour and its likely consequences for others. This would certainly explain why Freud and most subsequent psychoanalysts have found that the severity or otherwise of an individual's superego can't be traced to that individual's parents, or to any other conditioning influence, but seems to be an independent factor, just as it would be if it were an evolved, rather than an acquired character.

Such a view of the SuperEGO as having evolved by natural selection would also tally with Darwin's observations of it in one of his own children at a very early age: 'When 2 years and 3 months old, he gave his last bit of gingerbread to his little sister, and then cried out with his self-approbation "Oh kind Doddy, kind Doddy" ... A little later (2 years and 7½ months old) I met him coming out of the dining room with his eyes unnaturally bright, and an odd unnatural or affected manner, so that I went into the room to see who was there, and found he had been taking pounded sugar, which he had been told not to do. As he had never been in any way punished, his odd manner certainly was not due to fear, and I suppose that it was pleasurable excitement' – in other words, the pleasure principle – 'struggling with conscience.' Nor did the deceit to which our earlier discussion of consciousness opened our eyes escape the observant Darwin: 'A fortnight afterwards, I met him coming out of the same room, and he was eyeing his pinafore which he had carefully rolled up; and again his manner was so odd that I determined to see what was within his pinafore, notwithstanding that he said there was nothing and repeatedly commanded me to "go away", and I found it stained with pickle-juice; so that here was carefully planned deceit.'[12]

Self-observation is probably particularly efficient where the voice is concerned because it is heard by others in much the same way that it is heard by the speaker. Gesture or facial expression, on the other hand, can only be indirectly felt by the actor, not seen directly as they are by others. The fact that you never need a mirror to hear yourself in the way in which you always need one to see yourself is perhaps why the SuperEGO is so fundamentally related to speech and to its medium of communication, language. As Freud put it 'the ego wears a "cap of hearing".'[13]

This in turn must be one of the most important reasons why Freud found that verbal labels must be attached to things for them to become fully conscious, but are not so attached to things in the unconscious. To revert for a moment to the computer as a model, we could imagine words as being the icons, or file-names that were used to find data on a disk. A file with an icon or valid name would be a visible – and accessible – file. But hidden, invisible files would not have icons or names that appeared on the desktop, and so could not be identified.

Freud's discovery was that, for something to be fully conscious, it needs to be represented in words that serve to connect the thing with the term used to depict it. Where such connections are missing or compromised, consciousness of what they represent is also compromised to the point that the word does not correctly recall the thing. The inability of the EGO to link words directly and clearly to the unconscious would mean that it could not describe the contents of the unconscious anymore than a computer can normally display invisible files. (In the case of the subjects in the voice recognition experiments who failed to recognize their own voices, it was self-awareness at the verbal level that was lacking, not at that of the skin, where recognition could be detected.)

If consciousness is indeed a psychological interface with the psychology of others as I suggested earlier, this finding would make immediate sense. Denying a word-representation to a feeling, wish, thought or memory would render it incommunicable to others, and therefore put it outside the self-other interface that we call consciousness. Put in Freudian terms, we would say that denying something a verbal representation amounted to repressing it.[14]

Indeed, you could see the EGO acting as the Macintosh operating system does when the user wishes to delete a file. This is done by dragging the file to the trash-can on the desktop (see figure 13). However, the computer does not waste time and energy actually erasing the file. All that it does is to erase the trashed file's *name* from its directory. With its directory entry gone, the file is effectively erased, even if its data remains physically on the disk. Indeed, you could say that a file is deleted by being made invisible to the operating system, and is only physically destroyed by having fresh data written over it at some later time.

In practice this is very similar to Freud's view of the workings of repression, whereby the name of something is deleted from consciousness, leaving the thing it represents as an inaccessible entity in the unconscious. Like data-retrieval utilities in computers, which attempt to restore erased files by searching for the raw data despite the loss of its name by the operating system, Freud found that the repressed could indeed be retrieved to consciousness, but only if the missing word-representations could be restored. Indeed, his prime method of doing so, so-called *free association,* closely resembles methods used in computer data-retrieval.

If file names have been lost, but the data contained in those files still exists somewhere on a disk, one way to find it is to search the entire disk for key words or distinctive pieces of data that may have been contained in the lost files. For example, suppose that I accidentally trashed this chapter just after writing this paragraph. One way to get it back might be to run a program that would examine the entire disk on which it had been written for words or phrases that I knew it contained, such as 'free association' or 'data-retrieval'. This would probably throw up numerous files, but among them the lost ones might certainly be found. All that would then be necessary would be to give the newly-found files valid names, and my data would be restored.

Essentially, this is what free association attempts to achieve. By encouraging the patient to allow their thoughts to wander randomly and throw up chance associations of ideas, feelings, memories and thoughts, Freud found that the repressed unconscious could be retrieved to consciousness. Hence psychoanalysis is essentially a *talking cure* – one that attempts to make the repressed conscious once more by giving it a voice, rather than denying it one, which is what repression effectively does. Expressed in the terminology of the second topography, Freud remarks that 'Psychoanalysis is an instrument to enable the ego to achieve a progressive conquest of the id.'[15] Essentially it re-establishes the broken or distorted links between unconscious memories, emotions and thoughts with their verbal representations in the conscious. To this extent it is the opposite of repression: a process that enlarges consciousness and gives a voice to the repressed – a kind of data-retrieval for the human, psychological operating system.

A case recounted to me by Anna Freud illustrates the fundamental finding. She had been analyzing a woman who produced much material relating to infantile sexuality but who resolutely refused to accept that any such thing had ever existed in her case. Then one day she described a childhood pastime to which she had given a wholly innocuous name (which unfortunately I cannot recall, although Anna Freud did tell me), and which certainly had no sexual connotations whatsoever in its usual usage. Anna Freud then asked the woman to think what word she would find in a dictionary for what she had just described. The woman was astounded and horrified to realize that what she had described would normally be known as masturbation. She was particularly astonished that she had always known about that practice, but had never recognized its true meaning.

This example is a good one, because people often think that something has to be wholly and completely unconscious to be repressed in the Freudian sense. Often, repression is like that, as the voice-recognition experiments showed. In that case, recognition of the voice was wholly unconscious – known to the body, but completely unknown to the mind. When repression works like this, it is rather like a computer file that has been made completely invisible. But the case we are now considering is more like a file that remains visible, but with a misleading name – like a computer game hidden in a work folder and named as if it were a spreadsheet.

Because the woman always knew about the infantile practice, it remained conscious to that extent. But what had never been conscious – at least until Anna Freud pointed it out to her – was that this was what everyone else would call masturbation. Self-deception involved only the sexual aspect of what the woman had done, not the activity as such. This was made easier because she had not known the true, dictionary term in her childhood, and so had only known it under a name of her own choosing. Because the term she chose was a wholly innocuous one, it was easy later to sever any links that might have existed in consciousness between it and the reality it represented. The result was that she recalled the term and the practice it designated, but without connecting it to anything else that might have made her aware of its true significance. She did this by filing it in her memory under 'innocuous childhood pastimes' rather than where it should have been filed: under 'masturbation'. Only when Anna Freud required her to find a new name that would make sense to someone else did the truth dawn and the repressed return to consciousness.

Repression, in short, is how self-deception is carried out, at least if it demands that something should be excluded from consciousness. Freud's finding that the removal or sabotaging of verbal labels was critical to this process makes perfect sense if we view language as a pre-adaptation for consciousness and consciousness itself as an interface with the minds of others. But the last example raises a new issue to which we must now turn. This is the fact that if reproductive success is the bottom line for evolution by natural selection as we now know it to be, sexual motives should be of supreme importance, not least as candidates for repression. As we shall now see, this is exactly what Freud found.

SEX & THE SINGLE GENE

Everyone associates Freud with sex. Usually they do so disparagingly, so that Freud's theories remain as controversial today as they were almost a century ago. But Darwin also had his problems with sex – or, at least with his concept of 'sexual selection'.

Sexual selection was until recently a profoundly misunderstood term. Darwin introduced it to try to explain features that had evolved generally in relation to sex and specifically in relation to the competition between individuals – usually males – that seemed to be the critical factor. The tail of the peacock, to take a celebrated example, might not enhance the survival of the male that carried it (by providing a convenient handle on him for a predator), but it did seem to contribute to his reproductive success.

The misunderstandings primarily associated with 'fitness' that we discussed earlier were responsible for making many think that natural selection selected for individual health and survival, whereas sexual selection selected for reproductive success. This made the two principles seem in conflict with one another – so much so that Wallace, the co-discoverer of natural selection, saw himself as 'more Darwinian than Darwin' in rejecting sexual selection as Darwin understood it. Above all, Darwin's concept of *female choice* – the idea that peacocks have such tails because peahens prefer them – was almost universally ridiculed and ignored for the best part of a hundred years. To the extent that sex had to exist, it was assumed to do so 'for the good of the species'. In this way group selection was applied to sex in much the same way that it was also applied to co-operation (see above, pp. 40–2). Darwin's critics failed to realize that they were trying to get something for nothing in thinking that individuals would put the reproductive interests of the family, group or species before their personal self-interest in reproduction.

According to Konrad Lorenz, for example, sexual rivalry between males competing for reproductive success was 'irrelevant, if not positively detrimental to survival' and led to 'bizarre physical forms of no use to the species'. Female choice was equally bad, producing results 'quite against the interests of the species'. Argus pheasants, a highly sexually selected species, Lorenz insists, 'will never reach a sensible solution' and should 'stop this nonsense at once'! Julian Huxley denounced sexual selection as 'on the whole a biological evil' because 'useless or even deleterious to the species as a whole', while Haldane called it 'disastrous for the species', and Mary Midgley appeals to 'prudence and common sense' to limit the damage done by it. Ernst Mayr proclaimed that 'various forms of selfish selection (eg . . . many aspects of sexual selection) may produce changes . . . that could hardly be classified as "adaptations".'[1]

In short, Darwin's findings about sex were as controversial in their own way as Freud's were to be soon afterwards. But as we shall now see, this is by no means the only thing that Freud and Darwin have in common on the subject. When Freud's findings are placed in the context of modern Darwinism, some surprising new insights emerge into human sexuality that neither Darwin nor Freud could have foreseen.

Libido, language of the gene

The disparaging remarks quoted above about Darwin's concept of sexual selection all share the same fundamental error. This is the failure to realize that natural selection selects ultimately for reproductive success, and that the organism is nothing more than the packaging of its genes, at least as far as selection is concerned. By insisting on the reality of sexual selection Darwin showed that essentially he understood the prime rôle of reproductive success. His critics only showed that they did not. For them selection meant selected for 'fitness' understood as individual health or well-being, or for the 'advancement' or 'progress' of the species as a whole.

But as we saw, natural selection is nothing other than the differential reproductive success of individual genes. Genes are the ultimate agents on which natural selection acts. If it selects on this basis, individual health and survival can be seen as no more than a means to an end — that end being, inevitably, the reproductive success of the organism's genes. According to this view, the organism is only a means to an end as far as its genes are concerned, and it is these, and only these, that will be passed on to future generations.

This is because, strictly speaking, multicellular organisms do not have reproductive success *as organisms* – at least, not in the sense in which unicellular ones have it. Single-cell organisms like amœbas that simply split in two to reproduce do indeed reproduce as organisms. One amœba becomes two identical ones. However, multi-celled organisms like peacocks or human beings cannot use this method. Not only is splitting in two impossible, but such species also reproduce sexually, meaning that two parents always contribute to the offspring. This means that any and all offspring are never identical clones of their parents as are the 'daughter' cells of an amœba which reproduces by simple fission. Understood as an assembly of a vast number of genes, every human being is unique (identical twins only excepted – but even they are not identical to any one *parent*). As a consequence, we can't strictly speak of multi-celled organisms having reproductive success as individual, unique organisms.

What do have reproductive success are the genes for which those organisms provide temporary packaging, so to speak. We know from the way in which we choose things (for example in shops) that packaging needs to be adequate and robust enough to protect the contents, but it should also be attractive to the buyer. And so it is with Darwinian evolution. An organism needs to provide an adequate and durable container for its genes so that they can survive in competition with other such containers. But organisms may also have to be attractive – for example to the opposite sex – if those genes are to have any chance of reproductive success. Just like a packet on the supermarket shelf, the organism needs to be selected. But again like commercial packaging, it may need to be more than simply utilitarian if the selector favours other features – such as its aesthetic appeal. So natural selection for survival and for sexual success – what Darwin called 'sexual selection' – ultimately reduce to the same thing: the differential reproductive success of genes that, unlike the unique, never-to-be-seen-again organism in which they find themselves, really do get reproduced and are, in that sense, potentially immortal.

Although Sigmund Freud is often castigated for his errors where evolution is concerned (for example, his Lamarckism discussed earlier), his findings led him to a view of sexuality that anticipates the modern

Darwinian one. For a start, Freud is often accused of exaggerating the importance of sex. But if reproductive success, rather than individual 'fitness' is what evolution is all about, such an emphasis is as it should be. Had Freud been influenced by the 'correct' view of Darwinism in his own day, he would probably have emphasized aggression, rather than sex. This is because 'survival of the fittest' Darwinism put the emphasis on the struggle for survival rather than on the reproductive success that was central to the rejected concept of sexual selection. The fact that Freud emphasized the sexual over all other drives in motivating human behaviour suggests not only that his views were shaped much more by his findings than by contemporary ideas, but also that his findings were real.

This also applies to the other common error made about sex in Freud's time (and still often made today). This is the view that sex exists 'for the benefit of the species' – in other words, the group-selectionist mistake (see above, pp. 40–2). From the beginning, Freud was far too well informed about the real motives and feelings of people to fail to notice that there was often considerable conflict between the interests of the individual where sex was concerned and the interests of others. Indeed, so important was this finding that he devoted an entire book to the subject – *Civilization and Its Discontents*. At the time he published them, and right up until very recently, Freud's discoveries on sexual matters have been very much as he first described them: 'deliberately independent of the findings of biology'.[2]

Thanks to trusting his findings, rather contemporary theories, Freud adopted a strikingly correct and up-to-date attitude when he commented that 'The individual himself regards sexuality as one of his own ends; whereas from another point of view he is an appendage to his germplasm, at whose disposal he puts his energies in return for a bonus of pleasure. He is the mortal vehicle of a (possibly) immortal substance – like the inheritor of an entailed property, who is only the temporary holder of an estate that survives him.'[3] Indeed, it is notable that Freud uses the very term 'vehicle' that Richard Dawkins, author of *The Selfish Gene*, was to adopt sixty-odd years later to describe the view of the organism as little more than the temporary repository of its genes. The words of Freud quoted immediately above are strong grounds for thinking that, had he been alive today, he would have adopted the modern Darwinian view of evolution advocated here and regarded the organism as existing for the benefit of its genes, rather than the converse.

But however that may be, the fact remains that Freud's discoveries have been even less well received than Darwin's theory of sexual selection. Like Darwin, Freud has been regarded as having ideas about sex that made it seem anti-social, unnatural, maladaptive, perverse or bizarre. Here again it seems is an issue where Freud and Darwin are closely comparable: both entertained apparently ridiculous ideas about sex!

In the case of Freud, the protests mainly follow from the fact that the sexuality he has in mind is by no means always and exclusively that of the adult, related to the genitals, or directed to reproduction. On the contrary, Freud is notorious for his much wider interpretation of sexuality and his insistence on finding it in childhood, in relation to objects other than the genitals, and in matters remote from reproduction. It is for this reason that he adopted the term 'libido' to indicate this wider concept of sexuality. In Freud's writing, *libido* means the sexual drive in its most general form. He regarded it as arising spontaneously from *erotogenic zones* in the body, to which it always retains some attachment, even when such zones are far from the genitals and divorced from the purpose of reproduction. He found – at first to his own consternation, then later to everyone else's – that libido was operative from the beginning in childhood and that, in part thanks to this, it could take many strange forms in adult life by retaining *fixations* on its origins. Finally, he realized that, quite apart from its physical manifestations, the libido was predominantly a psychological force, and that the mind, every bit as much as the body, was charged and suffused with it.

Freud continues immediately after the quotation above to add that, 'The separation of the sexual instincts from the ego-instincts would simply reflect this twofold function of the individual.' The 'twofold function', of course, is that of being an organism with its own ends on the one hand, and being the 'mortal vehicle of an immortal substance' – what today we know is DNA – on the other. The 'separation of the sexual instincts' to which he refers is his finding that, if we allow ourselves to adopt a wider, less narrowly and genitally focused view of sex, we can distinguish between what Freud termed 'ego-libido' and 'object-libido'. *Object-libido* is libido directed towards outside objects, normally but not exclusively (thanks to the concept of libido) the opposite sex. The clear reproductive function of the latter raises no difficulties, at least in so far as its objects are members of the opposite sex. But the other category, *ego-libido* is one of the prime discoveries of Freud and the essence of what he came to call *narcissism*.

Today the concept of narcissism is so familiar to us that, like so much else that we have absorbed from Freud, we fail to see how original an insight it was. It is seldom realized, furthermore, that this is an idea that absolutely requires the concept of libido. This is because an individual can only become an object of love to themselves if we conceive of that love in a much wider context than merely that of its basic biological and reproductive function. Again, narcissism can be a wholly psychological phenomenon and may not require any kind of physical expression – another observation that demonstrates how unavoidable the concept of libido is. If the ego can become an object of sorts for the individual's own libido, the concept of ego-libido as opposed to object-libido becomes a necessary one.

At first sight this seems blatantly to contradict our expectations about sex from an evolutionary point of view. This is because reproductive success appears to demand only object-libido, if we insist on calling it that, and even then only if the object in question is a member of the opposite sex. Ego-libido, however, is another matter. If reproductive success is the bottom line, one could see any and all deviations of sex from objects other than the opposite sex as 'maladaptive', 'selfish', 'bizarre', 'ridiculous' and as much of 'a biological evil' as the products of sexual selection appeared to be to Darwin's critics (see above, pp. 104–5).

But a moment's reflection shows that things are not quite so simple. After all, there is a sense in which natural selection does indeed select for survival, rather than reproductive success. This is because an organism has to reach reproductive age before it can have any reproductive success. Up to that point, selection will act on the individual's survival potential, rather than on its reproductive potential, because it has to exist – and mature in most cases – before it can have any direct reproductive success of its own. So survival does matter as a means to the end of individual reproductive success, even if survival of the organism can never be an end in itself as far as evolution is concerned.

If this is so, we can begin to discern an unsuspected logic in Freud's otherwise strange finding that the libido, understood as a generalized, de-focused sexuality, could relate to the individual's own self, as well as to the outside objects on which the organism relies for its reproduction. We could begin to see how genes whose ultimate goal is reproductive success would have a self-interest in the organism itself prior to the age of sexual potency simply because such genes could not have any reproductive success until that time. Rather than appearing as a biological absurdity, libido – or, at least, ego-libido – would now appear to be an emotion that expressed the interests of the genes in their vehicle, the individual's mind and body. And as far as the mind was concerned, libido understood as a psychological drive would be the emotional language by means of which the self-interest of the individual's genes was expressed.

If this were true, we could immediately make one testable prediction. We could predict that, if what Freud called narcissism is a finding reflecting the value of the organism to its genes, then ego-libido should begin at a high level but decline, especially after sexual maturity, to be replaced by or transformed into object-libido. This is exactly what Freud reports. His finding was that at birth all libido was ego-libido and that only gradually did it transform itself into object-libido. Furthermore, this transformation of libido seemed to be a continuous process right up to the end of life, as if the declining value of the organism to its genes was directly reflected in the level of ego-libido remaining.

A second prediction we might make if we believed that narcissism expressed the value of the organism to its genes would be that the sexes ought normally to show some differences. A full consideration of the fundamentals of sexual differences must wait until the next chapter, but here we could make one or two simple observations. The first is that the sexes are not the same with regard to how critical the body is to reproductive success. For a man, only the act of successful fertilization is necessary for him to have offspring. But for a woman, nine months of pregnancy is necessary, normally followed – at least in the primal conditions in which our species evolved its current adaptations – by lengthy lactation and laborious child-care. This makes the body of a woman, and its day-to-day health and vitality, much more critical to her long-term reproductive success than might be the case if she were a man. Even a sick, crippled, or invalid man might be able to have many children, but much less so would a woman with comparable disabilities.

This means that, in general, we might predict that women would tend to be more narcissistic than men and that male narcissism would be more concerned with potency and virility than with general fitness and long-term health. Indeed, we might recall at this point that, not only could a man be less healthy than a woman in general and still have comparable reproductive success, but that evolution has actually reduced male life expectancy to a figure significantly less than that for women. Studies of castrated males of a number of mammalian species including human beings suggest that it is the male sex hormone testosterone that is responsible for this difference. However, the same sex hormone is also in large part responsible for a man's reproductive success, showing that in the case of males personal survival is not as critical to reproductive success as it is in the case of females.

This difference between the sexes is in fact so common that a more narcissistic attitude, particularly to appearance and general well-being, is often taken as evidence of effeminacy in a man. Freud certainly found a difference between the sexes in this respect. In his original paper on narcissism, where he first introduced the distinction between ego-libido and object-libido, he went on to say that object-love seems more charac- teristic of men than of women. He noted that this is especially the case in women who grow up with good looks, and that such narcissistic women often 'have the greatest fascination for men'. He compared this with the charm of young children and wild animals, who are also notable for their 'narcissism, self-contentment and inaccessibility'. The fascin- ation, Freud thought, is in fact a result of a male's envy of them 'for main- taining a blissful state of mind' – the unassailable self-sufficiency of narcissism. Although Freud noted that these differences between the sexes are by no means found in all cases, he realized that they 'correspond to the differentiation of functions in a highly complicated biological whole'.[4] To what extent he was hinting at the point I made immediately above about the differing rôles of the sexes in reproduction is hard to say, but his words do suggest that something of this kind was apparent to him.

Although non-psychoanalytic studies of narcissism are hard to come by, there is one independent source of verification of these predictions about differences between the sexes that we could look to. This is a collection of well-researched studies of *risk taking*. Clearly, a readiness to take risks is inversely related to narcissism because the more you value something, the less likely are you to hazard it. Similarly with the libido. If the self is highly valued, the self should not be risked by the EGO. Numerous studies of risk-taking in many different contexts consistently and reliably indicate a marked difference between the sexes. With few if any exceptions, women are much less likely to indulge in behaviour that risks life and limb by comparison to men. Indeed, a recent study showed that the predicted differences in risk-taking behaviour could still be found in Kibbutznics after three generations of socialization aimed at eliminating sex-rôle differences. Only in one respect were women ready to take greater risks than men, and that was in defence of their own children. With this one understandable exception, men remained the prime risk-takers.[5]

The selfless gene

If we regard narcissism as the expression of the genes' self-interest in the survival of the organism, critically to reproductive age, we might ask if such a reinterpretation of Freud's findings is really justified. After all, Freud like Darwin knew nothing of genes as such, and even today our knowledge of how genes influence human behaviour is extremely limited. As a result, speaking of narcissism as expressing the interest of genes in the preservation of their vehicle, the organism, may seem an arbitrary revision, designed to put a patina of biological respectability on an otherwise absurd idea. And how could such an assertion be proved?

In this respect Darwin may provide a model. Like Freud, he made many observations in his day that were either rejected as ridiculous (as in the case of female choice), regarded as factually wrong (for example, his correct insistence that the earth was much older than physicists allowed), or were simply ignored (the profusion of facts he marshalled to demonstrate sexual selection). Many if not most of these findings have since been vindicated, often in ways Darwin could not possibly have foreseen. Very often, his conclusions have been proved to be correct, even if the manner in which he arrived at them might not reflect current thinking and approaches to such problems.

Much the same may be true of Freud, and his findings about narcissism might be a case in point. Observing that self-love may serve the self-preservative interests of the organism is hardly a revolutionary discovery, and if Freud's findings regarding narcissism amounted to no more than this we would be justified in thinking that they proved little about their applicability to our modern understanding of selection at the level of the individual gene. What we would require, if we were to be convinced on this point, would be some non-obvious finding that could only be explained by the selfish gene model. The differences Freud observed between the sexes would certainly be a good start, but we might still wish for more.

What is so counter-intuitive about the selfish gene view of evolution is that, as we have already seen, it can explain social co-operation much better than the apparently more obvious group-selection view. In this respect it might more accurately be called 'the selfless gene', given that the essential fact is that genes for altruism in one individual can promote their own reproductive success in another. As we saw, children inherit half their genes from each parent in a sexually reproducing species like ours. Therefore, if narcissism is about the self-interest of genes in the preservation of their vehicles, we should expect Freud to have found that narcissism – love of the self – should include love of one's children, but not of unrelated individuals. 'Object-love', is the term he applied to love of unrelated others, and this raises no difficulties. But if my interpretation of his findings about 'ego-libido' is correct, we should find him claiming that such narcissism is not exclusively directed towards the self, but to children too. Significantly enough, this is exactly what Freud does find:

> If we look at the attitude of affectionate parents towards their children, we have to recognize that it is a revival and repro-duction of their own narcissism . . . Thus they are under a compulsion to ascribe every perfection to the child – which sober observation would find no occasion to do – and to conceal and forget all his shortcomings. Moreover they are inclined . . . to renew on his behalf the claims to privileges which were long ago given up by themselves. The child shall have a better time than his parents; he shall not be subject to the necessities which they have recognized as paramount in life. Illness, death, renunciation of enjoyment, restrictions on his own will, shall not touch him; the laws of nature and of society shall be abro-gated in his favour, he shall once more really be the centre and core of creation – 'His Majesty the Baby', as we once fancied ourselves.

We have seen Freud himself observing that what today we would call the gene is potentially immortal even if the individual is little more than

113

a 'vehicle' for it. But here too, 'At the most touchy point in the narciss-istic system, the immortality of the ego . . . security is achieved by taking refuge in the child' – or, in other words, in the fact that, if individual organisms age and die, their DNA can in principle go on for ever. 'Parental love,' Freud concludes, 'which is so moving and at bottom so childish, is nothing but the parents' narcissism born again.'[6]

But by far the most striking case of the coincidence of Freudian findings regarding ego-libido and modern insights into evolution at the level of the gene relates to the issue of altruism. If narcissism really is the expression of the self-interest of genes in their vehicles, then it ought to extend to acts of altruism directed towards other kin, apart from children.

We have already seen that altruism, like parental feeling, can indeed be based on shared genes, what we called 'kin altruism' (see above, pp. 43–58). We have also seen that altruism posed a severe test for Darwinian thinking because it seemed to violate the rule that only genes that promote the reproductive success of an individual could be selected. This was because, by definition, a gene for altruism would benefit the reproductive success of others. But we also saw that, because close relatives share their genes, the cost of an altruistic act in one individual may be less than the benefit to an identical copy of the gene for altruism in a near relative. Indeed, we can now see that, essentially, this is the explanation of what Freud calls 'parental love' above. It is because chil-dren share the genes of their parents, and usually constitute vehicles for them with a longer life expectancy, that it pays the genes of parents to have them make sacrifices for their children or for other close relatives (see figure 8, p. 47 above).

If narcissism is indeed the emotional expression of genes' self-interest in the survival of their vehicles, such narcissistic feelings should extend to near kin, as well as to the self and to children. Freud's finding was that this is exactly what does happen, but he found that it comes about by the process he called *identification*. Identification describes a subjective feeling of similarity with another person or thing. Specifically, Freud found that identification occurred in the EGO, and not in the ID. Furthermore, his own researches and those of Anna Freud established that this could come about in two, often overlapping, ways. Sigmund Freud's study of social groups based on psychological ties among the members established that the tie in question is one of identification.

But, surprisingly, his finding was that the primary identification was not with the other members, but with the leader, or leading principle of the group. Specifically, Freud found that members of such groups identify the leader with some aspect of their SuperEGO, and then form a secondary identification with one another. Abstract principles or idealizations can become focal points for identification of such groups because the SuperEGO enshrines such ideals and values. However, the parents are the models for the SuperEGO. This means that the leader is often seen unconsciously as a parent, with the implication that all the followers are the leader's children.

Individuals with the same parents are likely to share the same genes for altruism, at least to a fifty per cent probability. In the primal hunter-gatherer societies in which our ancestors evolved, most leaders with whom you might identify probably would have been relatives, perhaps most likely actual parents, given the small-scale, kin-based nature of such societies. So feeling that you had the same parent – or SuperEGO identification – as someone else would mean that you were likely to be their kin. *Identification with* the parental leader, then, would be *identification of* kin, solving the recognition problem by comparison, not merely with the self, but more importantly, with the common parent.

Of course, in modern societies individuals meet and interact with many more others than they would ever have done in primal societies. As a result, people today can form identifications with all kinds of others to whom they are not remotely related. But this is only because of modern conditions, unforeseen by natural selection. It seems that if natural selection did select for feelings of identification in the EGO as a means of identifying kin and mobilizing kin altruism, it did so because most individuals so identified in primal hunter-gatherer societies would normally have been kin. To this extent it is rather like the tendency for some organisms to co-operate with those they grow up with. Normally, those with whom they grew up would indeed be kin, so following a rule that indicated you should co-operate with them would serve the purposes of kin recognition even if it occasionally meant that one or two of your fellows were not in fact relatives. In the human case, the rule seems to be, 'act altruistically towards those with whom you can identify' where identification can often mean sharing a common Super-EGO, which in primal conditions would normally be based on a common parent. The result is that Christians are 'brothers and sisters in Christ', their priestly leaders are 'fathers' and Popes (from the same root as *papa*), while in heaven they worship God the Father and his Son, along with the Mary, Mother of God.

In this way what Freud termed ego-libido and what I am interpreting as feelings that serve the self-interest of an individual's genes would become attached to others, albeit through an indirect route made possible by sharing a common identification with the leader based on similarities in the member's SuperEGOs. If the common SuperEGO identification were normally based on common descent in primal societies, such identifications would direct the EGO's inherent narcissism to near relatives, such as siblings, cousins, uncles and aunts. A purely subjective emotion of self-love that included others like oneself would mirror latent but objective genetic identities underlying the mechanism of kin altruism in primal humans.

So too might another finding of Freud's, what he terms 'the narcissism of minor differences'. This he describes as the tendency for neighbouring peoples, families related by marriage and other groups otherwise intimately connected to one another, to engage in constant feuding and conflict, often over trivial issues. However, the fact that minor differences between people often assume major proportions, despite the greater amount that they have in common, could be part of the evolutionary heritage of primal hunter-gatherer existence. This is because primal hunter-gatherers were nomads, lived at very low population densities, and never could travel further than their feet could take them. The result would be that primal human beings would seldom if ever have encountered anything other than neighbouring groups who were in all probability much more like them in race, culture and language than they were different. The 'narcissism of minor differences' may have evolved to reflect the other side of the coin of identification. This would be discrimination based on relatively trivial apparent differences that would serve to represent more important genetic differences, for example those distinguishing blood relatives from relatives by marriage, or members of your own hunting and gathering group from neighbours. (Certainly, you can't help noticing that in the political, cultural and scientific world, the effect of the narcissism of minor differences is to produce tribal behaviour, and very often tribal warfare with the pen, if not with actual weapons.)

Findings reported by Anna Freud suggest that a further psychological mechanism involved in motivating altruism is *projection*. This is defined in psychoanalysis as the EGO's perception in others of something it has repressed in itself – noticing the mote in someone else's unconscious while overlooking the beam in your own. Anna Freud presents an example of 'a young governess' – now known to be herself – who as a child 'was possessed of two ideas: she wanted to have beautiful clothes and a number of children. In her fantasies she was almost obsessionally absorbed in picturing the fulfilment of these two wishes. But there were a great many other things that she demanded as well: she wished to have and to do everything that her much older playmates had and did – indeed, she wanted to do everything better than they and to be admired for her cleverness. Her everlasting cry of "Me too!" was a nuisance to her elders.' As an adult, however, her personality appeared to have undergone a total change: 'What chiefly struck one about her' – and this I can confirm from my own observation – 'was her unassuming character and the modesty of the demands which she made on life . . . she was unmarried and childless and her dress was rather shabby and inconspicuous. She showed little sign of envy or ambition . . .' However, analysis revealed that

> The repudiation of her own sexuality did not prevent her from taking an affectionate interest in the love life of her women friends and colleagues. She was an enthusiastic matchmaker and many love affairs were confided to her. Although she took no trouble with her own dress, she displayed a lively interest in her friends' clothes. Childless herself, she was devoted to other people's children . . . She might be said to display an unusual degree of concern about her friends' having pretty clothes, being admired and having children. Similarly, in spite of her own retiring behaviour, she was ambitious for the men whom she loved and followed their career with the utmost interest . . . Instead of exerting herself to achieve any aims of her own, she expended all her energy in sympathizing with the experiences of people she cared for.

This was possible because 'She projected her prohibited instinctual impulses onto other people . . . She showed her sympathy with their wishes and felt an extraordinarily strong bond between these people and herself . . . She gratified her instincts by sharing in the gratification of others, employing for this purpose the mechanisms of projection and identification.'[7]

Thanks to projection, one person's frustrated or inhibited narcissism can be vicariously satisfied in another with whom they identify. If, in primal conditions, subjects for identification would chiefly have been kin, the purely psychological projection of self-interest would follow lines of genetic relatedness. Anna Freud speaks of herself as living 'the lives of other people, instead of having any experience of her own', by this tendency to project her own wishes. But it is not just wishes that live in others. Copies of shared genes do so too, and it is almost certainly for this reason that the psychological mechanisms of identification and projection evolved in the first place. By these means, human beings in primal conditions may have been motivated to act altruistically towards those they felt were kindred spirits, and such kindred spirits in primal societies probably would have been their genetic kin.

The oral contraceptive stage

Freud introduced the term 'ego-libido' in his first, pioneering paper on narcissism, published on the eve of World War 1. Clearly, 'ego' here means the self as a whole, rather than the more restricted view of the ego as an agency elaborated by Freud later and further refined in my suggested acronym EGO. This approach led him to postulate a state of *primary narcissism* in which individuals began at birth and from which they gradually emerged in the course of development. It is here, perhaps more than anywhere else, that Freud's ideas have been controversial, thanks to his insistence on so-called 'infantile sexuality' – his finding that the libido was active in childhood, as well as in adult life.

However, just as modern research has cast a new and generally vindicating light on Darwin's almost universally rejected concept of sexual selection, so PsychoDarwinism can illuminate Freud's findings regarding infantile sexuality in a manner that could not have been foreseen even quite recently. As we shall see, there are some major surprises in store if we consider the issue of sex from this point of view.

The first phase of infantile sexuality discovered by Freud is known as 'the oral stage'. He regarded the mouth, lips and associated mucous membranes as a prime *erotogenic zone*, that is, an area of the body from which libidinal sensations arose spontaneously and from which sexual pleasure could be obtained. Freud's justification for regarding the oral zone as connected with the libido was threefold. First, he noted that the mouth was normally involved in sexual pleasure by kissing, licking or sucking. If this were not enough, he also knew that some individuals obtained their principal, orgasmic sexual fulfilment in this way. Thirdly – and this was crucial for his view that oral libido existed in childhood – he observed that young children will suck for sucking's sake, even when they are not hungry, and that they will use fingers, thumbs, comforters or whatever in so doing. Darwin too observed that 'It may be presumed that infants feel pleasure whilst sucking, and the expression of their swimming eyes seems to show that this is the case.'[8] Obtaining pleasure for its own sake from a region of the body that will later figure in some sexual perversions and that will normally constitute a part of adult sexual foreplay convinced Freud that his view of oral behaviour as 'sexual' in infancy was not far-fetched.

Perversion in Freud's writings is a technical term, not a pejorative one, and is defined as a *gratification of the libido derived from some other source than the genital of the opposite sex*.[9] The concept of ego-libido gradually differentiating itself into object-libido seemed to explain perversion by the fact that, if frustrated or inhibited in its ultimate achievement of attachment to the genital of the opposite sex, the libido could retreat to earlier phases in its development and to previous objects, such as the subject's own mouth. So-called 'oral perverts' would, then, be individuals whose libido had remained largely fixated on this zone and at this primary stage of libidinal development. In this way Freud was able to link his discovery of narcissism to later, more obvious phases of sexual development by the concept of libido as a broadly defined sexual drive. Additionally, this enabled him to argue that the libido evolved gradually from primary narcissism to adult object-love and from oral eroticism to genital orgasm.

Although this is a brilliantly conceived theory of the development of sexuality and has deeply penetrated modern ideas on the subject, recent discoveries cast a surprising new light on Freud's findings. For example, research shows that oral behaviour – sucking without being hungry – has important consequences for the mother in primal or Third World conditions. If the baby is kept constantly with the mother, and can have unrestricted access to her breasts, the effect of oral behaviour is to make the baby suck its mother's nipples very frequently, and for long periods of time (sometimes playing with the other nipple while doing so). The compulsive thumb- or comforter-sucking that we regard as normal in young children is not found in monkeys or apes, nor in hunter-gatherers like the !Kung of the Kalahari Desert, where babies are constantly with their mothers, day and night. The reason is simple: the babies can always suck their mother's nipples and so have no need of substitutes. Comparative studies of breast-milk show that species which suckle frequently, such as chimpanzees, have much thinner, less nutritious breast milk than those which suckle infrequently. The fact that human breast milk is very similar to that of chimpanzees in this respect suggests that we too are adapted for frequent suckling.

Research also shows that persistent stimulation of the mother's nipples by the baby inhibits her sexual cycles for something over two years after giving birth. Experiments in which the nipples of ewes were anæsthetized proved that it is the neurological stimulation of the nipple that is critical to the contraceptive effect, not the production of milk as such (which continued unaffected even when the ewes with the anæsthetized nipples began to cycle again). Many women notice that their breasts in general, but nipples in particular, are considerably desensitized in late pregnancy, but become extremely sensitive immediately after giving birth. Studies show that the total amount of milk obtained by the baby is more or less the same, whether suckling is very frequent, or limited to set periods. (Digestion could be a different matter, with relatively infrequently fed babies much more likely to regurgitate than more frequently suckled ones.) However, reduction in suckling rates dramatically affects the mother's sexual cycles, which will begin again if the rate of suckling declines, particularly if the night feeds are omitted. This explains why the contraceptive effect of breast feeding is not generally recognized in affluent cultures where supplementary feeding, especially during the night, is introduced early on.[10]

However, even without supplements, children will eventually begin to eat solid food, and mothers' sensitivity to nipple-stimulation begins to decline after approximately two years. Given that it may take a few months for a woman's sexual cycles to become re-established and for her to conceive, succeeded by nine month's pregnancy, it follows that the contraceptive effect of oral behaviour on women will tend to result in births being spaced approximately three to four years apart – a prediction confirmed by studies of birth-spacing among the !Kung, for example.

120

Freud was aware of the contraceptive effect of breast-feeding, which has been known to science since Aristotle, and was correctly informed about its duration in traditional cultures. However, he could never have realized its full significance, which only becomes apparent in relation to a much more recent and dramatic finding. This is that in Third World conditions the birth of a child within the first four to five years of the life of an existing child is the greatest single threat to the older child's life. Indeed, in West Africa a term has been coined to describe 'the disease of the displaced one' – gross protein deficiency in a child peremptorily weaned because of the birth of a sibling.[11] If such conditions are a guide to those that existed for the greater part of our evolutionary history, it may explain reports that Australian aborigines traditionally would allow new-born babies to starve to death rather than displace existing children at the breast. Such behaviour may seem callous and inexplicable to us, but makes considerable sense if the alternative were to be the death of the older child. A mother who persistently gave birth at short intervals and prematurely weaned an existing child would probably find very few of her children surviving to any later age if premature weaning usually meant death for the weaned child.

It begins to look very much as if what we are calling oral behaviour – compulsive sucking without being hungry – could be a Darwinian adaptation by means of which young children attempt to postpone the life-threatening birth of competitors for their mother's care and attention. Given that the birth of a sibling within the first four years of an existing child's life is such a critical factor for the existing child's survival, we can see that oral behaviour makes a great deal of sense when we look at it from the point of view of the child whose life is likely to be threatened.[12]

I mentioned this discovery at a scientific conference at the University of Edinburgh in 1989. Within a few days I received reports that students there were being told in lectures that 'Badcock has proved that Freud was wrong about the oral stage!' This in itself was an interesting illustration of the eagerness with which anything that seems to contradict Freud is seized upon, and is again something that makes him like Darwin, to whom the same applies. Hardly a few months seem to go by without the news media giving unwarrantedly full attention to some new 'disproof' of Darwin, and here was my interpretation of oral behaviour being used to discredit Freud! Apparently my suggestion was being interpreted to mean that oral behaviour was in fact an adaptation primarily concerned with the survival of children, rather than with their sexuality as such.

In a sense this is correct, but only very superficially. It is indeed true that my explanation of the evolution of oral behaviour claims that it was selected because the gene for it promoted the survival of babies who carried it by making them stimulate their mothers' nipples even when satiated, thereby postponing their mother's sexual cycles. But if we recall my earlier remarks about narcissism we can see that such a view is very superficial indeed. If, as I am suggesting, what Freud called narcissistic libido is in fact a current of emotions expressing the value of the organism to its genes, then oral behaviour, in so far as it protects the organism, ought to be narcissistic in quality. But as we have already seen, this is exactly what Freud found. My theory, if correct, vindicates the view that oral behaviour is narcissistic; it certainly does not contradict it. On the contrary, it gives a new, deeper meaning to Freud's concept of narcissism that is much more directly 'sexual' if we interpret that term to mean that, ultimately, genes are only interested in the organism to the extent that the organism is the means to their reproductive success. Only if we go back to the bad old days of 'survival of the fittest' Darwinism could we really believe that contributions to an organism's survival were quite different from those to its ultimate reproductive success. However, we can now see that Freud's discovery of narcissism as an aspect of the libido was based on a much deeper and much more recently realized truth: that the organism is ultimately nothing more than the vehicle – to quote Freud and Dawkins – of the reproductive success of its genes.

Finally, we can also begin to see how those genes may influence behaviour as well as other aspects of the organism. The simplest and crudest way of putting this would be to say that babies are 'programmed by a gene for oral behaviour' in much the same way that we might say that my word-processor software was programmed to make back-ups of my work every few minutes. But this does not mean that written somewhere in the DNA of a human being is a code that says, 'In order to ensure your best chances of survival, suck your mother's nipples as often as possible, even when you are not hungry, for about two years or so after your birth!' Indeed, there is not even a code in my word-processor program that says, 'Make a back-up every five minutes'. What the code actually contains is an indication that, after a certain number of cycles of the computer's clock, a standard subroutine will be called that saves files to disk. That standard subroutine is part of the computer's operating system, it is not part of the word-processor software as such. The latter only contains codes indicating when and how such functions as saving files should be carried out. The actual saving subroutine is standard because used by all kinds of different applications that the computer can run. Duplicating it in every such package would be both wasteful and unnecessary.

Freud's findings suggest that the 'gene for oral behaviour' probably works in the same way. Darwin's observation of his week-old son showed that 'a warm soft hand applied to his face excited a wish to suck,' suggesting that, 'This must be considered as a reflex or instinctive action.'[13] We can presume that sucking originally evolved because of its function in connection with food and that a standard feedback exists that rewards such activities as filling a hungry stomach with feelings registered subjectively as pleasure. Indeed, we have already seen that what Freud called 'the pleasure-unpleasure principle' almost certainly evolved as part of the standard human system to motivate behaviour favourable to the individual's reproductive success and to discourage behaviour contrary to it. We also saw that Darwin anticipated this finding, also noting the pleasure babies take in sucking (see above, pp. 94–5 and 119). With the pleasure principle already in place in regard to sucking activities connected with babies' intake of food, it would presumably only need slight modification somewhere to make sucking a pleasure in itself. For example, cell connections that inhibited sucking-stimulating neurones might be deleted in the course of embryonic development, or such neurones might be directly wired to pleasure centres. Alternatively, secretions of neurotransmitters or inhibitors at specific sites might achieve essentially the same results. A 'gene for oral behaviour' would then mean the heritable differences that resulted in that embryological effect. It would not have to say, 'Suck for the sake of it!', but that would be its consequence in practice.

However, such an effect would have to be heritable because, if not, its possessors could not pass it on to their descendants, and natural selection could not reward their reproductive success because of it. So the 'gene for oral behaviour' need not be imagined as springing into existence as a single, complete and complex instruction, but is much more likely to have evolved as a slight modification in the instructions that our genes give to us in the course of development before or soon after birth.

In terms of Darwin's three principles of the expression of the emotions, oral behaviour would appear to correspond to the first: serviceable associated habit. However, it is only now, thanks to Freud's insight into the wider emotion of narcissism, that we can see that oral behaviour is serviceable not merely to the individual child, but associated with the self-interest of its genes, and has become habitual thanks to natural selection.

We can now begin to see a deeper connection between Darwin's highly controversial insight into sexual selection and Freud's equally ridiculed and rejected libido theory. As we saw at the beginning of this chapter, Darwin's critics were so concerned with the survival and well-being of the organism – its fitness, to use the F-word – that they failed to realize that ultimately only reproductive success counts in natural selection. This error led them into a hasty rejection of sexual selection, and was compounded by their getting-something-for-nothing, group-selectionist assumptions about sex evolving 'for the good of the species' rather than the individual. Freud's findings regarding the libido in general and narcissism in particular have been rejected because his critics have only been prepared to see sexuality in a reproductive, adult, genitally focused context. But we can now begin to see that what Freud actually discovered about the libido and narcissism probably relates to what Darwin's critics thought was so important – the survival of the individual organism, at least prior to reproduction.

What both Darwin and Freud anticipated was that natural selection in fact selects on the basis of the reproductive success of individual genes. This insight explains both sexual selection and narcissism. Organisms understood as the vehicles of their genes are ultimately both expendable *and* initially critical for the reproductive success of the genes they carry. The first aspect – the expendability of the organism to its genes – explains why 'fitness' is only a means to an end. The second – the critical, even if declining, value of the vehicle to its genes – gives a new, Darwinian insight into narcissism.

ŒDIPUS SEX

The most notorious of Freud's findings is undoubtedly the Œdipus complex, so called after the mythical Œdipus, who unwittingly married his mother and murdered his father. What seems so preposterous about this is that it could have anything to do with normal behaviour, where parricide and incest are rare and singular occurrences. Again, there seems to be no obvious biological or evolutionary rationale for the Œdipus complex whatsoever, especially since father-murder violates the principles of kin altruism, and incest appears to be ruled out on genetic grounds. Furthermore, pointing out that Freud did not for one moment think that the Œdipus complex *actually* made people murder the same-sex parent and commit incest with the opposite-sex one does little to help. It is widely thought that he believed this is what people unconsciously *wanted* to do, and that cultural prohibitions, such as the incest taboo, only prevented this otherwise 'natural' behaviour. But as we shall now see, a new approach to the problem, based on the precedent set in the last chapter, may overcome many of these objections. We shall see that, when set against the right evolutionary background, some of Freud's seemingly most bizarre ideas begin to make considerable sense.

Setting the primal scene

We saw in the previous chapter that oral behaviour may have evolved as a means by which an existing child could manipulate its mother's fertility in its own interests. At first sight, both mother and child appear to have the same interest in this. Indeed, we could say that mother and child had 'co-evolved' in this respect, with the gene for oral behaviour in the child only able to promote its own reproductive success thanks to parallel evolution of a gene for sucking-induced infertility in the mother.

As far as it goes, this is correct, but it does not go far enough. To see why, let's consider what happens after about two years. We know that at this point the mother's infertility comes to an end, no matter how much the baby sucks. The reason is that the mother's evolutionary self-interest – her reproductive success, in other words – may be best served by her conceiving a new baby. But the existing child will not see it this way. As far as it is concerned, a few more months of undivided attention from its mother will probably promote its own reproductive success more than if the mother has another baby. If she does, she directs some of the resources that might have gone into milk for itself into nutrients for a fetus that at most shares half its genes. Although there will always be large areas of coincidence in self-interest, conflict between mother and child is likely at the margin. Parent and child both have a self-interest in the child eating, but the child will usually have a self-interest in slightly more food, or somewhat longer feeding than the parent would favour. This means that, as the mother's period of suckling-induced infertility comes to an end, conflict will break out over when she should conceive again, with the existing baby attempting to postpone conception.

But this is by no means the only example of conflict between a mother and her offspring. A striking case has recently been discovered at the very beginning of gestation. Although a fetus may appear to be in harmony with its mother merely because it is physically inside her body and dependent on her for its existence, we now know that fundamental conflicts occur between mother and fetus over the question of blood-supply. Cells from the fetus have recently been discovered to invade the mother's arteries close to the placenta, but not the veins. There they break down the arterial walls so that the blood vessels widen, allowing more blood to enter the placenta to the benefit of the fetus, which also releases toxins into the maternal blood supply to increase blood pressure, also to the fetus's, rather than the mother's benefit. The mother for her part fights back by similar bio-chemical means that aim to reduce the effects of such fetal intrusions, explaining why if either side fails serious illness usually results for fetus or mother or both.

Conflict can also break out over the content of the blood. Both mother and fetus need the glucose in the mother's blood, but the fetus needs more of it than the mother does. The fetus therefore secretes ever higher levels of the hormone *lactogen*. This makes the mother less sensitive to insulin and raises her blood sugar levels to the benefit of the fetus. But high blood sugar threatens the mother with diabetes, so she escalates her production of insulin. The result is that by the end of pregnancy the output of lactogen is two thousand times what it was at the beginning. Diabetes in pregnancy once seemed a simple case of illness. Now we see it as one of parent–offspring conflict over blood sugar, fought out inside the mother's body with dangerous chemical weapons.

Such conflicts are not limited to pregnancy. They can continue afterwards, with the conflict complicated by the fact that some genes can be marked, revealing from which parent they came. A gene from the mother has a fifty per cent chance of being in any other child that she may have and so has a vested interest in her reproductive future (see figure 8, p. 47). An example is Prader-Willi syndrome. It is caused by a maternal gene that lacks a corresponding paternal copy, and results in poor suckling, a weak cry, inactivity and sleepiness. Presumably this is because the mother's genes are selected to make the baby as undemanding as possible. However, a gene from the father has no necessary chance of being in another offspring of the same mother and so can be expected to make much greater demands on her. This is exactly what seems to happen in Angelman syndrome children, who are characteristically hyperactive, wakeful and given to prolonged suckling. Angelman is caused by a single paternal gene that lacks a maternal copy to counteract it and looks very like a 'gene for oral behaviour' of the kind that I mentioned earlier (see above, pp. 123–4).

These examples suggest a surprising insight into one of Freud's strangest and seemingly most biologically absurd findings. This is his insistence that young children, having passed through the oral stage, then enter a so-called 'anal' one in which pleasurable sensations are associated with the retention of urine and faeces. At first sight, this seems as pathological as diabetes does during pregnancy, because it is hard to understand how retaining excreta, rather than voiding them, could be adaptive in any way. Yet it is conceivable that anal behaviour, if I may call it that, might have a very similar explanation to gestational diabetes.

In the primal conditions in which we evolved, mothers probably carried their babies with them for most or all of the time. In such circumstances a mother can easily see what comes out of a baby. But if she is breast-feeding – and she would have been for up to four or five years – she cannot see what is going in. Unlike a glass feeding bottle, the breast does not allow visual inspection of its contents. However, as a general rule, what goes into a baby must come out in one form or another, and common observation shows that our intake of food and drink is roughly proportional to, and synchronized with, our output through excretion. Nevertheless, a toddler or baby that was not excreting would give the impression that it was not ingesting, perhaps indicating to the mother that she was not feeding it enough. Normally, retention of excreta is disagreeable to adults, but young children may have evolved a tendency to retain their faeces as a deceptive tactic in mother–child conflict over breast milk. If so, a 'gene for anal retention' may have evolved to influence the EGO of a young child in the way in which a 'gene for oral behaviour' may have done so. This would be by making the sensation produced by the behaviour pleasurable in itself. Once again the pleasure principle would be the means through which evolutionary forces had expressed themselves in human psychology. As in the case of gestational diabetes, an apparently pathological condition would in fact turn out to be an effect of an evolved parent–offspring conflict over food resources. And if so, one of Freud's seemingly most bizarre findings would at last have been explained.[1]

These considerations make one wonder how many other things there may be that we regard as pathological, not because they genuinely are, but merely because we are seeing them out of their evolutionary context. We have already seen that oral behaviour is probably an example. As long as you see it purely in a modern, Western context, where the contraceptive effect of suckling is masked by early termination of breast-feeding and where the birth of a sibling within the first few years of the life of an existing child is not such a threat, sucking for its own sake seems just that, and nothing more. But we have seen that once you take account of primal conditions, where the contraceptive effect of prolonged sucking would have been significant and where the birth of a sibling is indeed a mortal danger to an existing child under five, oral behaviour begins to have adaptive value, and genes for it seem to be able to pay their way in the only currency nature accepts: reproductive success.

More specifically, we might ask what further significance this might have for Freud, particularly regarding other aspects of 'infantile sexuality'. If 'the oral stage' now makes such good sense once we place it in its evolutionary context and remove the distortions introduced in our behaviour by modern living conditions, we might begin to wonder what else in Freud's findings would benefit from such a change of perspective. We could begin where we have left off, and ask what follows the oral stage. As we have seen, a child of two or three has a problem in primal conditions, because stimulating its mother's nipples will no longer prevent her conceiving. Is there anything else it could do?

It is here that one of the strangest of Freud's findings might begin to make considerable sense. This is what is usually referred to in psychoanalysis as *primal scene* material, and describes real or imagined observation or overhearing of parental intercourse by a young child. Almost always this is interpreted as a violent attack on the mother by the father and is accompanied by considerable anxiety, often linked to apparently irrational feelings that the child's own genital is threatened – so-called 'castration anxiety'.

At first sight, curiosity and anxiety on the part of a young child about the parents' sexual activities, and a desire to observe them, looks very much as Freud himself interpreted it. It seems to be evidence of precocious sexuality in a child, and seems to show unmistakable evidence of infantile voyeurism. This is especially the case if the parents and the child sleep in different rooms, and if the parents take normal precautions against disturbing the child. Then any such interest on the child's part in the parents' sexual activities invites direct comparison with adult voyeurism, and seems to corroborate Freud's view of the infant as 'polymorphously perverse'.

But things may not be as they seem. Just as anal behaviour ceases to look psychopathic and starts to appear positively adaptive in primal conditions, so primal scene material may make quite different sense if seen in the original context in which it evolved. Here, as among the Australian aborigines who pursued a primal hunting and gathering way of life until recently, families would not have slept in separate rooms. On the contrary, Australian aborigines routinely bedded down around camp fires at night, with children sleeping next to their parents. In such circumstances, and with the birth of siblings still a serious threat to its own survival, a child whose mother was no longer sensitive to nipple-stimulation as a means of postponing the birth of a sibling might be motivated both to monitor, and to feel certain anxiety about, its parents' attempts to engender one. A child who was watchful, anxious, and perhaps even ready to attempt to sabotage the act – perhaps by crying, or soiling itself or its parents – might indeed enhance its survival and ultimate reproductive success by comparison with one who passively accepted its fate.

If this interpretation of primal scene anxiety is correct, it is interesting to note that in his major case-history concerning primal scene material, that of the so-called 'Wolf Man', Freud remarks that 'his mother was so fond of him because he was the youngest, and this gave him good grounds for wishing that no younger child might come after him. His dread of this youngest child was revived under the influence of the dream which brought up before him his parents' intercourse.' Freud was able to date the Wolf Man's primal scene experience fairly accurately to the age of about one and a half years. This is approximately when we would predict that an infant in primal conditions should begin to become sensitive to its parents' sexual activities, given that the effectiveness of oral behaviour ends at about two years. Furthermore, we might also understand Freud's otherwise surprising finding that the infant Wolf Man defecated as a result of witnessing the primal scene. In primal conditions he might well have done so on or near his parents, and this might certainly have been enough to put them off their stroke, so to speak. Given the threat posed by siblings to its existence in such conditions and at such an age, a child who did something like this might enhance its chances of survival by comparison with one who did not.

Although this interpretation may strike some readers as ridiculous, I can report that it had a quite different effect on two distinguished anthropologists to whom I suggested it, both of whom had spent many years living with Australian aborigines. Both took it completely seriously, and one volunteered the information that the aborigines were so conscious of the interference of toddlers in parents' sexual activities that husbands and wives seldom attempted intercourse at night, but usually went off into the bush together during the afternoon siesta. The anthropologist reported that it is common to see toddlers try to follow their parents on such occasions, but that other adults in the camp usually distract and detain them, so that the couple can have some peace. Neither anthropologist thought that my suggested interpretation was in any way far-fetched, at least if you consider it in the appropriate conditions.[2]

Furthermore, it may be significant that the only taboo reported to be enforced on infantile sexuality by Australian aborigines in their traditional culture was one forbidding observation of parental intercourse. This is all the more telling because many other activities that would be highly disapproved of in most other cultures were openly tolerated in children, such as masturbation, exhibitionism, public urination and defecation and imitation of sexual intercourse.[3] My suggestion may provide an explanation of why infantile voyeurism was an exception and became an instance of parent-offspring conflict, even among the otherwise easy-going aborigines.

As far as the question of castration anxiety goes, this also seems absurd at first, but on further reflection it too makes some sense if we think back to our previous discussion of narcissism. If the individual is merely the vehicle for its genes, and if the birth of a sibling within the first four to five years of that vehicle's life is a mortal threat to it, then anxiety about its own reproductive success makes sense. And that is all that castration anxiety may be. It may simply be a narcissistic concern with future reproductive success concretely represented by anxiety about the organ most immediately concerned with it – the genital. This is because, although the individual may be a vehicle for its genes in general terms, the genital is the critical vehicle of its reproductive success. Indeed, the fact that male chimpanzees have been known to castrate other males suggests that the special importance of the male genital at least is perceived even by apes.

For the genes primal conditions would still apply, given that genetic change is so slow. As a consequence of this timelessness of the ID, primal scenes might still trigger the expression of an emotion that Darwin never attempted to explain, but that Freud did in terms of its evolutionary past: 'These scenes of observing parental intercourse . . . and of being threatened with castration are unquestionably inherited phenomena, an evolutionary heritage . . . a child catches hold of this evolutionary experience where his own experience fails him. He fills in the gaps in individual truth with prehistoric truth; he replaces occurrences in his own life by occurrences in the life of his ancestors.'[4]

The cupboard-love complex

In order to be able to understand conflicts between parent and child more clearly, we need a more abstract, general term for the many different ways in which parents may contribute things that their children want for their development. We need a single concept covering food, shelter, protection, transportation, instruction and so on, and one that is basic enough to apply however these things are provided (for example, nutrients both before and after birth). The concept in question we owe to the evolutionary biologist, Robert Trivers, and it is termed 'parental investment'. *Parental investment is defined as any contribution to the reproductive success of an offspring at a cost to the remaining reproductive success of the parent.* Like the definition of altruism that it so closely resembles, parental investment is a key concept in modern Darwinism and one that will be fundamental to the argument throughout the remainder of this chapter and the next. As we shall see, what the modern theory of altruism is to social behaviour, the theory of parental investment is to sexual behaviour.

The usefulness of the concept is illustrated by *crying*. As Darwin noted in *The Expression of the Emotions,* 'Infants, when suffering even slight pain, moderate hunger, or discomfort, utter violent and prolonged screams.' He interprets this 'partly as a call to their parents for aid, and partly from any great exertion serving as a relief.'[5] Robert Trivers follows Darwin in pointing out that crying is an expression of distress that young children can employ to solicit parental attention of all kinds along with the investment that may follow from it, whether in the form of food, protection, emotional reassurance or whatever. However, Trivers adds that, having once established the signal, there is nothing to stop a child employing it more intensively or more frequently than the parent might think fit. If the result of amplified or prolonged crying was to attract marginally more parental investment, it would be selected (recall that we have already defined parental investment in terms of contributions to an offspring's reproductive success).

Nevertheless, Darwin noted that 'Infants whilst young do not shed tears or weep.' Observation of one of his own children showed that at 67 days old only 'a slight effusion occurred . . . during a screaming fit. The tears did not run over the eyelids and roll down the cheeks of this child, whilst screaming badly, when 122 days old. This first happened . . . at the age of 139 days.' Darwin interpreted this to mean that the tear glands require 'some practice in the individual before they are easily excited into action.' He also noted that 'When the habit has once been acquired by an infant, it expresses in the clearest manner suffering of all kinds, both bodily pain and mental distress.' If we add to this Darwin's judgement that 'no expression is more general or more strongly marked than weeping' and that it is found only in human beings, these observations suggest that weeping is pressed into service as a distinctively human signal of distress as soon as a child can manage to produce tears.[6]

The result would be an 'arms-race' escalation in which infants amplified the crying signal in order to maximize the parental investment it might bring them, but parents became de-sensitized to it by seeing the behaviour described by Darwin as normal in children. Consequently adults show a double standard of sensitivity to crying. Relative indifference is shown to children, who are expected to cry for the slightest reason, but in the case of adults crying is usually taken to be a significant expression of disturbed emotions and is therefore taken much more seriously. This effect can be observed in any public place where people of all ages brush shoulders. Crying children will be ignored by most adults as long as they are not obviously lost or abandoned, whereas even slight weeping in another adult will be noticed, even if others take care not to become involved with them.

Another example that illustrates the usefulness of the concept of parental investment mentioned by Trivers is *regression*. In many species, human beings included, the amount of investment the offspring needs is proportional to its age, with younger ones needing more food, protection, help and so on from their parents than older ones. However, an offspring that appeared or behaved as if it were younger than it really was – who had, in another word, *regressed* – might solicit more parental investment than it would get if it seemed its true age. Of course, employing regression as a means of obtaining greater parental investment is a deceptive tactic, but we have already seen that deception can pay, especially if you can get away with it (see above, pp. 67–77). We have also seen that such deceptions tend to become unconscious, and so it is no surprise that regression figured prominently in the findings of Freud.

Regression might be taken as an example of Darwin's second principle of the expression of the emotions, antithesis, because it attempts to deny the infant's true age, as if the child were trying to say, 'Look I'm not this old, I'm younger!' Crying is also clearly related to his third principle, the involuntary overflow of emotion, as we saw above when Darwin commented on crying 'serving as a relief' as well as a call for parental attention. But even in this respect there is a considerable element of deception in relation to the cause of the outbreak of crying, which is seldom as great as the expression suggests. The first principle, serviceable associated habit, we have already noted in connection with oral behaviour (see above, pp. 118–24), but other examples may nevertheless be found. A possible one might be *smiling*.

In adults, a smile is a gesture of friendliness and recognition. We do not smile at strangers unless we want to attract their attention, and failure to smile in the course of interacting with a friend or loved one creates the impression that something is wrong. Essentially, smiles express pleasure, enjoyment and happiness – so much so that Darwin regarded the smile as 'the first stage in the development of a laugh'.[7] Normally we convey this to others by smiling *at* them. A smile reserved to oneself, however, often elicits enquiries from others as to what we are thinking, as if it were taken for granted that a smile was a social signal, and therefore one that others should understand. If executed as an isolated expression clearly directed to another person and unaccompanied by words or other gestures, a smile is often a way of saying 'Thank you', or of acknowledging something.

Darwin discussed smiling at some length in his book, and reported his observations of his own children, in whom he detected spontaneous smiling as early as six weeks old, and certainly by nine weeks. These findings are corroborated by modern research, which has also found a smiling reflex in prematurely born infants. Even a schematic oval with dots for eyes will elicit a smile response in four-month-old babies. Yet smiling involves a complex co-ordination of numerous muscles, as Darwin noted. These findings, along with the universality of the smile among human beings, suggest that there is, as a manner of speaking, a gene for smiling, and that it begins to influence behaviour almost from the beginning.

Nevertheless, Darwin observes that, as in the case of weeping, practice is necessary to perfect the smile and modern research suggests that children deprived of intimate and frequent contact with their mothers tend to smile less readily. This suggests that smiling involves a capacity to respond suitably to a stimulus, and is more than just a simple reflex, like blinking. Furthermore, and despite Darwin's observation that 'The art of screaming . . . from being serviceable to infants, has become finely developed from earliest days',[8] it is possible that the smile too is a serviceable habit, associated with the earliest interactions between mother and child.

Here it does not seem far-fetched to think that infants who produced smiles in response to the attentions of their mothers secured a better response from them than those who remained poker-faced and apparently insensitive. This is because a mother, already habituated to the smile as an expression of pleasure and gratitude in interactions with adults, would be bound to be gratified by a similar expression in an infant for whom she was doing so much. Whether the infant actually felt pleasure and gratitude as an adult might, who could say? But a smiling infant would certainly look as if the emotions expressed were much the same. If this strengthened and deepened the emotional tie of the mother to her baby, the gene for smiling might be selected simply because smiling babies were better loved, better fed and generally better cared-for than non-smiling ones. If such enhanced parental investment contributed to those infants having marginally improved reproductive success in adult life, their own offspring would be likely to inherit the gene for smiling, and so on.

But smiling may only be the start of it. We know that as infants mature they become capable of much more than merely smiling at their mothers. A smile, as Darwin noted, is the expression of an emotion, and in the case of smiling the emotions expressed are all positive ones, such as pleasure, gratitude, love and affection. If a mere smile can secure enhanced maternal care for an infant, then, clearly, the emotions expressed by it might achieve even better results. If an expression of distress, like crying, can be amplified in the way in which it evidently has been, then presumably the emotions underlying smiling could also be amplified. Those emotions, as we have already seen, are pleasure, gratitude and liking. A smile can say, 'I am pleased,' 'Thank you,' or 'I like you.' And what begins as smiling by the baby often develops into long periods of eye-contact which, in an adult would not merely imply, 'I like you', but 'I love you.'

In other words, if it paid infants to amplify distress signals, then the amplification of more positive signals might pay even more if the result was to secure enhanced parental investment from the mother. A smile that expressed liking might be serviceable in this respect, but a fond look of love might be more serviceable still. Indeed, if the infant showed that it loved the mother passionately, and reinforced the message not merely with facial expressions of its love, but with embraces, kisses and verbal expressions, the likelihood is that the benefit to its ultimate

135

reproductive success by enhanced parental investment in it would be even greater. Darwin reports of his son that signs of affection 'probably arose very early in life, if we may judge by his smiling at those who had charge of him under two months old . . . But he did not spontaneously exhibit affection by overt acts until a little above a year old, namely, by kissing several times his nurse who had been absent for a short time.'[9]

This may be at the bottom of one of Freud's most controversial findings, what we might call *Œdipal behaviour*. By this term I mean powerful feelings of love and affection for the mother and a tendency to see the father as a rival for the mother's affections. If my interpretation of Œdipal behaviour is correct, this would simply be an amplification of the expression of the positive response to the mother that is first found in smiling. It would amplify pleasure, gratitude and liking into a deep love for the mother that would show itself in all manner of ways and be expressed in every aspect of the child's relationship with her.

We could explain this by appeal to the fact that in primal conditions, and indeed in all human societies up to the present, the mother is the chief and often the sole agent of parental investment in the first few years of life. It is she who breast-feeds the infant (as we have seen, usually for two or more years), and it is she who cares for it throughout most of the early period of childhood. Traditionally the father has little or nothing to do with day-to-day child-care and seldom if ever carries out any significant tasks in this respect while children are very young. This would explain both why the mother is the target of early Œdipal behaviour and why the father is not, at least at first. Indeed, it might also explain why the father tends to be seen as something of a rival by the child. Even in our own, less traditionally sex-stereotyped societies, fathers often see new-born babies as competitors for the mother's attention, and clearly, if the father can see it this way, so too can the child. In claiming the maximum of its mother's time, care, attention, love and resources available for investment in itself, the child will almost certainly sometimes find itself in competition with its father. The father, for his part, is bound to notice that the child is effectively attempting to monopolize the mother, and to resent it, making the Œdipal picture of him as a jealous rival to some extent inevitably correct.

However, if this is the right interpretation, we can immediately see that both sexes ought to show Œdipal behaviour, at least in early child-hood. This is because the mother remains the prime source of parental investment in primal conditions, irrespective of the child's sex. Although Freud originally tended to think that the Œdipus complexes of the sexes were symmetrical, with both girls and boys feeling love for the opposite-sex parent and rivalry with the parent of the same sex at the same stage of development, he later abandoned that view. Further observation convinced him of something about which Anna Freud was adamant: that little girls too have an Œdipus complex centring on the mother as a love-object, at least in early childhood.[10] Indeed, Anna Freud would often point out that some little girls (although certainly not all) go through a definite stage of 'tom-boy' behaviour and act towards their mothers as if they were boys themselves, rather than girls.

This finding is important because, if it were not so, an attempt to interpret Œdipal behaviour as essentially concerned with soliciting parental investment from the mother would fail in the case of girls. The fact that Freud modified his view to include what is often rather confusingly called 'the pre-Œdipal phase'[11] of a little girl's Œdipal attachment to her mother suggests an astonishing possibility. This is that, rather than having dreamt up the whole idea of the Œdipus complex out of his own tortured imagination as he is often believed to have done, Sigmund Freud may in fact have observed something valid. Furthermore, it suggests that what he observed only begins to make real sense once we set it in the context of modern parental investment theory – something only conceived fifty years after this death.

Sexy sons, envious daughters

Robert Trivers's concept of parental investment is also applicable to the question of what constitutes the essential difference between the sexes. In modern biology the universally accepted convention is that the sex with the *smallest* sex cell is *male* and that with the *largest* is *female*. At first sight this may sound a slight difference. After all, a sperm and an egg cell are very small, and although the larger, female cell represents more parental investment, it does not seem so very much more. Nevertheless, eggs are usually several orders of magnitude (that is, powers of ten) larger than sperms and always produced in numbers that are also orders of magnitude less than the numbers of sperms.

One of the most important consequences of this fundamental asymmetry is that, with millions of sex-cells at his disposal and no further necessary parental investment to contribute, a man's reproductive success is only limited by the number of women he can fertilize. A woman, by contrast, can only have one pregnancy at a time. This could mean twenty or more children in one lifetime, but even this would be few compared to what one man could achieve, given enough wives. In principle, he could father twenty or thirty children in one month, and certainly in nine months! To put the matter another way: one man with twenty wives can have vastly more children than one woman with twenty husbands. She could have one child for each of her twenty husbands if she was lucky, but assuming twenty children per wife, the man with twenty wives could have three hundred and eighty more! However you look at it, individual men can have much more reproductive success than individual women. This is because, in principle, every viable sperm a man produces could fertilize an egg, whereas every fertilized egg a woman produces she must carry to term if it is to contribute to her personal reproductive success.

Although he did not put the matter in terms of parental investment, Darwin clearly realized that if one male could in principle fertilize large numbers of females, other males might not fertilize any at all. The result would be that successful males would have many offspring, whereas unsuccessful males would have few or none. The successful males would have been selected thanks to whatever it was that ensured their reproductive success. One possibility might be conflict between males for access to females. This Darwin believed explained the elaborate armaments and defences that males of many species acquire for the purposes of mating, such as antlers in the case of deer. However, another mechanism of sexual selection might be female choice: the possibility that some males might appeal to females more than others and therefore have greater reproductive success than those less preferred. This, Darwin thought, explained the ostentatious display of peacocks and many other species whose males are decorated in ways that seem to reduce their survival prospects (for example, in making them more conspicuous to predators) but might promote their reproductive success still more by their appeal to females.

The Expression of the Emotions originally began as a part of *The Descent of Man, and Selection in Relation to Sex,* but became so long and independent a work that Darwin published it separately a year later. In certain respects Darwin's concept of female choice comes close to the subject of the book on the emotions: for example, his observation that 'Sexual selection . . . implies the possession of considerable perceptive powers and of strong passions.'[12] The point is that female choice relies on a psychological mechanism, which is essentially one of the expression of the desires of females by their choice of mate. Furthermore, Darwin did not hesitate to draw a parallel between human and animal psychology in this respect: 'In regard to sexual selection. A girl sees a handsome man, and . . . admires his appearance and says she will marry him. So, I suppose with the peahen . . .'[13] It was probably this subjective, psychological basis for female choice – not to mention the attribution of such selective power over males to females – that made the concept appear so ridiculous to Darwin's critics.

Nevertheless, this aspect of Darwin's theory did have one important weakness. This was its inability to explain how and why females chose. As far as Darwin was concerned, female choice was a given, a matter of observation that had to be accepted. There seemed little point in asking why peahens like peacocks' tails – the fact is that they do, and that explains the evolution of the trait. However, it remained a mystery what was in the peacock's tail for the individual female, particularly in view of the enormous cost of it to males, an individual female's own male offspring included.

It was not until 1915 that a solution was found. R. A. Fisher suggested that if a female chose a mate who appealed to her, for whatever reason that might be, the chances were that her own male offspring would inherit some of the attractive traits of their father. This would be because a female would probably share the same tastes as other females when it came to choosing a mate. So choosing one who appealed to her would probably mean that her sons would appeal to others when their time came to find mates. In other words, if sons shared genes for attractiveness with their fathers in the way that females might share genes for being attracted to them with those sons' mothers, the mother's reproductive success would be maximized by her mating with the most attractive male she could find. This immediately made female choice look more comprehensible, because it showed how ostensibly absurd tastes in male decoration like peacocks' tails could promote the reproductive success of the females who favoured them. Furthermore, once started, the cycle of females choosing attractive mates and having more attractive sons as a result could run away with itself, producing the extremes that are so often seen in sexual selection. A slightly more attractive male would secure more reproductive success, passing his slightly more attractive trait on to his male offspring, and so on.

To put it simply, we might say that Fisher's theory held that, in choosing an attractive mate, a female was selecting genes for her son that would enhance his reproductive success when his turn came to mate. However, in a species like ours, with long periods of intense parental investment, especially by the mother, a Fisher-effect might evolve in the conflict over that investment. For example, suppose that a woman mates with an attractive man and has two children by him, a son and a daughter. If the son inherits his father's attractive traits, parental investment in him at the expense of the daughter might pay, all other things being equal. Admittedly, the mother's genes are equally invested in both son and daughter – fifty per cent in each (see above, figure 8, p. 47). But the half of her genes in the son with the right stuff may have much greater reproductive success than the half in the daughter. As far as her genes are concerned, there is absolutely nothing she can do about this, but her parental investment is a very different matter.

Here it is important to recall that we defined parental investment in terms of its contribution to the offspring's reproductive success. We assume that parental investment will, all other things being equal, usually promote reproductive success, rather than reduce it. In the situation imagined above, a mother might, admittedly, decide to invest preferentially in the daughter, on the grounds that this might make up for her shortcoming where future reproductive success was concerned. However, male reproductive success can be very great indeed even though highly variable, whereas female reproductive success is usually much more dependable, if also more modest for the reasons we have already seen (see above, pp. 137–8). This means that extra parental investment directed towards a son who showed signs of reproductive promise in childhood would probably add to his mother's reproductive success more than it might if directed to a daughter.

In any event, the suggestion that mothers might direct preferential parental investment towards 'sexy sons' who showed signs of unusual reproductive success in adult life is entirely in keeping with Fisher's principle, which is effectively one of reproductive success breeding more reproductive success. Furthermore, it has the advantage of explaining many of Freud's findings regarding the male Œdipus complex. It might work like this: women who chose attractive mates would tend to have sons who inherited part of their fathers' attractiveness. The result of such greater attractiveness would probably be greater reproductive success for the sons in question, and indirectly for their mothers. By this means infantile sexuality in little boys could evolve as a precocious expression of their sexual attractiveness that tended to attract parental investment from their mothers. This would certainly seem to explain Anna Freud's observation that what five-year old boys demand above all is the mother's admiration of their masculinity.[14]

We have already considered the possibility that both sexes may have amplified the expression of positive reactions towards the mother as a means of soliciting parental investment. For a son, this might provide the basis for further developments that he, being male, was uniquely equipped to exploit. For example, if the mother found that her son showed amorous feelings towards her and other evidence of sexual precocity she might sense that here indeed was a 'sexy son' who could have a promising sexual career ahead of him when he was an adult. Above all, a mother's own feelings in reaction to her son's infantile amorousness might suggest to her that, if he could make his own mother feel this way about him in childhood, how much more would other women react in adult life!

In short, it may be that, not only have both sexes evolved oral behaviour, primal scene anxiety, and Œdipal behaviour as a means of securing parental investment, but that males in particular have evolved an intensified form of Œdipal behaviour as a means of soliciting preferential investment from their mothers. If sons who successfully exploited this tactic matured into men who appealed in the same way to potential mates, then Fisher's principle would be operating in terms of parental investment in sons, by little boys giving some kind of advance notice of their future sexual appeal to their mothers. In this way, sexual selection might favour parental investment in 'sexy sons' who would make desirable mates for other women when they matured. The riddle of infantile sexuality would in part be solved — at least in little boys — and a form of behaviour that may once have seemed to lack a biological basis would now find an unexpected one in Darwin's most contentious concept — sexual selection by female choice.

But what of little girls? How does their behaviour evolve in a setting that seems so satisfactory for sons?

The first thing that a little girl could do would be to try a similar tactic to her brother's on her father. There would be at least two good reasons for this. The first is that if Œdipal behaviour on the part of a child exploits precocious sexuality as a means of seducing a parent into preferential investment in it, there is no reason why children of both sexes should not try it. Since the majority of parents will be sexually normal in preferring a partner of the opposite sex, it follows that although a little boy can maintain his mother as the object of his Œdipal behaviour, a little girl might do better to target her father. He should prove more susceptible to his daughter's charms than her mother would be, particularly as she grows older and her Œdipal behaviour becomes more subtle.

The second reason is that, as a child gets older, the father becomes a more significant agent of parental investment in all societies and in primal ones no less. Whereas only the mother can breast-feed a child and is likely to be the primary care-giver during infancy, fathers are well equipped to make the kind of parental investment that can be critical in later childhood. More adult food items, more secure protection in the more serious conflicts in which a child may be involved in later childhood, critical instruction and help in adult affairs, more widely ranging social and political contacts, exchangeable material items, weapons and wealth, and much more a father may be well placed to give to his children, often to the benefit of their ultimate reproductive success. For example, a study in a rural community in the Caribbean showed that father-daughter interactions peaked between ages eleven to fifteen and that girls with resident fathers married better than those without.[15] Indeed, in our own societies it is a commonplace to observe that a girl's social standing – and very often the range of partners for her – is usually much more critically dependent on her father than her mother. In primal societies, such as those of the Australian aborigines, it would be even more critical, with a girl's future husband largely determined by the kinship and political connections of her father. Clearly then, a female Œdipus complex could pay, somewhat as a male one might.

But it could not pay in the *same* way, thanks to the fundamental asymmetry between the sexes that we noted earlier (see above, pp. 137–8). The fact that male reproductive success is in principle only limited by the number of females a male can fertilize means that a father's personal reproductive success is usually likely to be greater than that of any daughter, simply because he is male and she is female. For this reason alone, preferential parental investment in a 'sexy daughter' by her father would seldom reward his reproductive success as much as investment by a woman in a 'sexy son' might reward her reproductive success. This probably explains why Freud found that the female Œdipus complex was so much less clear, less acute and less simple than the male one. It may also explain what must otherwise be the weirdest and most widely ridiculed of his findings about female psychology – penis envy.

In his original paper on parent–offspring conflict, Robert Trivers remarked that 'in many species sex is irreversibly determined early on . . . and the offspring is expected at the very beginning to be able to discern its own sex and hence the predicted pattern of investment it will receive.'[16] If parental investment is likely to be biased towards one sex rather than the other, then an offspring might also be expected to be able to determine the sex of its siblings, along with that of itself. In childhood, secondary sexual characteristics of the kind that adults often use to determine sex, such as depth of voice, facial appearance or figure, have not yet developed. Only the primary sex differences are present, and of these, the presence of the male genital is almost always much easier to determine than the female one, thanks to the effects of the evolution of upright posture on our species and to the fact that the penis protrudes from the body in a prominent position. So if a little girl needed reliably to diagnose her own sex and that of others – particularly in primal societies where children even more than adults usually go naked – she would need to do no more than look for a penis and assume that anything with one was male and anything without one was female. Indeed, this is effectively how the sex of a fetus is determined during an ultrasound scan. If a penis is visible, you can be sure you are going to have a boy, but if not, it is probably going to be a girl. This is also what Freud found in the unconscious of both sexes: an apparently unshakable unconscious conviction that a woman is a man without a penis!

To put the matter another way, you could say that in the unconscious the sexes are not registered as *male* and *female*, but as *male* and *not-male*. This idea is no more strange than Darwin's belief that tail-wagging and other reactions in friendly dogs express a comparable negative message ('not angry', see above, pp. 6–7). Indeed, it soon becomes apparent that, if Darwin was right about his second principle of the expression of the emotions – antithesis – then Freud's finding about the way 'female' is represented in child psychology and the human unconscious is probably another example. The idea that a woman is a castrated man is equivalent to the tail-wag where 'not angry' corresponds to 'not male'. In both cases antithesis is used to express a meaning. In the case of the human unconscious, where concepts have no words to represent them (see above, pp. 100–103), sex is seemingly represented by the presence or absence of a penis.

The critical importance that this gives to being male makes considerable evolutionary sense in terms of the fundamental asymmetry of the sexes and the consequences for parental investment – perhaps especially by the mother – that follow from it. Well may adults scoff at such an absurd concept of the sexes, and well may parents think that young children should have no concern whatsoever with sex. Nevertheless, a young child suffering sexual discrimination in the allocation of its parents' investment might well take a different view. Such a child ought to have some way of diagnosing its own sex and that of its siblings independent of parental ideology and, if it discovers that it is female, ought to expect to be discriminated against. Envy might not be an emotion of which we are normally very proud, but we all know we feel it from time to time. Nor is it hard to imagine how it might have evolved. Clearly, those whose envy motivated them to compete for what others were getting might enjoy greater ultimate reproductive success than more altruistic individuals who felt no such base, self-interested emotions. In childhood, envy might certainly be expected in rivalry between siblings, and if it were unconsciously associated with ideas about how to diagnose sex, Freud's strange finding of penis envy would follow naturally. Essentially, penis envy would be an emotion that evolved to mobilize little girls to compete with their brothers for the preferential parental investment that Fisherian sexual selection might win for them from their mothers. Effectively it would be a current from the unconscious ID that said, 'If you lack a penis, assume that you are being deprived of something important that anyone who has one may be getting!'

In the light of this interpretation it is worth pointing out that Freud remarks that penis envy often expresses itself as a reproach against the mother, who is somehow assumed to be responsible for the daughter's lack of a penis. He adds, however, that this is often followed by 'A second reproach' that Freud finds 'is a rather surprising one. It is that her mother did not give her enough milk, did not suckle her long enough . . . that she did not feed her sufficiently.'[17] Although this additional complaint may have surprised Freud, it is exactly as it should be if my suggestion about the evolutionary basis of penis envy is correct. Furthermore, it is a reproach that is fully justified in many cultures, where it is traditional to breast-feed boys longer than girls. And linking complaints about not having a penis with others about not getting sufficient food certainly suggests that penis envy may have something to do with parental investment. These findings suggest that this strangest of all forms of expression of the emotion of envy does make some sense, but only when set in the context of Darwinian theories of parental investment and sexual selection.

I have found that it also makes personal sense to some women, and over the years have collected a number of cases where the penis was not just envied, but procured, at least in fantasy. The prize for mechanical ingenuity should perhaps go to a woman who confessed that from very early on she realized that her parents had really wanted her to be a boy. She did her best to be one by wearing boys' clothes, having short hair and playing football with her father. But in secret she added something even more essential: a long thin shampoo bottle suspended between her legs from a piece of string. With a second piece she could make it stand up at will – something, she proudly pointed out, no boy could do!

Penis envy, in short, may have co-evolved with Fisherian sexual selection for preferential parental investment in sexy sons. A symmetrical envy of females on the part of males could not be expected to evolve for the simple reason that the sexes are not symmetrical where personal reproductive success is concerned. However, the fact that most females can be expected to have moderate reproductive success will mean that many of them will be descended from daughters whose brothers were favoured by preferential parental investment at their expense, and many of their female descendants will suffer the same fate. This will select for strategies such as penis envy to deal with preferential parental investment in brothers. Males, by contrast, will be disproportionately descended from the reproductively most successful males of the past. As a result, just as all male peacocks have gorgeous tails, simply because the most sexually successful peacocks of the past had them, so all human males will inherit adaptations for reproductive success, not for dealing with discrimination against them that would imply relative reproductive failure.

The co-evolution of male and female strategies in competition for parental investment might also explain Freud's finding that women appear to blame their mothers for their lack of a penis. Although this makes no biological sense on one level (because sex is actually determined by the father in human beings) it nevertheless might do in terms of another finding. This is Freud's observation that it is latent penis envy that often motivates mothers to discriminate in favour of their sons and against their own daughters. This is because the son is seen as possessing the attribute that the mother was denied – the penis. Through him she vicariously gratifies her frustrated wish for it and so favours him over her daughters, who, like her, lack it.

Expressed in such bald terms, this sounds crazy. But if we think back for a moment to our earlier consideration of kin altruism thanks to the mechanisms of projection and identification, we can see that this makes biological sense. Latent penis envy, Freud found, made a woman identify with her son, and project her own frustrated wish for a penis onto him. The possession of a penis does indeed equip a son in a way a mother or daughter never is equipped. It equips him for potential life-time reproductive success vastly in excess of anything his mother could achieve. Although penis envy in females and Œdipal behaviour in males may sound absurd to the conscious EGO, it could make the only kind of sense that the ID and evolution understands – reproductive success at the level of the individual gene.

THE RIDDLE OF THE SHRINKS

Incest is a key issue in any attempt to link biology, psychology and cultural behaviour because it touches on all these areas: biology in its genetic basis, psychology in terms of how people feel about it, and culture in relation to laws, taboos or other restrictions that are usually placed on it. However, incest is also one of those questions where, to quote Mark Twain, 'The researches of many commentators have already thrown much darkness on this subject, and it is probable that, if they continue, we shall soon know nothing at all about it.' Part of the controversy that surrounds incest arises from misunderstandings of Freud's writings on the subject. Further confusion stems from the fact that what has passed for a Darwinian approach to the problem for most of this century is very dubiously Darwinian in a modern sense, and certainly was not Darwin's own view.

With Freud's findings so widely misconceived, Darwin's own words ignored and an essentially un-Darwinian theory masquerading as the 'Darwinian' explanation, there is room for a new solution. In so far as it is a synthesis of Freudian findings and modern Darwinism, we might regard it as a PsychoDarwinist one. We shall see in the final chapter that what goes for incest may go for many other aspects of human behaviour, and that the model of the mind we considered earlier provides the basis for a general solution to the problem of how genes and the cultural environment interact in human psychology.

What Freud really said

Incest touches Freud's work directly, and remains one of the major stumbling blocks for many who take a Darwinian approach to human behaviour seriously. This is because it is widely thought that Freud found that incest was 'natural' and only prevented by cultural prohibitions. By contrast, his contemporary, Edward Westermarck (1862–1939) took the view that an innate aversion to incest was the result of natural selection. This was because 'self-fertilization in the case of plants and close in-breeding in the case of animals are, on the whole, injurious to the species.' In the case of human beings, Westermarck claimed that 'as in other cases, natural selection has operated, and by eliminating destructive tendencies and preserving useful variations has moulded the sexual instinct so as to meet the requirements of the species.'[1]

I have quoted Westermarck's own words here because they clearly show that his view of the matter was self-evidently group-selectionist (see above, pp. 40–2). According to him, incest was avoided, not for the good of the individual, but for that of the species as a whole. So emphatic was Westermarck that natural selection acted on species, rather than individuals as Darwin predominantly asserted, that he held that sexual selection was a completely different principle because 'it produces effects disadvantageous to the species.' The fact is that Westermarck, far from being a Darwinian in the modern sense, was a Social Darwinist who rejected Darwin's individualistic view of natural selection because it did not seem to serve the interests of the species. Consequently, he denied sexual selection, claiming instead that ornaments like the tail of the peacock should 'be explained by the principle of the survival of the fittest'. Fallacious, Social Darwinist reasoning like this led Westermarck to believe that 'The home is kept pure from incestuous defilement, neither by laws, nor by customs, nor by education, but by instinct which under normal circumstances makes sexual love between the nearest kin a psychical impossibility.'[2]

Despite – or perhaps because of – Westermarck's group-selectionist approach and old-fashioned Social Darwinism, his view of incest-avoidance has achieved the status of dogma among many who claim to take a Darwinian view of human behaviour. But like Wallace calling himself more 'Darwinian than Darwin' in rejecting sexual selection (see above, p. 104), believers in Westermarck's instinct theory of incest-avoidance have not in reality adopted Darwin's own approach to the problem. On the contrary, Freud – who is normally seen as the antithesis of Westermarck on the incest issue – was very much closer to the essentials of Darwinism in some significant respects. For a start, Darwin, like Freud, did not believe in any innate aversion to incest in human beings. On the contrary, Darwin held that 'it has been clearly shown . . . that there is no instinctive feeling in man against incest', and Freud explicitly followed Darwin in his belief that modern man was descended from ancestors perhaps comparable to modern gorillas. Rather than appeal to an instinct against incest as Westermarck felt compelled to do, Darwin believed that a mating system like that of the gorilla was in itself enough to prevent incest. This is because young males tend to be driven out of the breeding group as they become sexually mature and so do not have the opportunity to mate incestuously.[3]

Nevertheless, the fact remains that Freud's Œdipus complex suggests to many an instinct for incest in childhood, which is only 'repressed' by socialization. But if, as I argued in the previous chapter, precocious sexuality directed towards the mother by so-called 'sexy sons' were all about securing preferential parental investment rather than actual incest, one major difficulty would have been removed. If I am right, it now begins to look as if the incestuous element is only illusory and that what human nature in fact wishes to secure by Œdipal behaviour in infancy is not incest but personal reproductive success in adult life. Indeed, it has always been true that the Oedipus complex was about infantile – and therefore non-reproductive – sexuality and that considerations about its incestuous character were rather beside the point where adult behaviour was concerned.

But most people still think that Freud's view was that the incestuous tendencies of the Œdipal period were repressed by outside pressure that went against the grain of human nature. Incest was natural, according to this view. Its avoidance was cultural and the result, not of nature, but of nurture. It may come as something of a surprise, then, to learn that this was not in fact what Freud reported. I quoted Westermarck's own words above to bring out the Social Darwinism of his approach, so let me now quote Freud's own to show what his actual position was. Freud's paper of 1924, 'The Dissolution of the Œdipus Complex', begins with these words: 'To an ever increasing extent the Œdipus complex reveals its importance as the central phenomenon of the sexual period of early childhood. After that, its dissolution takes place; it succumbs to repression, as we say, and is followed by the latency period. It has yet to become clear, however, what it is that brings about its destruction . . .'

Having posed the problem, Freud then goes on to remark that analyses give the impression that it is the inevitable disappointment of

149

Œdipal wishes that constitutes an important part of the answer: 'In this way the Œdipus complex would go to its destruction from its lack of success, from the effects of its internal impossibility.' However, he immediately adds a further consideration:

> Another view is that the Œdipus complex must collapse because the time has come for its disintegration, just as the milk-teeth fall out when the permanent ones begin to grow. Although the majority of human beings go through the Œdipus complex as an individual experience, it is nevertheless a phenomenon which is determined and laid down by heredity and which is bound to pass away according to programme when the next pre-ordained phase of development sets in. This being so, it is of no great importance what the occasions are which allow this to happen, or, indeed, whether any such occasions can be discovered at all.[4]

If we add the point that he makes a few pages on that the dissolution of the Œdipus complex also constitutes the basis of the 'prohibition against incest', we can clearly see that the preceding quotation refutes absolutely those who have interpreted Freud as a believer in a purely environmental, acquired mechanism of incest-avoidance. On the contrary, Freud remarks that 'There is room for the ontogenetic view' – that is, personal experience – 'side by side with the more far-reaching phylogenetic' – or evolutionary – 'one', and refers to the whole process as 'this innate programme'.[5]

However, if we now ask what psychological factor Freud thinks brings about the end of the Œdipus complex, he has no doubts whatsoever: it is castration anxiety. At first, like so much in Freud, this sounds ridiculous, but not if we recall what I said about it earlier. We shall recall that I suggested that, since the organism is nothing more from the point of view of natural selection than a vehicle (to quote Freud's and Dawkins's term) for its genes, reproductive success is everything. Incest between parents and children, however, is not in general a good reproductive strategy for genetic reasons (see below, p. 157). Consequently, if our view of narcissism as the emotional expression of the reproductive self-interest of the gene is correct, we should expect to find narcissistic feelings in conflict with the incestuous aspects of the Œdipus complex. This is exactly what Freud found. He found that the Œdipus complex is normally resolved as a result of a conflict between narcissistic feelings and feelings of love for the parents, with the narcissistic feelings normally getting the upper hand over the incestuous ones.[6] Admittedly, these narcissistic feelings may express themselves in weird terms – in this case as anxiety about castration – but, translated into the language of the gene, it makes perfect sense: incest normally threatens reproductive success, just as castration does.

Nevertheless, Freud candidly concludes, 'But this does not dispose of the problem; there is room for a theoretical speculation which may upset the results we have come to or put them in a new light.'[7] Yet tantalizingly, Freud never says what he has in mind here, and his final, unfinished summary of his findings, *An Outline of Psychoanalysis,* adds nothing further.

Why we forget childhood

Although we may never know exactly what, if anything, Freud meant by these cryptic remarks, a conclusion drawn from our earlier considerations may at least shed some considerable new light on the issue, even if not upsetting his results as much as he may have feared. If we look back to my earlier account of Freud's findings relating to Œdipal behaviour in the context of modern evolutionary theory, we can see that it constitutes a clear case of parent–offspring conflict. I put forward the view that Œdipal behaviour in both sexes in earlier childhood and in boys throughout was fundamentally an adaptation that evolved to solicit parental investment. However, we saw that basic theory predicts that conflict will occur between the offspring's interest in consuming parental investment and in the parents' interest in providing it, especially at the margin, however that may be defined (see above, pp. 126–31).[8]

As far as it goes, this is alright, but there is a problem here. The problem is that those who are parents, and must be motivated to play the parent's rôle, will always have been children earlier, when they were motivated to play the child's rôle. Being able vividly to recall how you felt as a young child when your parents disciplined you would make being a parent yourself much more difficult. At the very least, you would feel ambivalent if parental feelings selected to favour your adult self-interest were in conflict with recollections of how you felt as a child.

Indeed, evidence of this can be seen in modern societies where conflicts between adolescents and parents are concerned. Thanks to a much earlier age of puberty and postponement of adulthood in modern industrial societies, adolescence has become a very protracted period by comparison to what it is in primal ones, such as the Australian aborigines or the !Kung. As a result, many parents become ambivalent about continuing to play a parental rôle, in part because they can recall so clearly how they felt when they were adolescents.

But early childhood is different, and the difference is that everyone forgets how they felt then. Yet we seldom notice how extraordinary this forgetting of the first five to six years of life is. In what other recording medium, apart from the human brain, are the first records the least likely to be retained? As many forgers learn to their cost, the norm is the opposite. And why should people be so easily able to recall so many later firsts when they cannot recall their first sight of the world, taking their first breath, or walking their first step?

Yet there is certainly every reason to think that even very young children are perfectly capable or remembering and recognizing people, places and things. Regarding his observations of his own son, Darwin comments that 'it is worth mentioning, as showing something about the strength of memory in a young child, that this one when 3 years and 23 days old on being shown an engraving of his grandfather, whom he had not seen for exactly six months, instantly recognised him and mentioned a whole string of events which had occurred whilst visiting him, and which certainly had never been mentioned in the interval.'[9] Nor is there any reason to think that Darwin's son was exceptional. On the contrary, it is entirely normal to find that events from age two and a half that had been clearly recalled at age three have been totally forgotten just a few years later.

The reason for this universal forgetting of childhood may be that children need to forget memories of their own feelings as children so that they can play an unambivalent rôle as parents. Loss of memories of early childhood, in other words, might have evolved as a Darwinian adaptation to deal with the problem of ambivalence on the parent's part in later parent-offspring conflicts over the critical factor of parental investment. To some extent such forgetting may be a consequence of the critical rôle that words play in consciousness. If the SuperEGO needs to issue a pass for consciousness, so to speak, in the form of a word-representation for something that would otherwise remain unconscious, it follows that memories from before the time we learn to speak competently may be lost for this reason alone. Indeed, the example of Anna Freud's I mentioned earlier, where something was excluded from consciousness by not being represented by the dictionary term for it illustrates the process very well (see above, pp. 102–3).

Nevertheless, in this connection it is interesting to note that Freud insists à propos the dissolution of the Œdipus complex that 'the process we have described is more than a repression. It is equivalent, if it is ideally carried out, to a destruction and an abolition of the complex.'[10] To revert for a moment to my earlier computer analogy, we might see this as amounting not merely to making the Œdipus complex file inaccessible (that is, repressed) but to completely erasing it. This is precisely what happens with many installers, for example. An installer is a piece of software that installs a program in a computer. Almost always this involves the erasure of old files or the creation of temporary files that are erased when the installer quits. Something like this seems to be what Freud has in mind when he asserts that 'the complex is not simply repressed, it is literally smashed to pieces . . . in ideal cases, the Œdipus complex exists no longer, *even in the unconscious*'.[11] Indeed, he adds that 'If the ego has in fact not achieved much more than a repression of the complex, the latter persists in an unconscious state in the id and will later manifest its pathogenic effect.'[12]

This statement is interesting in drawing attention to a common misunderstanding of Freud's concept of repression. This is that Freudian repression is both carried out at the wish of others and is something that in itself causes illness by excluding something from consciousness. In fact, we can see that where the Œdipus complex is concerned, repression is actually a cause of psychological problems because it is so notoriously inefficient. Indeed, Freud's view of psychopathic symptoms was that they represent a partial failure of repression and a return of the repressed. Psychoanalysis achieved its therapeutic results, not simply by liberating the repressed, but by substituting conscious, rational resolutions of mental conflict for the unconscious, irrational and inconclusive repressions of the unconscious.

In the light of this realization, the fact that Freud goes out of his way to insist that the Œdipus complex ideally ends in more than a mere repression – that is, a defensive fending off from consciousness by the

EGO – suggests that he found that its resolution involved more than merely the EGO's efforts, and perhaps drew on an evolved, 'innate programme', 'laid down by heredity'.[13] If so, such an event occurring at such a time in childhood could hardly be unaffected by parent–offspring conflict. Furthermore, since Freud himself pointed out that it is the psychoanalyst 'who has to raise his voice on behalf of the claims of childhood',[14] it follows that the repression of the Œdipus complex must correspond to the claims of the parent. This statement would have been a commonplace in the past, and a basis for the widespread misunderstanding of repression as something that parents routinely do to children. But now we can begin to see that it in fact reveals a surprising truth, one of which even Freud was unaware (although he may well have vaguely intuited it and this could be the reason for his references to 'speculations' and 'new light' on the subject). This is the realization that the extra, annihilating factor at work in the dissolution of the normal Œdipus complex may well be an evolved, 'innate programme' aimed at obliterating memories of having been the child so that, when the time eventually comes, you could competently play the rôle of the parent.

However, such a solution yields an unexpected bonus, because this biologically-mediated, evolved resolution of the normal Œdipus complex also provides what Westermarck required, but could never supply – a naturally selected mechanism for incest-avoidance. This comes about simply because a 'gene' (or any heritable tendency) for forgetting childhood of the kind I have suggested would also be a 'gene for incest-avoidance' if its effect were what Freud found it to be. This was that a child of either sex would tend to turn away from the parent of the opposite sex and accept the incest prohibition by identifying with the parent of the same sex.

Indeed, Freud's theory is like Westermarck's to the extent that both insist that incest-avoiding behaviour in adult life results from exposure to other family members during a critical period of childhood lasting up to about age six. Freud's findings suggest that incest-avoidance is the result of a complex process of childhood psychological development comparable to that which takes place during embryological development in the body. The Œdipus complex ought normally to 'self-destruct', rather as cells in four triangular wedges at the end of the limb buds of an embryo self-destruct, leaving the precursors of the five digits. The

154

Œdipus complex would be one critical stage in this developmental process, not the 'natural', 'true' state of human sexuality that had to be repressed by culture in order for civilized life to be possible.

The widespread confusion that exists over this issue is in part the result of psychoanalysts' therapeutic concern with abnormalities in this development that almost always involve the persistence of the Œdipus complex, rather as abnormal development of the fingers results from failure of the normal pattern of cell death in the embryonic hand. Indeed, it would not be going too far to say that, as a rough generalization, much of the therapeutic value of psychoanalysis lies in bringing about a destruction of an Œdipus complex that has not destroyed itself at the appropriate point in childhood. Like old or temporary files that were not erased when an installer quit but remain to cause trouble in a computer later, the Œdipus complex might be seen as something that the psychoanalyst has not merely to retrieve, but to erase. Only then could the human psychological operating system return to its normal pattern of development.

Nevertheless, Freud's findings regarding the dissolution of the Œdipus complex only deal with one aspect of the problem: the termination of the infantile relationship with the parents, along with its 'incestuous' overtones. This does not amount to an 'aversion' so much as to an erasure of an earlier stage of development. However, Freud did find that more positive – or should I say negative? – reactions against the idea of incest were to be found, somewhat as Westermarck also believed.

In the closing pages of his book of 1913, *Totem and Taboo,* Freud advanced a Lamarckian evolutionary scenario to explain how this may have come about. According to Freud, incest was at first avoided by the means mentioned by Darwin and found in so many other mammals: sons were driven out of their fathers' mating group when they reached sexual maturity. But eventually the excluded sons banded together, murdered the father and raped the mothers and sisters. Having done so, they gratified the negative, hating side of their ambivalent feelings about the father. But then the other, positive, loving side of those feelings asserted itself as guilt and remorse for what they had done. So traumatic was this event in human evolution and perhaps repeated so often, that Freud, following a clear precedent set by Darwin (see above, pp. 12–13), assumed that such originally voluntary expression of guilty emotion about incest and parricide would become eventually fixed by inheritance. What Freud, writing at the very end of his life, called 'the psychical precipitates of the primeval period became inherited property which, in each fresh generation, call not for acquisition but only awakening'. 'I have no hesitation in declaring', concluded Freud, 'that men have always known (in this special way) that they once possessed a primal father and killed him.'[15] Assertions such as these – and there are many more I could quote – prove conclusively that Freud's view of the Super-EGO in general and of specific aspects of it such as guilt about incest and parricide was one that assumed genetically-fixed, inherited causes much more than is generally realized.

This is where Freud falls victim to the Catch–22 logic of his twentieth-century critics. They dismiss his insistence on an evolved basis for incest-avoidance by pointing to the Lamarckian terms in which it is expressed. Then, having disposed of the evolutionary aspect, they assume that what Freud really meant was that incest was natural and its avoidance wholly cultural. They then appeal to evolution to prove this wrong and that incest-avoidance is natural, *not* cultural. So whatever Freud said, he is wrong: wrong if his view is taken to be an evolutionary one, and wrong if it is not.

There is, however, an alternative. This is to consider the possibility that Freud was right in general terms about an evolved basis for incest-avoidance, even if wrong in terms of the particular scenario he suggested for it. It is certainly true that, were Freud alive today, he could draw on much better knowledge than was available to him in 1913, when evolutionary thinking was adulterated with Lamarckism and a true understanding of evolutionary genetics only just about to emerge. So let's conclude this discussion of incest with a brief review of our best recent insights into the essential issues and compare them with Freud's findings.

Having it both ways

Darwin's scepticism about an innate aversion to incest may have had something to do with the fact that he married his first cousin, Emma Wedgewood. Marrying a first cousin is regarded as incestuous in many societies, and even today is a criminal offence in several states of the USA. Such marriages are banned because it is believed that they do genetic harm, and Darwin was concerned enough to try to get questions on cousin marriage included in the 1871 Census of Great Britain and Ireland. When he failed in this, his son George tried to obtain estimates of the prevalence of cousin marriage by counting unions between couples with the same surname. Then he studied oarsmen at Oxford and Cambridge to evaluate the effects of inbreeding on physique.[16]

The reasons for Darwin's concern go back to our earlier observations about genetics (see figure 8, p. 47). There we saw that a person inherits two complete sets of genes, one from each parent. The second copy acts as a back-up, so that if a gene is defective, the corresponding one can make up for it, so to speak. However, inbreeding (marrying a relative) works against this because there is a chance that a child of a couple who share a common ancestor will inherit that ancestor's gene from both parents. If the gene is a good one, there is no problem. But if the gene is defective or confers some ill effect, there is no back-up to compensate, and so the illness or disability shows itself. A good example is Queen Victoria, who carried a gene for the blood-clotting disorder, hæmophilia. She did not suffer from the disease herself, thanks to having a healthy back-up gene. Unfortunately, some members of the Russian royal family had Queen Victoria as an ancestor on both sides, and they suffered from hæmophilia as a result of inheriting her hæmophilia gene from both parents.

Nevertheless, modern insights into the evolution of co-operation like those I summarized earlier show that, whatever the genetic cost of inbreeding may be, it can also confer significant social benefits. Termites are an interesting example. Like ants, bees and wasps, they live in huge colonies with a strict division of labour that results in the majority of workers forgoing reproduction. In some species, the founding kings and queens commonly get replaced by secondary breeders from within the colony. The new parents are likely to be brother and sister, and their offspring can become highly inbred. This in itself tends to predispose termites to co-operation. Like cells in a multi-cellular organism, the high degree of relatedness between individuals means that a sacrifice by one can benefit identical copies of genes for such sacrifices in others (see above, pp. 43-8). As in the case of the bees, wasps and ants, offspring end up more closely related to their brothers and sisters than they would be to any offspring they were to have themselves. Because individuals can only pass on half their genes to their offspring, but share more than half of their genes with their siblings, it pays those genes to farm the queen for siblings. That way, more of them are copied than otherwise.

Mammals as a whole are not characteristically social, at least by the standards of termites. But there is an exception: the so-called naked mole rat (which, although a rodent, is neither a mole nor a rat, and more graphically described as 'the sabre-tooth sausage'). This mammal has evolved a strikingly similar system of reproductive division of labour to the insect one, with castes of sterile workers and soldiers altruistically helping a 'queen' to reproduce. But here again, DNA fingerprinting has shown that colonies are highly inbred, with an average eighty per cent identity of genes. This is a result of an estimated eighty-five per cent of matings being between parents and offspring or siblings – rampant incest, in other words, along with extreme social co-operation.[17]

If doing good to others is the essence of altruism, then avoiding harming them in one's own interest is also altruistic. Statistics relating to homicide suggest that relatives do indeed avoid killing one another. For example, in 1972 seventy-five per cent of all murders of relatives in Detroit were by non-blood related persons. Whereas thirty per cent of people who carried out a murder together in Miami were found to be blood-relatives, only two per cent of murder victims were blood-relatives of their murderers. Nor are such figures in any way exceptional. The degree of genetic relatedness between collaborative killers is far higher than that between victim and murderer in all societies for which data are available. Furthermore, they are thrown into tragic relief by the finding that, where parental murder of children is concerned, an adopted child living in the USA, Canada or Great Britain is one hundred times more likely to be killed by a step or substitute parent than by a natural one.[18] Here again, the basic reason is that if genes find identical copies of themselves in near kin, it does not normally pay those genes to wipe themselves out.

These statistics are significant because they have been used to discredit Freud, on the grounds that they show that evolution would not select for the murder of fathers by sons, for example. Had Freud claimed that the outcome of the Œdipus complex normally was murder of the father by a son or the mother by a daughter, these criticisms would have been reasonable. But as we have seen, this is not in the least what Freud actually found. He found that the Œdipus complex came to a pro-grammed end in childhood, and certainly did not involve actual incest or parricide. Furthermore, he concluded in *Totem and Taboo* that guilt about family violence was fixed by heredity, and an outcome of evolution, just as these statistics would suggest. Indeed, given that a true understanding of the evolution of kin altruism would not come for another fifty years, Freud's evolutionary scenario of 1913 should be seen as anticipating it, rather than violating its fundamental principles. With no true scientific insight into how inhibitions of aggression against relatives could evolve by natural selection, Freud's admittedly antiquated evolutionary scenario ought to be appreciated for its essential finding, rather than ridiculed for its specific errors.

The statistics relating to murder of step-children in particular suggest why relatedness is critical in child-rearing and why marrying someone with whom you already share genes may be an advantage as far as their likely degree of altruistic co-operation is concerned. Presumably this is the point of the Provençal adage, 'Marry within your village; if you can, on your street; if you can, within your house.' Furthermore, practice seems to have followed precept because eighty per cent of rural French marriages traditionally were contracted within a five-kilometre radius.[19] Indeed, the great popularity of marriage to first cousins found throughout the world suggests that some degree of inbreeding can have advantages.[20]

Recent research into first-cousin marriage like that contracted by Darwin shows that although the death-rate of the resulting children rises slightly along with the incidence of congenital abnormalities, it is more than offset by the greater fertility of cousin marriages. This research suggests that, although inbreeding may impose some genetic cost in terms of death and abnormality, it also confers real benefits measurable in reproductive success.[21]

We appear to be driven to the conclusion that not one, but two factors are important. On one side would be sex, which is essentially a question of reproducing by exchanging genes with others. Sexual reproduction produces high rates or genetic recombination, particularly in large, multi-cellular organisms whose lifespan is much longer than that of the disease micro-organisms and other parasites that infest them. By ensuring that offspring are not identical genetic clones of their parents, sex appears to produce a variation in individuals which means that disease parasites and other kinds of stresses never meet the same organism in two generations, thanks to the constant recombination that sex produces. Indeed, this may explain why naked mole rat colonies appear to be particularly susceptible to being wiped out by new diseases. It may be that the intense inbreeding they practise reduces genetic variability to dangerously low levels where disease resistance is concerned. This would be the genetic cost that such colonies paid for the social benefits that inbreeding also brings.[22]

Over and against the genetic benefits of outbreeding, for example for superior disease-resistance, we would have to set the social benefits of inbreeding. This is the basis on which multi-cellular organisms were able to evolve in the first place, given that their cells are predisposed to co-operate with one another by their genetic identity. Among sexually reproducing multi-cellular organisms like human beings, termites or mole rats, inbreeding promotes kin altruism by the high chances that any particular gene for altruism will be present in the beneficiaries of its effects. As we saw earlier, a gene for self-sacrifice can increase its reproductive success if its effects are to save more copies of itself in near kin (see above, pp. 43–8 and figure 8). The result is two contradictory factors, each pushing in a different direction: one towards inbreeding, one towards outbreeding.

If, in the spirit of Darwin's book on the emotions we ask what the psychological expression of this is likely to be, the answer is: *ambivalence* – that is, contradictory feelings about the same thing. As David Spain, an anthropologist who is an authority of the Freud-Westermarck controversy, has pointed out,

> it was Freud, not Westermarck, who directed our attention to the centrality of *ambivalence* in human affairs. Freud's genius does not lie in his claim that there is an "aversion" to incest in humans; rather, it lies in his claim that incest is something which people can find both attractive and repelling. Only when this is incorporated into our explanatory models can we expect to understand our . . . data.[23]

Anyone who reads *Totem and Taboo* in its entirety soon realizes that the central, recurrent theme of the book is ambivalence. Freud gives a number of examples of it, including ambivalence about enemies, rulers, and the dead. In each case he finds elaborate taboos, which Freud interprets as collective defence measures against the contradictory emotions that people feel towards the object in question. Incest is simply another case, albeit the most important. Freud concludes that the existence of elaborate taboos and restrictions on incest suggests that human beings are fundamentally ambivalent about it – that is, that they feel strong attractions to it *and* deep revulsions from it at one and the same time.

As far as the ID is concerned, ambivalence is of no consequence. As we saw earlier when we discussed Freud's model of the mind, he found it a complete chaos. Indeed, ambivalence, contradiction and irrationality is the norm for the ID, rather than anything else (see above, pp. 93–4). However, we also saw that ambivalence caused severe problems for the EGO, whose chief function is control of voluntary thought and action. This is because satisfying contradictory demands is always difficult in the real world, where you just can't keep your cake and eat it at one and the same time (see above, pp. 95–103). Consequently, Freud found that the EGO typically creates defence measures against ambivalence, and tries to deal with it by imposing rules and observances on itself that serve to avoid and diffuse the conflict.

For example, suppose that you like cakes, but also need to watch your weight. This makes you ambivalent about them: the pleasure principle says, 'Eat cake, enjoy!' The reality principle says, 'Don't eat cake – you'll get fat!' Compromise might work, but only if you could find non-fattening cakes that satisfied your taste buds as much as your need to stay thin. Failing that, you could try to solve the conflict in a number of ways. An obvious one would be by avoidance. You could look the other way when cakes are around, or cross the street to avoid walking past a cake shop. Another method might be an arbitrary rule. You could say, 'I'll eat cake only on Fridays' or 'only on the third Friday in a month that ends with an "r"', or whatever. Finally – and especially if neither avoidance nor a rule worked – you might become phobic about cakes and convince yourself that they were wholly bad for you and that you ought never so much as think of eating one.

Where incest is concerned, examples of all these reactions can be found, especially in pre-industrial societies. Avoidances are very common, and sometimes prevent tabooed individuals from even meeting one another, let alone speaking. Rules are practically universal, and can become astonishingly arbitrary, often taking in non-genetic relatives as well as genetic ones. For example, figure 15 illustrates one of the simplest rules found among Australian aborigines (and in fact represents groups of kin defined by the same term, brother, mother, etc.). As the

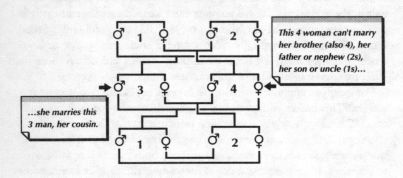

- •A 1 man marries a 2 woman, and the children are 3s
- •A 2 man marries a 1 woman, and the children are 4s
- •A 3 man marries a 4 woman, and the children are 1s
- •A 4 man marries a 3 woman, and the children are 2s

If the marriage rule above is represented as a genealogical diagram, incest is avoided and cousins marry:

This 4 woman can't marry her brother (also 4), her father or nephew (2s), her son or uncle (1s)…

…she marries this 3 man, her cousin.

♀ Females   ♂ Males   ⊔ Marriage   ⊓ Siblingship   ⌐ Descent

FIGURE 15: Australian aborigine marriage-class rules.

genealogical diagram shows, the rule is in fact a simple one preventing many forms of incest and prescribing marriage to a cousin. However, eight-class systems are also very common among Australian aborigines, and these are much more complex and exclude many more classes of kin (including the very first cousins you are supposed to marry under four-class systems). Furthermore – and as is typical of arbitrary rules, even where cake-eating is concerned – such regulations tend to be both frequently broken and reduplicated and reinforced. Among Australian aborigines, for example, marriage-class rules are backed up and overlaid by totemic and other laws that mean that if near kin are not excluded by one, they almost certainly will be by another. This is because simple, straightforward rules can cope with simple situations, but complex, con-

162

tradictory motives call for correspondingly complicated means to resolve them. Having several different rules about the same thing suggests having more than one feeling about it. Indeed, as Freud pointed out, such psychological defences in depth suggest a challenge from deep in the psyche.

Finally, a phobic attitude to incest appears to be one of the most common of all. This is what Freud called 'the horror of incest', and certainly seems to have been the attitude of Westermarck, at least if phrases like 'incestuous defilement' are anything to go by (see above, p. 148). Indeed, looked at from this point of view, Westermarck's aversion theory, so popular with Darwinists even in recent years, seems much more an expression of the emotions involved in controlling human inbreeding than a scientific explanation of them. Westermarck's theory may be Darwinian to that extent – the expression of an emotion – but Freud's findings understood on the basis of our modern insight into evolution at the level of the individual gene – PsychoDarwinism – could be a much more fruitful scientific approach to the issue of inbreeding. Indeed, as we shall see in the final chapter, it could solve a number of other fundamental problems too.

THE PSYCHODARWINIST SOLUTION

In my experience the major objection that many people have to the modern, organisms-are-the-vehicles-of-their-genes view of evolution is that they fear it means rigid determinism, with genes being the drivers of those vehicles, regardless of anything else. This raises the issue of the rôle of environmental factors, like upbringing and culture, as well as that of free will. We are seldom conscious of being driven by our genes, whereas all of us know how difficult it can sometimes be to make our minds up about something. If our genes are in the driving seat, such indecisiveness seems perplexing. Even if we grant that our consciousness may be cryptic in hiding more than it reveals (see above, pp. 59–77), the fact of choice and inner conflict still remains, at least at the conscious level.

In this last chapter, I want to look briefly at ideas about causality in science and then to take a particular example: the determination of sexual behaviour in human beings. As I hope to show, PsychoDarwinism has something important to offer in solving what is perhaps the deepest and most troubling problem of science – the interaction between genes and human behaviour. Finally, I shall return to the fraught topic of incest as an illustrative example of what the new perspective can achieve.

Life, but not as Thomas Hobbes knew it

The scientific revolution of modern times began with physics and astronomy. Perhaps that is the reason why our ideas about causality in natural systems have tended to be heavily influenced by those sciences, and by Isaac Newton's supreme achievement in particular. Before the scientific revolution of the sixteenth and seventeenth centuries, most people accepted a view of the universe based on scripture and, ultimately, on divine law. The earth was taken to be the centre of the universe, and the sun, moon and stars were believed to circle it in paths ordained by God. Only the wandering planets seemed to sound a discordant note in this harmony of the spheres, but even they could be fitted, more or less elegantly, into the divine order. The revolution in astronomy and physics associated with Newton (1642–1727) changed this picture profoundly, but in certain respects it remained very similar to the original world-view. Admittedly, now the sun, rather than the earth, occupied the centre. The crystalline spheres were now replaced by empty space that the planets traversed in elliptical orbits, and the three laws of motion and the principle of universal gravitation rather than the actions of the angels now controlled the whole. But God remained the Prime Mover who had set the whole impressive structure in motion in the first place and remained forever the spirit who had devised the clockwork cosmos that Newton's laws kept running so smoothly.

The universe ruled by Newton's laws was predictable, regular and mechanistic. It became a paradigm, or exemplary model, for ideas about order in other spheres, such as biology and society. Here too, thinkers like Thomas Hobbes (1588–1679) invoked the central power of the state to play a rôle like the sun in Newton's universe. In Hobbes's view, a central authority was necessary to save human beings from the 'state of nature' that he graphically described as 'nasty, brutish and short'. Like planets without a sun to hold them in their orbits, society would dissolve into anarchy, 'the war of all against all', unless the central power of the state were there to guarantee the safety and security of all.

Today, such ideas still affect us, even though recently they have been deeply compromised by developments in physics itself – principally relativity and quantum mechanics. But we still tend to think of social order as having to be imposed on recalcitrant human nature. And much of the difficulty that many people today find with the ideas that genes may influence human behaviour lies in mechanistic, rigidly deterministic assumptions about how such influences would work. There is still a widespread feeling that if science is going to try to explain human behaviour it can only do so in terms of a clockwork, mechanistic model reminiscent of Newton's universe, with rigid laws that would predict behaviour in the way in which astronomers predict solar eclipses.

Some modern Darwinists seem to encourage such a mechanistic view. For example, Edward O. Wilson (whose book, *Sociobiology*, did much to establish the term as synonymous with modern Darwinism), writing with Charles Lumsden argues that 'genes and culture are held together by an elastic but unbreakable leash. As culture surges forward . . . it is constrained and directed to some extent by genes.' This results in 'a tight linkage between genetic evolution and cultural history.' Their favourite example is incest-avoidance: 'when children are raised together in close domestic proximity during the first six years of life, they are automatically inhibited from full sexual activity at maturity.' Consequently, 'It is natural – in the full, biological sense – for people to be opposed to brother-sister incest.'[1]

Occasionally you see this idea graphically illustrated in connection with books or articles on evolutionary biology. People are represented as puppets with strings being pulled by strands of DNA, or some other representation of genes. Although Darwinists often complain about such crude images, they do seem to represent the spirit of the elastic leash model, at least if writers like Wilson are to be taken seriously. He, at least, certainly does seem to believe that we are at the end of an elastic leash that deters us from committing 'unnatural' acts like brother-sister incest. This may not be rigid Newtonian determinism, but it does seem to be elastic determinism, with the gene playing the rôle of the sun in keeping behaviour in its 'natural' orbit.

By contrast to Newtonian clockwork – elastic or otherwise – consider 'Life'. This is what is termed a 'cellular automaton'. It consists of 'cells' that occupy a position on a computer-screen 'world'. A cell can be 'alive', in which case it is showing, or 'dead', in which case it is not seen. Each cell touches eight neighbours at its faces and corners, three in the row above it, three below, and one either side of it. A simple set of rules – every bit as rigid as those of mechanics – determines the fate of cells. A lone cell, or one with just one neighbour, dies. If a cell is in contact with more than three other live cells, it will die. If a dead cell is touched by exactly three live cells, it is born – becomes live itself. These rules are applied to all cells, alive and dead, each 'generation'. Then the cycle is repeated, creating a new 'generation'. It is this repetitious application of a set of basic rules to the cells that make it a 'cellular automaton'.

Patterns of live cells are sometimes given names, and have interesting properties. Consider, as an example, the arrangement resembling a small 'r' in figure 16. This configuration bursts into life, and continues to evolve for over a thousand generations before stabilizing in a set of regular – although not necessarily static – figures. In the course of this

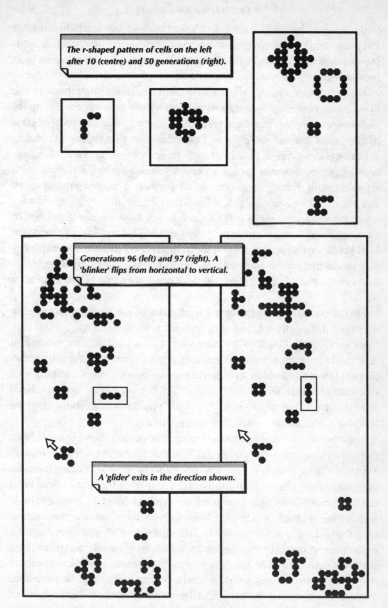

FIGURE 16: Life.

evolution it throws out six 'gliders' that travel in a definite direction at a regular rate. On a wrap-round screen they return to interfere with the patterns that gave birth to them, leading to more complex and ever-changing patterns.

The forms that emerge out of Life contrast starkly with those in the Newtonian universe. Gravitation and Newton's laws tend to simplify and compound parts into larger, more regular wholes. The present state of the solar system, which was assembled out of trillions of smaller particles, is the direct result of such forces operating for five billion years. Life, by contrast, tends to create ever-changing diversity, with astonishing, if fleeting, symmetries, contrasts and sudden explosions of activity. Yet the rules of Life show that, essentially, its order is of a social kind, because the status of a cell is wholly determined by that of its neighbours – lone cells are simply dead. The resulting patterns of living cells are those of dynamic, social interaction that show complexity and symmetry far beyond that of the individual cells which make up the pattern. Social order, it seems, does not have to be Newtonian after all.

On the contrary, the gravitating tendencies of the Newtonian universe work out differently where living organisms are concerned. To simulate this effect, let's go back to EVOLV-O-MATIC. Imagine that we have a new kind of critter, a predator that eats other critters when it encounters them. However, we also let other, non-predatory critters have an 'eye' that enables them to see each other and the predators, and to move accordingly. What is likely to happen? The answer is: bunching, or herding – the social equivalent of gravitation.

Look at it this way: any lone critter can be attacked by a predator from 360° (figure 17). We could call this its 'angular vulnerability'. However, if two critters see each other and bunch, so that each moves alongside the other, their individual angular vulnerability has been halved to 180°, because any predator coming from its partner's side will hit the partner first, not it. Four critters bunched together reduce individual angular vulnerability by half again, to 90°, and once we have more than about six, that figure can drop in principle to 0°, because one individual can hide inside a ring of its fellows. If the total reaches forty or so, the majority are protected by those on the periphery, whose angular vulnerability declines the larger their number becomes.

This is not just an abstract model, or something that only happens

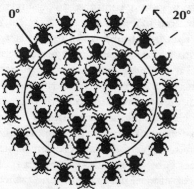

FIGURE 17: Social geometry.

on computer screens. You can see it happening whenever sheep see a dog, and slow-motion films of shoals of fish show that they hold together thanks to hundreds or thousands of individuals trying to reduce their angular vulnerability to 0° in three dimensions. Social gravitation, it we may put it like this, does not require a central authority or governing body in the way in which the Newtonian solar system requires the sun.

Thomas Hobbes may have believed that the state of nature was murderous anarchy, but Hobbes was wrong. At the very least, individuals grouping with others for their own safety will not generally be motivated to antagonize their fellows. Modern studies of animal behaviour show that order and not chaos is the norm in animal societies, and we have already seen that Tit-for-Tat co-operation can spread through populations of selfish Defectors, establishing social order (figure 12, p. 56). Contrary to Hobbes, we now know that social order can evolve spontaneously, motivated solely by self-interest and driven by natural selection at the level of the individual gene (see above, pp. 38–58).

Four sexual politics

A commonly-heard objection to taking selection at the level of the individual gene seriously is the assertion that single genes cannot possibly influence behaviour. It is said that behaviour is the outcome of the whole organism, and therefore of thousands of genes. But this can be misleading. Take sex as an example. Today we know that sex in mammals like human beings is indeed controlled by a single gene. The gene, which has recently been mapped, acts as a switch that turns on other genes whose net result is to transform an individual who would otherwise be female into a male. Many genes may indeed be involved in making a mammal male, but they appear to be under the control of a single, master gene controlling sex. Furthermore, sex is hardly something you could dismiss as irrelevant to behaviour.

This makes the gene in question seem rigidly deterministic, just like something in Newtonian mechanics. But the case of alligators, crocodiles and turtles shows a very similar gene for sex determination in a completely different light. In all these species, sex is determined by the temperature of incubation of the eggs in the nest where they are left by the mother. In the case of crocodiles, alligators and the snapping turtle, higher temperature produces males, a lower one females, whereas in other turtles the reverse is true, and higher temperature produces females. But why? The answer appears to be that higher incubation temperature favours larger final body size, thanks to more rapid growth. In alligators and crocodiles this promotes the reproductive success of males, who compete for females during mating. However, in turtles larger body size is advantageous to females, who can produce more eggs as a result. The exception is the snapping turtle, and here again, males compete for matings with females, making large body size more advantageous to a male.

Natural selection, in other words, is applying the principle that if an environmental factor like incubation temperature can be important in relation to an organism's reproductive success, it should be exploited. As a result, a rule that effectively says 'set sex in accordance with incubation temperature' can evolve simply because those organisms that had the right gene for it would indeed have more reproductive success than others. So in the case of alligators, crocodiles and turtles a single gene seems to allow sex to be set in accordance with environmental factors. This is single-gene determinism, but determinism that allows the environment to decide the outcome.

Environmental sex determination does not apply to mammals, whose sex is determined by a sex chromosome. If you have a Y-chromosome with the male sex-determining gene you develop as a male; whereas if you have no Y-chromosome, you have no male sex-determining gene and develop as a female. Nevertheless, sexual behaviour in human beings is often claimed to be effectively under environmental control. Sociologists often point to social conditioning as the chief determining factor in people's behaviour, sexual behaviour not excepted. So even if biological or chromosomal sex is determined by a single gene, it is claimed that behavioural sex is not. On the contrary, the social environment of upbringing – so-called *socialization* – determines that. Sex is consequently referred to as 'gender' by analogy with language, where nouns can have one of three genders: masculine, feminine or neuter. Here the assumption is that, just as a noun's gender is not always strictly tied to sex, so the 'gender' of an individual human being is not strictly determined by the sex chromosomes. On the contrary, the use of 'gender' to refer to a person's sex implies that it is as arbitrary as the convention that in English a ship is feminine and the overwhelming majority of nouns are neuter.

It seems that the only way you could settle the nature/nurture question as applied to sex would be to carry out an experiment in which a group of chromosomal males was socialized as females and a corresponding group of chromosomal females was socialized as males, and then compare the outcome with control groups socialized in accordance with chromosomal sex. You could then see which factor predominated in the final behaviour: was it biological, chromosomal sex, or socialized sex? However, this looks like idle speculation, because ethically you could never carry out such an experiment.

Nevertheless, nature has carried it out for us – or at least one half of it. In the Dominican Republic a rare genetic disorder exists whose effect is to make chromosomal males appear to be females at birth. At puberty, however, the biological sex asserts itself and ostensible girls transform into men. A study found eighteen individuals unambiguously raised as girls by parents who had no idea that they might be chromosomal males despite their female appearance. They all had girls' names, wore girls' clothes, and some were engaged to be married to men at the time the sex change began to show itself. None received medication or hormone treatment of any kind (as often happens elsewhere). Nor was this a culture in which sex rôles were fluid or extensively overlapping. On the contrary, it was one of typical Latin American *machismo* with a clearly defined difference between the sexes. The study showed that eighty-nine per cent (sixteen of eighteen) adopted a male sex rôle, despite parental consternation and initial social pressure to the contrary. The outcome was conclusive: where chromosomal and social sex are in conflict and medical intervention does not occur, chromosomal sex wins about nine times out of ten![2]

It seems that environmental sex-determination in crocodilians contradicts the idea of rigid, mechanistic sex-determination by genes, but the Dominican Republic case also questions belief in an equally deterministic rôle for the social environment in human sexual behaviour. If one case shows genes letting environment decide sex, the other shows genes contradicting environmental determinants of sexual behaviour – and this in human beings, the species allegedly most emancipated from genetic determinism and most susceptible to social conditioning!

Of course, there is no real contradiction from the point of view of reproductive success, which is what matters in evolution. The reason why socialization cannot usually change sexual behaviour into that of

172

the opposite sex is that individuals normally enjoy greater reproductive success if they stick to their biological, chromosomal sex, rather than try to imitate the opposite sex. Indeed, several of the men in the Dominican Republic study went on to father children. None of them could have given birth to babies, however rigidly they had stuck to the sex-of-socialization. Although people often talk as if evolution and environmental influences where mutually exclusive and fundamentally opposed factors, the fact remains that an organism can only be capable of responding to the environment if it has evolved to do so. Environmental sex determination in crocodiles and the Dominican Republic case both illustrate the point: the crocodiles how evolution allows the environment to fix sex, the human example how it does not.

Nevertheless, those who argue for environmental influences on human sexual behaviour have a point that needs to be examined more closely. Furthermore, it is one where Freudian findings are as important as Darwinian ones, and so will serve as an excellent example of what PsychoDarwinism can achieve.

Although there are only two chromosomal sexes and only three 'genders', Freud discovered long before it was fashionable to have done so that there are at least four sexes from the psychological point of view. Along with masculine males and feminine females, there are masculine females and feminine males. According to his findings, adult sex rôle is not entirely fixed, but influenced by identifications that occur at the critical time of the dissolution of the Œdipus complex (see above, pp. 149–51). Normally, a boy gives up his mother as a love-object and identifies with his father, accepting the incest taboo as part of this identification. A girl correspondingly abandons her father as an object and identifies with her mother. However, this is not invariable. Quite often a boy may reject his father, cling to his mother in his unconscious and identify with her, becoming feminine in psychology, if remaining male biologically. Similarly, a girl may end up identifying with her father to become psychologically masculine, if chromosomally female. The details of this process are subtle and complex and far from fully understood, with many intermediate and mixed positions, so that the actual outcome is often unique to each individual. Although there are certainly many exceptions, Freud concluded that 'it almost seems as though the presence of a strong father would ensure that the son made the correct decision in his choice of object, namely someone of the opposite sex.'[3]

More recent research by Robert Stoller, an analyst who has specialized in the study of so-called 'transsexuals', also leads him conclude that 'in boys. . .the more mother and the less father, the more femininity.' As far as girls are concerned, Stoller adds that 'if an excessively close mother-child symbiosis and a distant and passive father produce extreme femininity in males, too little symbiosis with mother and too much father could produce very masculine females.'[4]

Such findings are not limited to psychoanalysis. In academic, statistical psychology too, there is a surprisingly vast literature on the alleged effects of father absence, most of it strongly corroborative of the psychoanalytic findings. According to a recent review of this literature, 'several studies have shown relationships between the father's role in the family and the son's masculinity. Thus fathers who are seen as heads of households have more masculine sons and the masculinity of sons is lower when the father plays a feminine role at home.' Fifteen separate studies showed that boys raised without fathers were less masculine and six others suggested that they may alternatively exhibit 'compensatory' hypermasculinity and aggressiveness. As psychoanalytic theory would predict, 'when the age of father–child separation is considered, studies show that father absence has the greatest effect on the masculinity of boys separated from their fathers in early childhood.'[5]

Clearly, the question we are considering has much to do with homosexuality, and here numerous studies come to the same conclusion as psychoanalysis: 'An inadequate father-child relationship often appears to be a major factor in the development of homosexuality in males . . . There is much evidence that male homosexuals do not usually develop strong attachments to their fathers . . . homosexuals who take a passive, feminine role in sexual affairs have a particularly weak identification with their fathers and a strong one with their mothers.'[6]

Home environment then, does seem to be important for adult sexual behaviour, perhaps especially in males. But why should this be so? As is so often the case, Freud and other psychologists report the finding, but have little in the way of an explanation. The simple answer is that no-one knows why. Some may be tempted to interpret these findings as contradicting the Dominican Republic study and supporting the view that human sexual behaviour is largely a product of the social environment. However, Darwinian insights suggest a number of possible alternative explanations.

A first suggestion might be that it is not accidental that *fathers* seem to be so critical, especially in relation to *sons*. This could be because *paternity* – who your father is – is always much more doubtful than *maternity*. Children issue from their mother's body physically, and experiment shows that breast-fed babies can learn to identify their mothers by taste and smell within about a week of being born. However, because the father's contribution to the child is only a single sperm that normally fertilizes a woman within her own body, there is a possibility of doubt – it could always have been the milkman!

This is where identification may come in. Freud found that identification *with* the father was critical. But as I suggested earlier, identification *of* relatives like fathers might come about by self-comparison because that would normally have reflected genetic relatedness in primal, kin-based conditions (see above, pp. 114–18). So identification with a father would amount to a means of judging paternity in conditions where it is always in principle uncertain. By comparing himself with a putative father, a son may be unconsciously assessing the likely extent to which that man is indeed his father. If the self-comparison is confirmed, the result would be not merely a positive identification of the father, but also of the son *with* the father.

This in its turn could explain why sons appear to be more critically affected by non-identification with an adequate father than do daughters. As we saw earlier, male reproductive success can always be vastly greater than female reproductive success (see above, pp. 137–8). However, by the same token it can also be much less. The result is that males are normally selected, both to take more risks in achieving it, and in trying different ways of being reproductively successful. If a single sperm is a male's only contribution to an offspring, any method of delivering it will do, as long as it succeeds. As a result, natural selection has produced many different types of males pursuing many different strategies for reproductive success, often in the same species.

My favourite example is the blue-gill sunfish, which I mentioned earlier as an example of deception in the interests of reproductive success (see above, pp. 67–8). In this species three distinct types of male are found. The majority is made up of regular males. However, there is a minority of 'little sneaks' – small males who hang about near a nest, wait for a female to start to lay eggs in it and then dart in, ejaculate and escape – all within one tenth of a second! Such sneaks grow into the 'transvestites', or 'female mimics' I mentioned before who closely resemble real females and promote their own reproductive success by mimicking them. Normally a regular male would never tolerate another male in his nest, but the transvestites succeed by appearing to be female and thereby duping the resident male.

Many other examples could be quoted that teach the same lesson: that there are many different routes to reproductive success, especially for males. It may be that in human sexual behaviour too, males may have a number of options. One might be to be a regular, masculine male. But another might be to seem feminine, so that masculine males discount you as a rival and females take your sexual designs on them less seriously. If the result were fertilizations where otherwise there would not be any, natural selection would take a hand, selecting 'deviant' sexual strategies as long as they conveyed some measure of reproductive success, just as they do in the case of the blue-gill sunfish. In short, some forms of homosexual behaviour may be examples of what we might call *cryptic sexuality:* reproductive success by subterfuge. This would certainly make sense of Freud's finding that 'the man who gives the appearance of being susceptible only to the charms of men is in fact attracted by women in the same way as a normal man'[7] – not so much a homosexual as a cryptic heterosexual.

There is certainly a wealth of evidence to suggest that, whatever may be the appearance and however much it may consciously be denied, homosexuals of both sexes show typical behaviour for their sex if you disregard its object. Lesbians, for example, are much more likely to form long-term, stable relationships with just one other woman, sometimes lasting a lifetime. Similar behaviour is seen in some species of gulls, where females who lack a male mate have to find a female one to share their nest, since nests left unattended are attacked by other gulls. This suggests that it is the prime female preoccupation with parental invest-ment that causes lesbianism, because it amounts to monogamy with a female instead of a male mate. Male homosexuals, however, are much less likely to form stable, quasi-monogamous relationships with other men. Indeed 'sex differences in the behavior of homosexuals . . . seem to match or exaggerate those in heterosexuals. The men are ardent consumers of pornography, whereas there is no such market among women. Men judge the attractiveness of potential partners by their physical beauty, and especially by their youth, to a far greater extent than do women.'[8]

With a number of options for his future sex rôle, a boy may need to be able unconsciously to assess his prospects by self-comparison – in another word, *identification* – with his father. If he is sure that he has a father who has himself made a success of a regular male sex rôle, a boy may feel some confidence that he can do so himself and can mature as a masculine male, just like his father. However, lacking such an identification, and given the considerable costs that sexual competition with other men can entail, a boy might unconsciously opt for a less regular, 'deviant' sex rôle. Indeed, what Freud discovered about identification with the father on the part of the son may be based on a genetic mechanism – the likelihood or otherwise that a boy had inherited genes for a successful male sex rôle from his father. If so, it is interesting to note that there is a study that suggests that homosexual men are lighter in weight and have less muscular strength than heterosexual men.[9] Paradoxically then, a finding of Freud's also widely confirmed by academic psychology that appears to lay emphasis on an environmental influence may turn out to be based on a genetic factor. And even though the key mechanism – identification – is purely psychological, it in turn may be based on a fundamental biological factor: the perennial uncertainty of paternity. Once again we see that Freud's finding may be much less about environmental, social influences, and much more about evolved behaviour than has been believed in the past.

Another possibility might be that the presence of an adequate father indicates the likely level of parental investment, which as we saw is defined in terms of contribution to an offspring's ultimate reproductive success. Fathers are important providers of parental investment, especially in later childhood. This may mean that just having one who seems to be doing his job is an important indication to a child of either sex, but perhaps a boy especially, that his ultimate reproductive success could be good. Again, a child's future marriage prospects in primal societies like those of the Australian aborigines are often critically dependent on his father's social and political connections (as, indeed, they are in most societies, our own not excepted). So having a clearly identifiable father might be critical in indicating marriage prospects for children of both sexes.

Of course, none of this environmental influence need be conscious.

177

We have already seen that human beings have evolved a cryptic form of consciousness that serves to hide much more than it reveals. Furthermore, the Darwinian assumption implicit in these suggestions is that reactions to environmental cues like the presence of a father would have evolved to promote reproductive success in normal circumstances and all other things being equal. Identification may be a process that occurs in the unconscious regions of the EGO, but ultimately it serves the interests of the ID, like most things the EGO does. The ID in turn is a creature of the individual genes packaged within the organism, and if some of these prompt identifications that promote their own ultimate reproductive success, this is all a Darwinian explanation requires.

Again, we do not have to assume that adaptations like father-identifications or their absence that might result in homosexuality *always* promote an individual's reproductive success. Environmental sex determination in crocodiles, for example, certainly does not mean that an individual crocodile's reproductive success is maximized *every* time. On the contrary, environmental sex determination sometimes will produce far from optimum results. Our only assumption is that, in normal conditions and all other things being equal, it will promote its own reproductive success by comparison with alternatives, like chromosomal sex-determination (which can also have its drawbacks).

This is an especially important point in relation to the Darwinian explanation of homosexuality, because on the surface any kind of deviation from normal reproductive behaviour seems maladaptive. But if homosexuals enjoy more reproductive success than they might otherwise have done without the genetic predispositions that ultimately produce that behaviour, those genes will have been selected. The fact that important environmental influences (like the presence of father) contribute to the outcome makes no difference because what is being selected is the sensitivity to the environmental conditions in the first place. Since some studies of modern male homosexuals suggest that at least half of them do indeed have children, the contribution to males' reproductive success of homosexuality as an adaptation should be taken seriously. Like temperature-sensitive sex-determination in alligators and crocodiles, what Freud discovered about environmental influences on sexual constitution in human beings may be an evolved mechanism in itself, rather than a case of nurture appearing to contradict nature as has so often been supposed up until now.

Strange attractions

Quite apart from psychological considerations like these, recent developments in genetics may be about to make a major contribution to how the problem of genes and behaviour is regarded in the future. One such development is the Human Genome Project. This is likely to be the biggest single international scientific effort of the early twenty-first century, and in scale could rival the great programmes of the twentieth century, such as the Manhattan project that built the atom bomb, or the Apollo programme that landed men on the moon. The *genome* is the totality of genetic information in an organism. The aim of the Genome Project is to identify and map all the genes found in a human being. Effectively it boils down to trying to find a number, some three billion digits long, written in the four-base code of DNA (see above, pp. 35–6). This three billion-digit number could be seen as the ultimate personal ID-number, because it specifies the complete set of genetic information necessary to make a human being and is unique to each individual (identical twins apart).

But mapping the human genome, although a worthwhile scientific aim in itself, will raise many more questions than it answers. One of the most urgent and basic of these is likely to be the question of how identifiable, mapped genes become translated into observed human behaviour. This is what we might term the 'gene-behaviour interface' problem. An interface is the region where two systems meet and exchange information. An example from an earlier chapter was the graphic user interface used in some computers (see above, pp. 79–80). Most people who have thought about the gene-behaviour problem in human beings come to the obvious conclusion that the brain and central nervous system are the 'hardware' of the interface, so to speak, and that the mind is what we might call the software interface.

To date, there have been two rival approaches to the problem: one, which we may term *biological determinism,* has assumed that, since the brain clearly develops as a result of a genetic program, so does behaviour. This is the school of thought to which Westermarck's instinct for incest-aversion has so much appeal and one that also appears to be vindicated by the Dominican Republic experiment. On the other hand is what we might term *cultural determinism.* This approach concedes that brain development may ultimately be controlled by genes, but argues that behaviour is largely under environmental, cultural control and is pre-dominantly the outcome of socialization. According to this school of thought incest-avoidance is not 'natural' in any sense, but wholly the result of a cultural rule.

Although Freud is not often thought of in this context, we have already seen that a number of modern Darwinists have pointed out that his findings offer an alternative to these two, perhaps over-simple approaches (see above, p. 91). This is because the Freudian model of the mind appears to get the best of both, without the drawbacks of either. For example, it takes the biological, evolved basis of behaviour very seriously. Indeed, we have seen that Freud himself – by contrast to recent psychoanalysis – repeatedly emphasized innate, evolved factors, for example in the resolution of the Œdipus complex and the institution of the SuperEGO. The ID understood as the human ID-number written in genetic code is the basis of his model of the mind, and as I have tried to suggest can easily be reconciled with our best modern insights into evolution at the level of the individual gene (see above, pp. 88–95).

As we have seen, Freud found that the main influence of the ID on the EGO was through the pleasure principle. We also noted that Darwin realized that feelings of pleasure and pain had probably evolved by natural selection (see above, pp. 94–5). According to the Psycho-Darwinist model, genetic determinism would primarily show itself in the extent to which human behaviour was influenced by subjective sen-sations of pleasure and pain, and everything in between. We may not feel very often that we are 'driven by our genes', or held on an 'elastic leash' by them, but most people would recognize pleasure and pain as powerful influences on their behaviour. Furthermore, if it were explained to them that pleasurable sensations normally result from behaviour that (all other thing being equal, and in primal conditions) tended to promote reproductive success and painful ones from the con-trary, most people would probably accept that here, at least, was a credible idea about how genes might influence them.

So the Freudian approach both takes biological determinism seriously and provides a realistic picture of how it works. But a drawback of biological determinism has been its tendency to ignore or fail to explain other influences on behaviour, such as cultural or environmental ones. Here too, Freud has much to offer because his approach also gives cultural factors due weight, thanks to the rôle of the SuperEGO, which is in part heavily influenced by factors such as the cultural environment. 'What it amounts to', Freud concludes, 'is that in the formation of the superego and the emergence of a conscience innate constitutional factors and influences of the real environment act in combination.'[10]

Conflicting demands from the ID and the SuperEGO impinge on the EGO, which then must choose programmes of action that serve to reduce the stress to which it is subjected by these agencies to the minimum, taking into account further demands originating in reality and perceived through the senses. Freud found that he could classify mental illness according to where failures in the EGO's attempts to accommodate these conflicting demands occurred: neuroses originated in failure to accommodate the demands of the ID, manic-depressive disorders in relation to the SuperEGO, and psychoses such as paranoia and schizophrenia in failures to relate to reality. However, the overall affect of his model is one that takes all three inputs to behaviour seriously, and gives due weight to each: the biological, genetic basis of the ID, the cultural and social foundations of the SuperEGO, and the external, environmental factors perceived through the senses.

The outcome is a solution to the problem of how genes relate to behaviour that is neither one of biological or cultural determinism, but one of *psychological* determinism. It finds that the EGO – a purely psychological agency – ultimately chooses. But the EGO chooses within parameters laid down by evolution: principally the pleasure principle in relation to the demands of the ID and the partly socially-determined sanctions of the SuperEGO. Furthermore, what the EGO chooses ideally are real solutions that satisfy the reality principle too. So cultural, biological *and* environmental determinism are the major inputs to the psychologically determined outputs of the EGO – actual behaviour.

The resulting system does not appear to act like a simple, Newtonian one, or even one where behaviour is at the end of an elastic leash. Even in Newtonian physics, interactions between three or more bodies become very complex and can never be exactly predicted. Furthermore, situations analogous to those faced by the EGO are now known to produce results that are anything but Newtonian and certainly not mechanistic, predictable and repetitive.

For example, imagine a magnet suspended in such a way that it can swing towards two fixed, repelling magnets. When this magnetic pendulum is released, it traces out a complex series of paths that are rigidly determined by interactions with the magnets, ultimately based on the laws of motion and magnetic repulsion. But now start the experiment again, with the pendulum just slightly displaced from its original starting point. The result is a totally different pattern of motion for every slight change in starting position. The motion, in short, is 'chaotic', and obeys principles of non-linear mathematics very different from those of Newton's linear laws. Rather than simple, rigid attraction and repulsion seen in a clockwork pendulum, 'strange attractors' and other non-linear, turbulent effects appear – or, at least, they do if you can observe the system for long enough, and study its overall effects. (Strange attractors are abstract, looping mathematical patterns describing the state of the system in space and time that never exactly repeat themselves or close.) Such non-linear effects give an order to what otherwise seems like chaos. But it is not the linear, rigid, clockwork order of Newton. On the contrary, it is closer to the complex patterns seen in weather systems, turbulent fluids or the pendulum example above. Chaotic systems also resemble human behaviour, which seldom repeats itself exactly, but nevertheless often seems to run in stable, if complex and open-ended patterns.

The suggestion I made about incest in the last chapter could be closely compared with this non-Newtonian behaviour. There I proposed, not one, but two selective pressures influencing behaviour, rather like the two magnets in the pendulum set-up. One effectively says, 'Inbreed for the sake of the greater co-operation you can get'; the other, 'Outbreed because of the genetic benefits.' Freud's findings suggest that the inbreeding, incestuous 'gene', if we can call it that, is part of the ID, and that the outbreeding motivation comes predominantly from the SuperEGO, expressed by feelings of guilt and shame. Both attempt to influence the EGO, but the EGO can't be expected to respond in a simple, deterministic way. With two antithetical currents of feeling operating in opposite directions, the EGO, like the pendulum, will not necessarily settle down to a simple pattern of compliance with the demands of both or either.

Indeed, we cannot even assume that these two selective pressures, for and against inbreeding, are at all the same in the way in which they act on the EGO. On the contrary, Freud – by contrast to Westermarck – found that the default setting, so to speak, was for inbreeding, rather than outbreeding. We saw earlier that the default sex for mammals is female rather than male. But whereas masculinity in mammals is caused by a single gene (see above, pp. 170–1), Freud's findings do not suggest that a single gene causes incest-avoidance as Westermarck effectively assumed in claiming an 'instinct' for it.

Psychoanalytic case materials are full of evidence for Freud's conclusion even though they are routinely ignored by most writers on the subject. A striking example is the case of a nineteen-year-old female college student who had had regular intercourse with her father and three brothers since the death of her mother six years earlier. She remained oblivious of any wrongdoing on her part, and regarded her incest as just another duty she owed the family in the absence of her mother. According to her therapist, she was well-adjusted and without guilt until, on reading in a textbook at college that incest was considered criminal and pathological, she suffered an attack of anxiety and was referred for psychotherapy.[11] Anna Freud recounted a case to me of a man who had been having sexual relations with his mother since he was five years old. When I asked her what effect it had had on him she replied, 'Oh, he's completely normal – for a five year-old!'

Of course, these are just isolated cases, and might be dismissed as merely anecdotal. Nevertheless, data exist which show that although legalized brother-sister marriage is very rare, it existed among Greek immigrants in Roman Egypt during the first three centuries after Christ. Evidence of it can be found as early as 136 BC, but detailed and highly accurate household census-returns taken every fourteen years between AD 20 and AD 258 show that brother-sister marriage was both common and conventional. 'It is worth stressing that we are dealing here not with occasional premarital sex between siblings, abnormal but condoned, but with lawful, publicly celebrated marriages between full brother and sister, replete with wedding invitations, marriage contracts, dowries, children, and divorce.' Brother-sister marriages recorded in the meticulous returns accounted for between fifteen and twenty-one per cent of all ongoing marriages, despite the fact that only about forty per cent of all families had a son or daughter of marriageable age. This means that at least a third of all marriageable brothers and sisters married within the family by preference to marrying out of it.[12]

These findings, and the wealth of material discovered by psychoanalysts, strikingly contradict Westermarck's assertion that incest is a 'psychical impossibility' for family members brought up in the same household. 'The brothers and sisters concerned seem ordinarily to have been co-resident members of "normal" family/household units throughout their childhood (with little or no evidence that would indicate substantial physical separation during the formative period of their upbringing).'[13] This remarkable case supports Freud's finding that the inbreeding tendency of the ID is the default, and that inbreeding-avoidance is much more likely to be influenced by environmental and social factors.

Furthermore, this makes considerable Darwinian sense. This is because some reproductive success is better than none at all. Faced with a choice between no possibility of having an offspring for 'the good of the species' and the chance of a closely inbred one to the benefit of your own reproductive success, natural selection would be much more likely to favour incest rather than its avoidance, if that were the only reproductive success conditions allowed. In other words, the college girl who committed incest with her father and brothers was not necessarily perpetrating the 'unnatural' act that Lumsden and Wilson claim it to be (see above, pp. 165–6). Had her mother been present in her home, her SuperEGO's innate guilt and shame may well have prevented her from doing what she did, thereby effectively motivating outbreeding. Contrary to Lumsden and Wilson, who claim that incest-avoidance 'is unresponsive, or at most weakly responsive, to choices made by other members of society',[14] Freud's view was that environmental and social factors seem to be critical in setting the degree of guilt about incest and that the SuperEGO, although resting on an evolved, innate basis, is heavily influenced by environmental factors.

This makes inbreeding/outbreeding behaviour seem more like environmental than chromosomal sex determination, with local conditions determining the eventual outcome. But the difference would be that, whereas environmental sex determination of the kind we saw in crocodilians is a straight choice between male or female, inbreeding as opposed to outbreeding would present a gradation, running from one extreme to the other. And this gradation would express itself in the EGO as ambivalent feelings whose shifting outcome would determine the exact point at which the balance of forces was resolved.

But if the EGO faces an internal conflict reminiscent of the non-Newtonian pendulum, then in relation to the external environment it faces a situation something like Life. In the case of inbreeding and outbreeding, for example, the range of possible sexual partners is likely to be heavily influenced by the relationships that exist between them. Like Life cells, either 'on' or 'off', members of the opposite sex may either be 'on' or 'off' as sexual partners as far as local conditions are concerned. Although the rules of sexual relationships are different from the rules of Life, they are comparable in determining which individuals any one may have contact with, what the consequences are for the birth of new individuals, and so on. Complex patterns of interaction are likely to arise in much the same way, and certainly cannot be expected to resemble Newtonian clockwork.

Royal families, to take an instructive example, are likely to find that, thanks to dynastic considerations, wealth, inheritance and so on, very few individuals in the general population are likely to be 'on' as marriage partners, and so such families may amend incest-avoiding behaviour accordingly. Indeed, they will probably amend it in the manner suggested by our theory since, if social factors are much more important than anything else – and that they certainly will tend to be, given the prominent social rôle of monarchs – genetic considerations are likely to play a less prominent part. The inbreeding gene's appeal to the EGO will grow, and the outbreeding incentive will lessen. An example of the consequences might be the Russian royal family, whose hæmophilia was a consequence of inbreeding, as we saw earlier. A contrasting case of the ill-effects of out-breeding might be the current plight of the British royal family, torn apart by conflicts and embarrassments that would have been much less likely if its members had married among themselves.

The theory also suggests that the benefits of inbreeding may have been underestimated in the past, and/or the costs exaggerated. The recent research I mentioned earlier into first-cousin marriage is a case in point (see above, pp. 156–7). Fatalities and congenital abnormalities did increase, but had less effect on the overall reproductive success of such marriages than did the advantages of marrying a cousin (earlier marriage and more pregnancies). The same study concluded that 'the adverse effects associated with inbreeding are experienced by a minority of families.'[15]

Indeed, it is possible that inbreeding is yet another of those issues where 'survival of the fittest' thinking has contaminated true Darwinian insights. This is because inbreeding obviously does reduce 'fitness' understood as personal health and survival. But we have also seen that social co-operation can promote reproductive success at the expense of individual survival (see above, pp. 46–8). Here again, royal families provide an excellent example. This is because, although some inbred royal families may pay a price in terms of individual member's health, it is also true that male royalty sometimes achieve phenomenal levels of reproductive success. This often comes about by having hundreds of wives or concubines. But even ostensibly monogamous male monarchs often have 'unofficial' offspring by mistresses, female slaves or servants, and so on. Polygyny on this scale involves much outbreeding because male monarchs simply could not find enough sisters or cousins to fill all the reproductive opportunities that they generally have. So although inbreeding may indeed reduce the 'fitness' of some royal families, the concentration of wealth and power that inbreeding generally brings may amplify the wider, less obvious reproductive success of their male members, to the overall benefit of the royal family's genes.

A similar explanation has recently been put forward for the otherwise seemingly inexplicable case of legalized brother-sister incest in Roman Egypt. Here an 'exiguously small governing élite, with privileged access to land and other economic resources' had 'the sense of almost "royal" distinction'. This exclusive, caste-like group had 'close vertical linkages with their own dynastic rulers', the Ptolemaic dynasty, among whom ten or eleven out of fifteen marriages of male rulers were with full sisters.[16]

But whatever may be the truth about inbreeding royalty or Greek settlers in Roman Egypt, the fact remains that both inbreeding and outbreeding incur costs and confer benefits. In the past, 'survival of the fittest', group-selectionist thinking of the kind indulged in by Westermarck probably exaggerated the costs of inbreeding, while ignoring the cost to some individuals' reproductive success of avoiding incest 'for the benefit of the species'. Such thinking also probably underestimated the benefits of inbreeding for reproductive success rather than personal 'fitness', and certainly ignored the benefits of close genetic relatedness for the evolution of co-operation.

Understood as a model of gene-behaviour interaction, the view of inbreeding and outbreeding suggested here leads us to expect exactly what we find. This would not be a universal optimum of outbreeding similar in all societies, with rigid and reliable incest-avoidance by instinct, as Westermarck's theory predicts. Rather we would expect a range of behaviour from pure incest at one extreme (Roman Egypt or the college girl mentioned above), to exaggerated avoidances at the other. Most behaviour would fall somewhere in between, with a tendency to cluster towards the middle, round about the first-cousin level of inbreeding that is found in so many societies. While the equivalent of strange attractors or other non-linear effects might be suspected underlying the selective forces concerned, we would certainly not expect them to show themselves by the kind of clockwork regularities produced by Newtonian physics or implied by the elastic leash model.

Similar observations apply to co-operation. Once again, we would not expect 'a gene for kin altruism' to evolve in such a way that human beings were always and in every way co-operative with their kin. On the contrary, close proximity and reliance on the same or similar resources can throw organisms into competition and conflict as much as it creates an environment for co-operation. Furthermore, there is every reason to think that the same applies to human beings. If family life were a picture of monotonous harmony and tranquil co-operation we might believe in a simple aversion to conflict among kin similar to that which Westermarck believed existed to prevent incest. But we all know that the truth is very different and that, notwithstanding the findings relating to family violence set out above (see above, p. 158), conflict and competition are the norm, rather than the exception in all families.

The truth is that human beings are not single-mindedly altruistic towards kin, any more than they are simply predisposed to aggression against them, as some have claimed. Freud's much more realistic view was that human beings are highly ambivalent about all close relationships, genetic ones not excepted. In this fundamental ambivalence, feelings of love and co-operation, hate and selfishness, mingle in unequal and constantly changing amounts. As in the case of incest, he found that the ID appeared to be unheeding of environmental factors like the presence of others, their values and expectations. But in the cases of both co-operation and incest he found that the SuperEGO appeared to be specifically evolved to represent the social environment to the EGO and to be as ready to punish it with guilt or reward it with self-esteem as the ID was to sanction it with pain or entice it with pleasure. In other words, if we want to speak of 'a gene for kin altruism' in human beings, Freud's findings would locate its effects in the psychological institution of the SuperEGO and explain ambivalence in terms of its conflict with the more selfish drives of the ID.

The general picture that emerges from these cases is one of the EGO caught uncomfortably between the conflicting demands of the ID, SuperEGO and sensed environment. Like a non-Newtonian pendulum or other chaotic system, the EGO would oscillate in turbulent patterns: now attracted by the pleasure principle to gratify this need of the ID, now repelled from it by that demand of the SuperEGO, then constrained by reality to attempt a compromise, and so on. Furthermore, since other EGOs with which it comes into contact are likely to be responding in the same way and will sometimes be important factors in influencing its own decisions, the final outcome is likely to be complex indeed. Given that such turbulent, chaotic complexity is exactly what we observe in ourselves and others, it argues strongly for such a model of human nature. When we include in this picture the recognition of the importance of environmental factors in development suggested in the earlier discussion of sex rôles, we can see that PsychoDarwinism has much to offer as a solution to the problem of how genes and human behaviour interact.

CONCLUSION

Darwin, Freud and the Hysteria of Science

In the course of this book I have tried to present as clearly and coherently as I can the new synthesis of Darwin and Freud that I call Psycho-Darwinism. In doing so, I have not treated Darwin and Freud in exactly the same way. I have interpreted 'Darwin' to mean modern, 'selfish gene' Darwinism in the main. Only in talking about psychology have I 'gone back to Darwin', so to speak. This has not involved any major change in our view of Darwin's work – save, I hope, a new and deeper appreciation of his psychological writings. But with this one exception, the Darwin that emerges from this synthesis is very much the Darwin that the best informed of modern Darwinists already know.

However, things are very different in the case of Freud. Few if any psychoanalysts would recognize the Freud presented here as familiar from modern psychoanalysis. On the contrary, my failure to mention any post-Freudian figure save Anna Freud and my insistence on returning to the most rejected and widely amended of Freud's ideas will make this book seem totally without precedent in present-day psychoanalysis. The view of Freud's findings that I have presented is nothing short of revolutionary, particularly in its rehabilitation of universally ridiculed ideas such as the Œdipus complex, castration anxiety and penis envy, to quote but three of the most outstanding. Even in the case of less inflammatory issues, such as Freud's final view of the resolution of the Œdipus complex, or the rôle of language in the mechanism of repression, I have returned to findings that have been widely neglected or largely forgotten in recent psychoanalysis. Such a complete reversal of conventional wisdom may seem totally unprecedented and most unlikely to come about. It may seem like folly to ignore fifty years of 'progress' in psychoanalysis. Nevertheless, plenty of precedents for the far-reaching and much more positive reappraisal of Freud that I have argued can be found in the history of science. Nor is it true that progress in science is a uniformly ever-up-and-onward process.

On the contrary, Freud himself suggested that scientific revolutions often follow the pattern of hysteria: 'Early trauma – defence – outbreak of neurotic illness – partial return of the repressed.' Freud takes Darwin's theory of evolution as a case in point: 'At first it met with embittered rejection and was violently disputed for decades; but it took no longer than a generation for it to be recognized as a great step towards truth. Darwin himself achieved the honour of a grave ... in Westminster Abbey. A case such as this,' says Freud, 'leaves us little to unravel. The new truth awoke emotional resistances' – the trauma – 'these found expression in arguments by which the evidence in favour of the unpopular theory could be disputed; the struggle of opinions took up a certain length of time' – the defence. 'From the first there were adherents and opponents; the number as well as the weight of the former kept on increasing till at last they gained the upper hand' – the partial return of the repressed. 'We are scarcely surprised that the whole course of events took a considerable length of time . . .'[1]

In fact, what we might term 'the latency period' of Darwinism was both longer and more complicated than Freud appears to have realized. Far from taking no longer than a generation, the process of full acceptance of Darwin's essential insights took at least a century and is still not fully complete to this day. The facts are these: Darwin published *The Origin of Species* in 1859. But 'the long period when Darwinism was most widely rejected ... stretched from soon after Darwin's death in the 1880s right up until the 1940s.' If we restrict our attention to Darwin's principal work on evolution by natural selection, we find a book of 1907 entitled *Darwinism Today* asserting that Darwinism does 'not satisfy present-day biologists', a judgement that modern research substantiates as 'undoubtedly true taking all biologists world-wide' into account. Indeed,

> Darwinism itself ... typically was condemned for being unscientific. From the end of the nineteenth century right up until several decades into the twentieth, Darwinism was quite commonly castigated for hindering scientific progress by insisting on asking the wrong questions. These were the days

when biology was finding its feet as a respectable science. And respectable was commonly interpreted to mean laboratory-based, no-nonsense fact-gathering, experimental in the narrowest sense (as, shamefully, 'scientific' is still all too often taken to mean today). In this light, Darwinian theory was stigmatized as speculative, untestable, inexact. . .[2]

Darwin's second major book, *The Descent of Man, and Selection in Relation to Sex,* was, if anything, worse received and more vehemently rejected than *The Origin of Species:* 'for almost a century . . . sexual selection remained on the Darwinian sidelines, neglected, distorted or misunderstood. Natural selection suffered a partial eclipse for almost half a century after Darwin's death. Sexual selection suffered an almost total eclipse for almost twice as long.' In 1907 sexual selection was regarded as 'now nearly wholly discredited', while twenty years later still, hostile authors confidently asserted that the 'doctrine of sexual selection . . . is nowadays embraced by hardly any true scientists' adding dismissively that only 'popular literature shows traces of it'. Even when good evidence was forthcoming, it tended to be ignored. One naturalist writing in 1913 complained that 'I did everything, within my power, to further scientific truth, and have indeed produced immensely strong evidence in favour of the Darwinian theory of sexual selection. It would seem, however, that, since the theory itself is (officially) out of favour, such evidence is not wanted.'[3]

Earlier I suggested a Darwinian explanation for such anti-Darwinian prejudices. I pointed out that natural selection may have shaped human psychology to express emotions that serve the self-interest of the individual's genes in the survival and success of their temporary vehicle (see above, pp. 23–4). Narcissism, in short, may have evolved along with the immune system and other mechanisms to protect and safeguard an individual's mind and body, at least for as long as they are useful to the individual's genes. One consequence of that may be a prejudice against scientific insights that place the organism in the wider scheme of nature and that subjectively seem to devalue its importance. If so, the trauma Freud attributes to scientific revolutions is their implicit insult to human narcissism and their tendency to show that objectively there is no basis for the subjective feelings that we have about ourselves and our place in the cosmos.

But if true of Darwin, Freud felt that this was even more the case where his own work was concerned. 'Human megalomania', wrote Freud, 'will have suffered its . . . most wounding blow from the psychological research of the present time which seeks to prove to the ego that it is not even master in its own house, but must content itself with scanty information of what is going on unconsciously in its mind.' In other words, if Darwin's discovery was an insult to our feelings about ourselves, Freud's findings were even more of a trauma. This was because they challenged our subjective awareness itself, and revealed it to be no more than superficial, with a deep, unknown unconscious beneath. To the extent that our consciousness is cryptic and has evolved to hide and disguise our more self-interested thoughts, wishes and emotions (see above, pp. 59–77), Freud's discovery constitutes a direct threat because of the way in which it unmasks the self-deceptions on which consciousness rests. Little wonder then, that Freud even more than Darwin has encountered intense opposition. Freud continued, 'We psychoanalysts were not the first and not the only ones to utter this call to introspection; but it seems to be our fate to give it its most forcible expression and to support it with empirical material which affects every individual. Hence arises the general revolt against our science, the disregard of all consideration of academic civility and the releasing of the opposition from every restraint of impartial logic.'[4]

Just as biologists widely rejected Darwin from soon after his death right up until the Second World War, so psychologists have tended to disparage Freud since the time of his death in 1939. Like Darwinism, psychoanalysis has also been widely condemned for being unscientific, for hindering scientific progress by insisting on asking the wrong questions, and has even more repeatedly been stigmatized as speculative, untestable and inexact. Indeed, just like biology during Darwin's period of latency, psychology was finding its feet as a respectable science. And in the case of psychology even more than that of biology 'respectable' was commonly interpreted to mean laboratory-based, no-nonsense fact-gathering – experimental in the narrowest sense.

As far as psychoanalysts themselves are concerned, there appears to be a parallel between their embarrassment about Freud's sexual theories and older Darwinists' rejection of sexual selection (see above, pp. 104–7). Early defections from Freudian psychoanalysis by Adler and Jung, and many more since, were in the main caused by objections to the libido theory. Later ones by Klein and the 'object-relations' school disputed the central importance of the Œdipus complex. Today many reject the concept of infantile sexuality altogether and attribute it instead to 'sexual abuse' of children by adults. Just as 'survival of the fittest' Social Darwinists hijacked Darwin's scientific revolution and turned it into a political ideology, so socialists have appropriated what they imagine is Freud's concept of 'repression' and attempted to portray Freud as one of themselves. So single-minded has the emphasis on social conditioning become in modern psychoanalysis and so neglected is Freud's insistence on innate, constitutional and evolved factors that it would not be straining the parallel with Darwin too far to describe much modern psychoanalysis as 'Social Freudianism' and to see it standing in relation to Freud's work as Social Darwinism stood in relation to Darwin's.

Throughout, Freud has been subjected to numerous character-assassinations, even more vituperative and absurd than those earlier directed against Darwin. Indeed, so negative and lacking in objectivity have attitudes towards Freud and his work become in some places that you could be forgiven for thinking that any nonsense is publishable about Freud as long as it finds fault with him. The following extract, for example, is part of a two-volume work, *The Non-Authentic Nature of Freud's Observations,* published in 1993 by the University of Uppsala:

> *Freud's theories are thoroughly unoriginal ... Numerous psychoanalytic observations are faked* ... As regards THE RELATION BETWEEN THE THEORY AND OBSERVATIONS ... *No psychoanalytic interpretation is supported by any clinical observations ... It is simply not possible that any pattern of observations could be encountered in the real world, which would supply evidence for any psychoanalytic interpretation or proposition* ... As for PSYCHOANALYTIC PROPAGANDA ... *Freud was perfectly aware of the fact that he had never discovered anything, nor ever cured any patient* ... Concerning THE PERSONALITY OF PSYCHOANALYSTS ... *All psychoanalytic writers reveal an unusually low degree of knowledge of human nature ... empathy ... capacity for clinical observation* ... (sic)[5]

Hysterical, obsessive attacks like this one (whose author threatens twenty further volumes) reveal the emotional nature of the rejection of Freud very clearly. Their authors are often so concerned with subjective issues that they seem to forget that a person's character has nothing necessarily to do with the objective truth or falsity of their findings or theories. Isaac Newton, for example, was not a man with whom I would have wanted to share an office. But this does not prevent him having been one of the greatest scientists who ever lived or his work ranking among the supreme achievements of science. The numerous character-assassinations to which Freud has been subjected can be no substitute for reasoned argument and hard evidence against his findings. As Albert Einstein once remarked when told of a book entitled, *Fifty Against Einstein,* 'one would have been enough!'

If we pursue the analogy between the typical course of a hysteria and revolutions in the history of science, the period of latency that follows the original trauma is itself followed by the resurgence of the rejected idea – the return of the repressed. It seems that human narcissism, no matter how deeply insulted by scientific insights it may be, is not a permanently insurmountable obstacle. Science, the supreme expression of the reality principle, can make progress, albeit slowly and gradually, against the narcissism rewarded by the pleasure principle. In the case of Darwin a period of almost exactly a hundred years elapsed between the publication of *The Origin of Species* in 1859 and the rediscovery of authentic Darwinism in the early 1960s. Exactly a century separates the publication of *The Descent of Man, and Selection in Relation to Sex* and the volume commemorating its centenary that included a paper by Robert Trivers marking the renaissance of sexual selection in the theory of parental investment.

This return to consciousness is perhaps no better symbolized than in the fact that today the edition of *The Origin of Species* that remains in print is the first – not, as you might expect, the sixth and final one to be published in Darwin's lifetime. The reason is simple: Darwin was so conscientious about noting and responding to criticism that by the sixth edition his theory had become watered-down and amended to the point that, with the benefit of hindsight, it seems corrupted and obscured.

Perhaps this sets a precedent for Freud, who is currently under every bit as dark a cloud as Darwin was earlier this century. It is certainly true that Freud's standing has fallen progressively since the 1950s. Today, fifty odd years after his death, it would be tempting to see him in a complete eclipse, comparable to the eclipse of Darwin half a century after his death. But even then, in the 1930s, the modern resurgence of authentic Darwinism – Darwin's return from the repressed – was already beginning with the decisive synthesis of his findings with those of Mendel. Although another generation had to pass before the discovery of the genetic code paved the way for our modern understanding of evolution at the level of the individual gene, the fact remains that Darwin's fortunes reached their lowest ebb round about fifty years after his death, but triumphed within a century or so of their original publication. For Darwin, eclipse was purely transitory, and following the first gleams of a return in the 1930s, today his work shines brighter than ever before.

If this is a precedent for Freud, the worst may soon be over, given that he died in 1939. The eclipse into which he seems to have fallen may have already passed the moment of totality. If so, the next fifty years could see an astonishing development: a return of Sigmund Freud on a par with that of Darwin since the 1930s. Freud's first major work, *Studies on Hysteria,* was published in 1895. Most people would regard the psychoanalytic revolution as beginning somewhere between this date and 1905, when Freud's *Three Essays on the Theory of Sexuality* was first published. *The Interpretation of Dreams,* which Freud regarded as his masterpiece, came out in 1900, exactly midway between these two, making it the most obvious point from which to date the Freudian era. This suggests that, if the precedent of Darwin is anything to go by, the beginning of the new millennium may see the third and final part of the pattern that Freud discerned: the return of the repressed following a period of latency and occurring approximately a century after the initial trauma.

By comparison with Darwin, Freud was much more stubborn, and was nothing like as ready as Darwin was to amend his views in response to criticism. As a consequence Freud has looked like an isolated, reactionary figure, sticking obstinately to outmoded views and dated attitudes. Darwin would doubtless have looked the same had he insisted on adhering to the original, more clear-sighted statement of his theory in the first edition of *The Origin of Species,* and for a century he definitely did look that way where sexual selection was concerned. But just as modern Darwinism has gone back to the earlier, less apologetic Darwin and vindicated his belief in sexual selection, so it is possible that the future will return to the authentic Freud, largely ignoring fifty or more years in which his findings have been diluted, denied and distorted by later developments in psychoanalysis. The consequence could be that Freud will eventually be seen as Darwin is today: not so much behind his times as a century ahead of them. If so, this book will not only have made the prediction, but perhaps begun to fulfil it.

REFERENCES

Preface

1. Trivers, R., 'Sociobiology and Politics', in *Sociobiology and Human Politics*, E. White, ed. 1981, Lexington, Ma.: Lexington Books, p. 39.

Introduction

1. Barash, D., *Sociobiology: The Whisperings Within*. 1979, London: Souvenir Press.
2. Darwin, C., *The Expression of the Emotions in Man and Animals*. Facsimile reproduction of the first edition of 1872 with an introduction by Konrad Lorenz, ed., 1965, Chicago: University of Chicago Press, pp. 50–1.
3. *ibid.*, pp. 32–3.
4. Freud, S., *An Autobiographical Study*. The Standard Edition of the *Complete Psychological Works of Sigmund Freud*, ed. J. Strachey *et al.* Vol. 20. 1925, London: The Hogarth Press and the Institute of Psychoanalysis.
5. Breuer, J. and S. Freud, *Studies on Hysteria*. The Standard Edition of the *Complete Psychological Works of Sigmund Freud*, ed. J. Strachey *et al.* Vol. 2. 1895, London: The Hogarth Press and the Institute of Psychoanalysis, pp. 180–1.
6. Darwin, C., *The Expression of the Emotions in Man and Animals*. Facsimile reproduction of the first edition of 1872 with an introduction by Konrad Lorenz, ed. 1965, Chicago: University of Chicago Press, p. 51.
7. Breuer, J. and S. Freud, *Studies on Hysteria*. The Standard Edition of the *Complete Psychological Works of Sigmund Freud*, ed. J. Strachey *et al.* Vol. 2. 1895, London: The Hogarth Press and the Institute of Psychoanalysis, pp. 91–2.
8. Darwin, C., *The Expression of the Emotions in Man and Animals*. Facsimile reproduction of the first edition of 1872 with an introduction by Konrad Lorenz, ed. 1965, Chicago: University of Chicago Press, p. 348.
9. Breuer, J. and S. Freud, *Studies on Hysteria*. The Standard Edition of the *Complete Psychological Works of Sigmund Freud*, ed. J. Strachey *et al.* Vol. 2. 1895, London: The Hogarth Press and the Institute of Psychoanalysis, p. 91.

10. Cronin, H., *The Ant and the Peacock: Altruism and Sexual Selection from Darwin to Today*. 1991, Cambridge: Cambridge University Press, p. 346.

11. *ibid.*, p. 328.

12. Freud, S., 'The Moses of Michelangelo'. The Standard Edition of the *Complete Psychological Works of Sigmund Freud*, ed. J. Strachey *et al.* Vol. 13. 1914, London: The Hogarth Press and the Institute of Psychoanalysis, pp. 211–39.

13. Ritvo, L., *Darwin's Influence on Freud: A Tale of Two Sciences*. 1990, New Haven: Yale University Press, p. 49.

14. *ibid.*, p. 72.

15. Darwin, C., *The Descent of Man, and Selection in Relation to Sex*. Facsimile reproduction of first edition with an introduction by John Tyler Bonner and Robert M. May. Princeton University Press, Princeton, 1981 ed. 1871, London: John Murray, pp. 37–8, 57.

16. Darwin, C., *The Expression of the Emotions in Man and Animals*. Facsimile reproduction of the first edition of 1872 with an introduction by Konrad Lorenz, ed. 1965, Chicago: University of Chicago Press, pp. 42, 29.

17. *ibid.*, p. 42.

18. Darwin, C., 'A Biographical Sketch of an Infant'. *Mind: A Quarterly Review of Psychology and Philosophy*, 1877. 2: p. 285–94.

19. Darwin, C., *The Expression of the Emotions in Man and Animals*. Facsimile reproduction of the first edition of 1872 with an introduction by Konrad Lorenz, ed. 1965, Chicago: University of Chicago Press, pp. 39, 41.

20. Ritvo, L., *Darwin's Influence on Freud: A Tale of Two Sciences*. 1990, New Haven: Yale University Press, p. 69.

21. Dawkins, R., *The Blind Watchmaker*. 1986, Essex: Longman, pp. 298, 300.

22. Darwin, C., *The Descent of Man, and Selection in Relation to Sex*. Facsimile reproduction of first edition with an introduction by John Tyler Bonner and Robert M. May. 1981 ed., Princeton University Press, Princeton, 1871, London: John Murray, p. 118.

Chapter 1

1. Gould, S.J., *Wonderful Life: The Burgess Shale and the Nature of History*. 1990, London: Hutchinson Radius, pp. 257–8.

2. Coghlan, A., 'Survival of the Fittest Molecules', *New Scientist*, 1992. (3 October).

3. Darwin, C., *The Descent of Man, and Selection in Relation to Sex*. Facsimile reproduction of first edition with an introduction by John Tyler

REFERENCES

Bonner and Robert M. May 1981 ed., Princeton University Press, Princeton, 1871, London: John Murray, pp. 59–61.

Chapter 2

1. Axelrod, R., 'The Evolution of Strategies in the Iterated Prisoner's Dilemma', in *Genetic Algorithms and Simulated Annealing*, L. Davis, ed. 1987, Pitman: London. p. 32–41.
2. Axelrod, R., *The Evolution of Cooperation*. 1984, New York: Basic Books.

Chapter 3

1. Darwin, C., *The Expression of the Emotions in Man and Animals*. Facsimile reproduction of the first edition of 1872 with an introduction by Konrad Lorenz, ed. 1965, Chicago: University of Chicago Press, p. 37.
2. Darwin, C., *The Descent of Man, and Selection in Relation to Sex*. Facsimile reproduction of first edition with an introduction by John Tyler Bonner and Robert M. May 1981 ed., Princeton University Press, Princeton, 1871, London: John Murray, p. 57.
3. Aitchison, J., *The Articulate Mammal: An Introduction to Psycholinguistics*. 1989, London: Unwin Hyman, p. 5.
4. Ekman, P., *Telling Lies: Clues to Deceit in the Marketplace, Politics, and Marriage*. 1985, New York: W. W. Norton, pp. 84–5.
5. Darwin, C., *The Expression of the Emotions in Man and Animals*. Facsimile reproduction of the first edition of 1872 with an introduction by Konrad Lorenz, ed. 1965, Chicago: University of Chicago Press, p. 208.
6. Ekman, P., *Telling Lies: Clues to Deceit in the Marketplace, Politics, and Marriage*. 1985, New York: W. W. Norton, p. 84.
7. *ibid.*, pp. 85, 81.
8. Freud, S., 'Fragment of an Analysis of a Case of Hysteria', The Standard Edition of the *Complete Psychological Works of Sigmund Freud*, ed. J. Strachey *et al*. Vol. 7. 1905, London: The Hogarth Press and the Institute of Psychoanalysis, pp. 77–8.
9. Trivers, R., *Social Evolution*. 1985, Menlo Park, California: Benjamin/ Cummings, p. 417.
10. Gur, R. and H. Sacheim, 'Self-Deception: A Concept in Search of a Phenomenon', *Journal of Personality and Social Psychology*, 1979. 37 (2): p. 167.
11. Darwin, C., *The Descent of Man, and Selection in Relation to Sex*. Facsimile reproduction of first edition with an introduction by John Tyler

Bonner and Robert M. May 1981 ed., Princeton University Press, Princeton, 1981 ed. 1871, London: John Murray, pp. 333–6.

Chapter 4

1. Freud, S., 'A Note upon the "Mystic Writing-Pad"', The Standard Edition of the *Complete Psychological Works of Sigmund Freud*, ed. J. Strachey *et al.* Vol. 19. 1925, London: The Hogarth Press and the Institute of Psychoanalysis, p. 228.
2. Freud, S., *Inhibition, Symptoms and Anxiety*, The Standard Edition of the *Complete Psychological Works of Sigmund Freud*, ed. J. Strachey *et al.* Vol. 20. 1926, London: The Hogarth Press and the Institute of Psychoanalysis, p. 163.
3. Freud, S., 'Repression', The Standard Edition of the *Complete Psychological Works of Sigmund Freud*, ed. J. Strachey *et al.* Vol. 14. 1915, London: The Hogarth Press and the Institute of Psychoanalysis, p. 147 (Freud's emphasis).
4. Rancour-Laferriere, D., *Signs of the Flesh: An Essay on the Evolution of Hominid Sexuality*. 1985, Bloomington: Indiana University Press, p. 9.
5. Barash, D., *Sociobiology: The Whisperings Within*. 1979, London: Souvenir Press.
6. Trivers, R., *Social Evolution*. 1985, Menlo Park, California: Benjamin/Cummings, pp. 146–7
7. Rancour-Laferriere, D., *Signs of the Flesh: An Essay on the Evolution of Hominid Sexuality*. 1985, Bloomington: Indiana University Press, p. 9.
8. Freud, S., *An Autobiographical Study*, The Complete Psychological Works of Sigmund Freud, ed. J. Strachey *et al.* Vol. 20. 1925, London: The Hogarth Press and the Institute of Psychoanalysis, pp. 32–3.
9. Young, R., *Darwin's Metaphor: Nature's Place in Victorian Culture*. 1985, Cambridge: Cambridge University Press, p. 59.
10. Freud, S., 'On Narcissism: An Introduction', The Standard Edition of the *Complete Psychological Works of Sigmund Freud*, ed. J. Strachey *et al.* Vol. 14. 1914, London: The Hogarth Press and the Institute of Psychoanalysis, p. 95.
11. Trivers, R., 'Sociobiology and Politics', in *Sociobiology and Human Politics*, E. White, ed. 1981, Lexington Books: Lexington, Ma. p. 18.
12. Darwin, C., 'A Biographical Sketch of an Infant', *Mind: A Quarterly Review of Psychology and Philosophy*, 1877. 2: pp. 285–94.
13. Freud, S., *The Ego and the Id*, The Standard Edition of the *Complete Psychological Works of Sigmund Freud*, ed. J. Strachey *et al.* Vol. 19. 1923, London: The Hogarth Press and the Institute of Psychoanalysis, p. 25
14. Freud, S., 'The Unconscious', The Standard Edition of the *Complete Psychological Works of Sigmund Freud*, ed. J. Strachey *et al.* Vol. 14.

1915, London: The Hogarth Press and the Institute of Psychoanalysis, pp. 161–215.

15. Freud, S., *The Ego and the Id*. The Standard Edition of the *Complete Psychological Works of Sigmund Freud*, ed. J. Strachey *et al*. Vol. 19. 1923, London: The Hogarth Press and the Institute of Psychoanalysis, p. 56.

Chapter 5

1. Cronin, H., *The Ant and the Peacock: Altruism and Sexual Selection from Darwin to Today*. 1991, Cambridge: Cambridge University Press, pp. 238–40.

2. Freud, S., *Three Essays on the Theory of Sexuality*. The Standard Edition of the *Complete Psychological Works of Sigmund Freud*, ed. J. Strachey *et al*. Vol. 7. 1905, London: The Hogarth Press and the Institute of Psychoanalysis, p. 131.

3. Freud, S., 'On Narcissism: An Introduction', The Standard Edition of the *Complete Psychological Works of Sigmund Freud*, ed. J. Strachey *et al*. Vol. 14. 1914, London: The Hogarth Press and the Institute of Psychoanalysis, p. 78.

4. *ibid.*, p. 89.

5. Lampert, A. and J. Yassour, 'Parental Investment and Risk Taking in Simulated Family Situations', *Journal of Economic Psychology*, 1992. 13 (3): pp. 499–507.

6. Freud, S., 'On Narcissism: An Introduction', The Standard Edition of the *Complete Psychological Works of Sigmund Freud*, ed. J. Strachey *et al*. Vol. 14. 1914, London: The Hogarth Press and the Institute of Psychoanalysis, p. 91.

7. Freud, A., *The Ego and the Mechanisms of Defence*. Revised Edition, 1968, London: Hogarth Press and Institute of Psychoanalysis, pp. 123–6.

8. Darwin, C., 'A Biographical Sketch of an Infant', *Mind: A Quarterly Review of Psychology and Philosophy*, 1877. 2: pp. 285–94.

9. Freud, S., *Three Essays on the Theory of Sexuality*. The Standard Edition of the *Complete Psychological Works of Sigmund Freud*, ed. J. Strachey *et al*. Vol. 7. 1905, London: The Hogarth Press and the Institute of Psychoanalysis, pp. 149–50.

10. Short, R., 'The Biological Basis for the Contraceptive Effects of Breast Feeding', *International Journal of Gynæcology and Obstetrics*, 1987. 25(Supplement): pp. 207–17.

11. Thapa, S., R.V. Short, and M. Potts, 'Breast Feeding, Birth Spacing and their Effects on Child Survival', *Nature*, 1988. 335: p. 679.

12. Blurton Jones, N. and E. da Costa, 'A Suggested Adaptive Value of

Toddler Night Waking: Delaying the Birth of the Next Sibling', *Ethology and Sociobiology*, 1987, 8: pp. 135–42.

13. Darwin, C., 'A Biographical Sketch of an Infant', *Mind: A Quarterly Review of Psychology and Philosophy*, 1877. 2: pp. 285–94.

Chapter 6

1. Haig, D., 'Genetic Conflicts in Human Pregnancy', *Quarterly Review of Biology*, 1993, 68(4): pp. 495–523.
2. Personal communications from David MacKnight and Warren Shapiro.
3. Róheim, G., 'Psycho-Analysis of Primitive Cultural Types', *International Journal of Psycho-Analysis*, 1932. 13.
4. Freud, S., 'From the History of an Infantile Neurosis', The Standard Edition of the *Complete Psychological Works of Sigmund Freud*, ed. J. Strachey *et al*. Vol. 17. 1918, London: The Hogarth Press and the Institute of Psychoanalysis, pp. 82, 36 and 97.
5. Darwin, C., *The Expression of the Emotions in Man and Animals*. Facsimile reproduction of the first edition of 1872 with an introduction by Konrad Lorenz ed. 1965, Chicago: University of Chicago Press, pp. 147 and 174.
6. Darwin, C., 'A Biographical Sketch of an Infant' *Mind: A Quarterly Review of Psychology and Philosophy*, 1877. 2: pp. 152–3.
7. Darwin, C., *The Expression of the Emotions in Man and Animals*. Facsimile reproduction of the first edition of 1872 with an introduction by Konrad Lorenz, ed. 1965, Chicago: University of Chicago Press, p. 208.
8. *ibid.*, p. 210.
9. Darwin, C., 'A Biographical Sketch of an Infant' *Mind: A Quarterly Review of Psychology and Philosophy*, 1877. 2: pp. 152–3.
10. Freud, S., 'Female Sexuality', The Standard Edition of the *Complete Psychological Works of Sigmund Freud*, ed. J. Strachey *et al*. Vol. 21. 1931, London: The Hogarth Press and the Institute of Psychoanalysis, pp. 223–43.
11. Laplanche, J. and J.-B. Pontalis, *The Language of Psychoanalysis*. The International Psychoanalytic Library, ed. M. Khan. Vol. 94. 1973, London: The Hogarth Press and the Institute of Psychoanalysis.
12. Darwin, C., *The Descent of Man, and Selection in Relation to Sex*. Facsimile reproduction of first edition with an introduction by John Tyler Bonner and Robert M. May, Princeton University Press, Princeton, 1981 ed. 1871, London: John Murray, p. 377.
13. Cronin, H., *The Ant and the Peacock: Altruism and Sexual Selection from Darwin to Today*. 1991, Cambridge: Cambridge University Press, p. 171.

14. Freud, A., *Studies in Passivity*, in *Indications for Child Analysis*. 1969, Hogarth Press and Institute of Psychoanalysis: London, p. 254.

15. Flinn, M., 'Parent–Offspring Interactions in a Caribbean Village: Daughter Guarding', in *Human Reproductive Behavior*, L. Betzig, M. Borgerhoff Mulder, and P. Turke, eds. 1988, Cambridge University Press: Cambridge. pp. 189–200.

16. Trivers, R., 'Parent-offspring Conflict', *American Zoologist*, 1974. 14: p. 257.

17. Freud, S., 'Female Sexuality', The Standard Edition of the *Complete Psychological Works of Sigmund Freud*, ed. J. Strachey *et al*. Vol. 21. 1931, London: The Hogarth Press and the Institute of Psychoanalysis, p. 234.

Chapter 7

1. Westermarck, E.A., *The History of Human Marriage*. 1925, London: Macmillan, Vol. II p. 218.

2. *ibid.*, Vol. I pp. 478–9.

3. Ritvo, L., *Darwin's Influence on Freud: A Tale of Two Sciences*. 1990, New Haven: Yale University Press, pp. 106, 103–4.

4. Freud, S., 'The Dissolution of the Oedipus Complex', The Standard Edition of the *Complete Psychological Works of Sigmund Freud*, ed. J. Strachey *et al*. Vol. 19. 1924, London: The Hogarth Press and the Institute of Psychoanalysis, pp. 173–4.

5. *ibid.*, p. 174.

6. *ibid.*, p. 176.

7. *ibid.*, p. 177.

8. Trivers, R., 'Parent-offspring Conflict', *American Zoologist*, 1974. 14: pp. 249–64.

9. Darwin, C., 'A Biographical Sketch of an Infant' *Mind: A Quarterly Review of Psychology and Philosophy*, 1877. 2: pp. 285–94.

10. Freud, S., 'The Dissolution of the Oedipus Complex', The Standard Edition of the *Complete Psychological Works of Sigmund Freud*, ed. J. Strachey *et al*. Vol. 19. 1924, London: The Hogarth Press and the Institute of Psychoanalysis, p. 177.

11. Freud, S., 'Some Psychical Consequences of the Anatomical Distinction between the Sexes', The Standard Edition of the *Complete Psychological Works of Sigmund Freud*, ed. J. Strachey *et al*. Vol. 19. 1925, London: The Hogarth Press and the Institute of Psychoanalysis.

12. *ibid.*, p. 177.

13. *ibid.*, p. 174.

14. Freud, S., 'A Child is Being Beaten', The Standard Edition of the *Complete Psychological Works of Sigmund Freud*, ed. J. Strachey *et al*.

Vol. 17. 1919, London: The Hogarth Press and the Institute of Psychoanalysis, p. 184.

15. Freud, S., *Moses and Monotheism*. The Standard Edition of the *Complete Psychological Works of Sigmund Freud*, ed. J. Strachey *et al*. Vol. 23. 1939, London: The Hogarth Press and the Institute of Psychoanalysis, pp. 132 and 101.

16. Bittles, A. *et al*., 'Reproductive Behavior and Health in Consanguineous Marriages, *Science*, 1991. 252: pp. 789–94.

17. Sherman, P., U. Jarvis, and S. Braude, 'Naked Mole Rats', *Scientific American*, 1992. 267 (2): pp. 42–8.

18. Daly, M. and M. Wilson, *Homicide*. 1988, New York: Aldine de Gruyter, pp. 87–8.

19. Eribon, D., *Conversations with Claude Lévi-Strauss*. 1991, Chicago: University of Chicago Press, p. 101.

20. van den Berghe, P., 'Human Inbreeding Avoidance: Culture in Nature', *Behavioral and Brain Sciences*, 1983. 6: pp. 91–123.

21. Bittles, A. *et al*., 'Reproductive Behavior and Health in Consanguineous Marriages, *Science*, 1991. 252: pp. 789–94.

22. Sherman, P., U. Jarvis, and S. Braude, 'Naked Mole Rats', *Scientific American*, 1992. 267 (2): pp. 42–8.

23. Spain, D., 'Incest Theory: Are There Three Aversions?' *Journal of Psychohistory*, 1988. 15 (3): p. 250

Chapter 8

1. Lumsden, C.J. and E.O. Wilson, *Promethean Fire: Reflections on the origin of mind*. 1983, Cambridge, Mass: Harvard University Press, pp. 60, 20, 133, 176.

2. Imperato-McGinley, J. *et al*., 'Androgens and the Evolution of Male-gender Identity among Male pseudohermaphrodites with a 5α-reductase Deficiency', *New England Journal of Medicine*, 1979. 300 (22): pp. 1233–7.

3. Freud, S., *Leonardo da Vinci and a Memory of his Childhood*, The Standard Edition of the *Complete Psychological Works of Sigmund Freud*, ed. J. Strachey *et al*. Vol. 11. 1910, London: The Hogarth Press and the Institute of Psychoanalysis, p. 99.

4. Stoller, R., *Presentations of Gender*. 1986, New Haven: Yale University Press, pp. 25, 57.

5. Lamb, M., ed. *The Role of the Father in Child Development*, Second Edition 1981, Wiley: New York, pp. 490, 19, 27.

6. *ibid.*, pp. 335–6.

7. Freud, S., *Leonardo da Vinci and a Memory of his Childhood*, The Standard Edition of the *Complete Psychological Works of Sigmund Freud*, ed.

REFERENCES

    J. Strachey *et al*. Vol. 11. 1910, London: The Hogarth Press and the Institute of Psychoanalysis, p. 100.

8. Daly, M. and M. Wilson, *Sex, Evolution and Behavior*, Second ed. 1983, Boston: PWS Publishers, pp. 308–9.

9. Evans, R., 'Physical and Biochemical Characteristics of Homosexual Men', *Journal of Consulting and Clinical Psychology*, 1972. 39: pp. 140–7.

10. Freud, S., *Civilization and Its Discontents*, The Standard Edition of the *Complete Psychological Works of Sigmund Freud*, ed. J. Strachey *et al*. Vol. 21. 1930, London: The Hogarth Press and the Institute of Psychoanalysis, p. 130.

11. Arens, W., *The Original Sin: Incest and Its Meaning*. 1986, New York: Oxford University Press.

12. Hopkins, K., 'Brother-Sister Marriage in Roman Egypt', *Comparative Studies in Society and History*, 1980. 22, pp. 303–4.

13. Shaw, B., 'Explaining Incest: Brother-Sister Marriage in Graeco-Roman Egypt', *Man*, 1992. 27 (2): pp. 275–6

14. Lumsden, C.J. and E.O. Wilson, *Genes, Mind, and Culture: The coevolutionary process*. 1981, Cambridge, Mass: Harvard University Press, p. 148.

15. Bittles, A. *et al*., 'Reproductive Behavior and Health in Consanguineous Marriages, *Science*, 1991. 252: pp. 789–94.

16. Shaw, B., 'Explaining Incest: Brother-Sister Marriage in Graeco-Roman Egypt', *Man*, 1992. 27 (2): pp. 275–6.

Conclusion

1. Freud, S., *Moses and Monotheism*, The Standard Edition of the *Complete Psychological Works of Sigmund Freud*, ed. J. Strachey *et al*. Vol. 23. 1939, London: The Hogarth Press and the Institute of Psychoanalysis, pp. 80, 66–7.

2. Cronin, H., *The Ant and the Peacock: Altruism and Sexual Selection from Darwin to Today*. 1991, Cambridge: Cambridge University Press, pp. 37, 49–50.

3. *ibid.*, p. 243.

4. Freud, S., *Introductory Lectures on Psychoanalysis*, The Standard Edition of the *Complete Psychological Works of Sigmund Freud*, ed. J. Strachey *et al*. Vol. 16. 1916, London: Hogarth Press and The Institute of Psychoanalysis, pp. 284–5.

5. Scharnberg, M., *The Non-Authentic Nature of Freud's Observations*. Uppsala Studies in Education, Vols. 47 and 48. 1993, Uppsala: University of Uppsala, Vol II, pp. 64–5.

INDEX